Preface

The term "cybercrime" is also commonly referred to as "Internet crime," "electronic crime," "e-crime," "hi-tech crime," or "computer crime." Regardless of which of the aforementioned terms is used, cybercrime generally refers to criminal activity where a computer or network is the source, tool, target, or place of a crime. To put it simply, our world has changed considerably since the advent of the Internet. We have since come to rely on the Internet as an invaluable tool to explore and gather what appears to be an infinite amount of data on every topic imaginable, but more importantly, the Internet has enabled us to swiftly communicate with virtually anyone, anywhere, at anytime across the globe. The anonymity, accessibility, and ever-present availability of the Internet, coupled with its relatively low cost, have made it incredibly attractive and appealing to everyone from the villager in Ghana to the corporate executive in New York City. However, there is a darker, more sinister side of the Internet for those who have turned to it for deviant, unlawful purposes. The Internet has essentially led to the formation of new, previously unheard of crimes that transcend all geographical boundaries and borders, and continue to evade law enforcement and prosecutorial measures that have traditionally been used to investigate, prosecute, and punish criminal activity. Not only have we seen the emergence of new crimes, we have also witnessed the evolution of what were once considered traditional crimes now being committed in cyberspace - creating an entirely new breed of criminal offenders.

The cybercrime articles included in this reader will undoubtedly appeal to students, or anyone for that matter, who is interested in learning about cybercrimes and the offenders who engage in such crimes. The reader is divided into six sections that cover a wide and diverse array of cybercrimes. The first section introduces students to the concept of cybercrime by providing an in-depth overview starting with Gene Stephens' article, "Cybercrime in the year 2025." In 1981, Stephens wrote an article for The Futurist on "Crime in the Year 2000," and in 1995, an article on "Crime in Cyberspace." In both, he suggested the role the computer and Internet would play in crime and crime fighting in the future. Well, the future is here and society is still inadequately prepar changing and continuously growing number cybercrimes.

Section two deals specifically with Internet pornography. The emphasis is on the criminal activities of the pedophile who has taken his crimes to an entirely new level – from the playground to cyberspace. Some, including this writer, believe that the Internet has an addictive quality to it, as evidenced by how easily many people become addicted to Internet pornography. With a simple click of the mouse, virtually every deviant fantasy comes to life. User behaviors range from simple curiosity to compulsive behaviors that can consume every waking minute in a continuous cycle of uploading, downloading, sending, viewing, and printing pornography. The Internet has made it much easier to share and send files containing child pornography and other illegal material with limited risk of exposure or detection.

Section three introduces students to transnational terrorist and extremist groups who have turned to cyberspace. We are all very familiar with the tragic events of 9/11, however, many are not as familiar with the activities of the cyberterrorists and other extremist groups who turn to the Internet not only to inflict terror, widespread damage and destruction, but also to recruit new members who may be sympathetic to their cause. Are we adequately prepared for a cyber attack? What is the US Department of Homeland Security doing to prevent a cyberterrorist attack? The answers to these questions and more can be found within the articles that follow. Domestic and foreign extremist groups have looked to YouTube and other popular websites as tools for terrorist recruitment, propaganda, and planning attacks. These sites have the ability to reach hundreds of thousands of people instantly and are difficult to remove once they have been posted, making the threat of transnational crime a major concern for all nations, not just the United States.

Section four focuses primarily on the criminal activities of the cyberstalker and the cyberbully, perpetrators of once traditional crimes that have become more sophisticated, more difficult to detect, and more complicated to prosecute because most of the criminal laws in existence today do not address such crimes. Bullying is often erroneously perceived to be a harmless rite of passage that many children and adolescents do their best to endure; however, it has a profound psychological and social impact on not only the victim, but also the perpetrator and bystanders of such acts. The cyberbully is even more threatening than the traditional bully because cyberbullies can inflict fear without directly interfacing with the victim. The cyberstalker shares many common characteristics with the cyberbully, in that the offender and victim profiles are similar. The difference is mostly in age, as the cyberbully and his or her victim tend to be adolescents, whereas the cyberstalker and his or her victim tend to be adults.

Section five delves into the technical side of cybercrime by focusing on what I have labeled computer hackers, crackers, and fraudsters. This particular offender preys upon individuals as well as businesses and organizations. Throughout most of the articles, you will notice a heavy emphasis on the financial implications of fraudulent activity whereby the computer or network is the source, tool, target, or place of a crime. Some hack into computers or computer networks for sheer fun and enjoyment. Regardless, the behaviors and actions of computer hackers are unethical and illegal.

Lastly, section six deals exclusively with the current efforts to combat cybercrime. To avoid becoming a victim of cybercrime, most security professionals recommend that private citizens and organizations educate themselves and remain cautiously aware of potential cyber scams. In his article, "Ten Tips to Combat Cybercrime," James Leon recommends ten simple yet effective ways to avoid falling prey to cybercrime that apply to both private citizens and organizations. Leon recommends that individuals be aware of suspicious or fraudulent emails, especially those that are not personally addressed to you. Second, he recommends not opening suspicious links that could contain viruses or malware from criminals attempting to gain access to private information stored on your computer. If at all possible, consider an email encryption program to protect against hackers from retrieving your emails, even those that you thought had been deleted. Leon also recommends disallowing permanent cookies and disabling scripts in web browsers. One of the most important recommendations is to install a firewall to screen and filter information coming into your computer from email, instant messaging, or HTML pages. It is also imperative that you secure wireless connections and use only secure websites for financial transactions. However, the most important recommendation is to be cautious and stay on the defensive. I always say, "If it's too good to be true, it's likely a scam." Law enforcement organizations in particular need to be more proactive in providing education and awareness about existing and emerging cyber crimes, because nearly all the literature studies to date indicate that cyber crimes are on the rise and will continue to evolve as criminals find new ways to outsmart, outwit, and otherwise prey on those who are perceived to

ix

be vulnerable targets. Remember, criminals are opportunistic and therefore search for the easiest target that provides the least amount of resistance.

Michael Pittaro

1

An Overview of Cybercrime

1

Cybercrime in the Year 2025

Gene Stephens

In 1981, criminal-justice scholar Gene Stephens wrote an article for the futurist on "Crime in the Year 2000," and in 1995, an article on "crime in cyberspace." in both, he suggested the role the computer and Internet would play in crime and crime fighting in the future. Here, he reviews what he got right, what he got wrong, and why, and he suggests the types of cybercrimes and cybercrime fighting that will occur by the year 2025.

In a 1981 article for THE FUTURIST, I wrote, "Data from all areas of the [criminal justice] system will be computerized and cross-referenced. Computers will store the modus operandi of convicted felons, and when a crime occurs, police may call on the computer to name the most likely suspects, or, in some cases, the exact offender" ("Crime in the Year 2000," April 1981).

It seemed quite logical at the time, but the forecast turned out to be overly optimistic; I underestimated the antipathy to change and the turf protection within the system.

The first paragraph of a subsequent article was more on target: "Billions of dollars in losses have already been discovered. Billions more have gone undetected.

G. Stephens, "Cybercrime in the year 2025 (2008), The Futurist, July-August 2008, p. 32-38. Reprinted by permission of the World Future Society, 7910 Woodmont Avenue, Suite 450, Bethesda, Maryland 20814, USA. Telephone: 301-656-8274.

3

4

Trillions will be stolen, most without detection, by the emerging master criminal of the twenty-first century—the cyberspace offender" ("Crime in Cyberspace," September-October 1995). Admittedly vague, it still seems to be a fairly accurate evaluation of the evolution of cybercrime.

In the same article, I correctly forecast an explosion of cellular phone time theft and phone fraud; increased cyberattacks and fraud against government and business; massive credit card theft and fraud; internal theft of clients' identities by financially struggling and/or greedy financial service employees; more cyberporn, cyberstalking, cyberharassment, and cybervengeance; and the use of biometrics and encryption as methods of protecting data in cyberspace.

In some other areas, my forecasts weren't as accurate. My fascination with the embryonic field of nano-technology led to a prediction of organic nanocomputers implanted in citizens' brains by the early twenty-first century.

Related forecasts included terrorists sending subliminal messages directly to the brain implants of potential recruits, cyberextortion by hacking into brain implants and scrambling or threatening to scramble information in it, and the problem of people with brain implants being unable to a separate virtual reality created by cyberoffenders in flesh-and-blood reality. This forecast may yet come true, however, for it's still early twenty-first century, and there is plenty of time for this technology and these disturbing crimes to begin to appear.

In the 1995 article, I was rather pessimistic about the short-term capacity of police to cope with emerging cybercrime:

The outlook for curtailing cyberspace crime by technology or conventional law-enforcement methods is bleak. Most agencies do not have the personnel or the skills to cope with such offenses.... Cybercrime cannot be controlled by conventional methods. Technology is on the side of the cyberspace offender and motivation is high—it's fun, exciting, and profitable (p. 28).

My suggested solution, unfortunately, seems even more "Pollyanna" today than it did then: "the only real help is ... conscience and personal values, the belief that theft, deception, and invasion of privacy are simply unacceptable."

According to Ray Kurzweil's "Law of Accelerating Returns," technological change is exponential rather than linear; thus, "we won't experience 100 years of progress in the twenty-first century—it will be more like 20,000 years of progress (at today's rate)." Predicting advances and their impacts on crime and crime fighting by 2025, then, is analogous to reviewing the next 5,000 years of technological progress in society.

Kurzweil himself made several forecasts that could have major implications for cybercrime; for instance, he said that by 2010 personal computers will be capable of answering questions by accessing information wirelessly via the Internet (this is one prediction that arrived a little early). By 2019, he held, a $1,000 personal computer will have as much raw power as the human brain; possibly more important, he believed that computer chips will be everywhere, embedded in furniture, jewelry, walls, clothing, and so on. Also by 2019, computers and humans would communicate via two-way speech and gestures rather than keyboards. Virtual sex via computer will become a reality, and education, business, and entertainment will also be increasingly computer based. Roadways would be automated and computer controlled, while human—robot relationships will be commonplace.

Possibly the most renowned of Kurzweil's predictions is the coming of "the Singularity"—when computers become self-aware—and the melding of humans and machines. Kurzweil sees this process well under way by 2025 as nanobots begin to surf the human bloodstream on search-and-destroy missions to combat pathogens and data nanobots augment human intelligence and access to information. Transhumans will be on their way to having an internalized capacity to communicate and interact with humans, machines, and other transhumans.

TECHNOLOGY'S POTENTIAL IMPACTS ON CRIME

What follows are my forecasts for how these developments might affect crime and crime fighting over the next two decades.

Computer and Internet use will become increasingly seamless, as hands-free, voice-activated communications and data entry and retrieval will be commonplace by the early teen years of this new millennium (the 2010s). The world community will have moved a long way in a few short years, since by late 2007, 1.25 billion people already had access to the Internet, though only about 2% of the world population regularly accessed it. Science-fiction writer William Gibson, who coined the term cyberspace in his 1982 short story, "Burning Chrome," forecasts that a fully wired world—a single unbroken interface without need for computers—will complete the evolution to full access of all Earth's citizens.

6

The Defense Advanced Research Projects Agency (DARPA) set up the Internet and fostered its early development, but DARPA will likely over haul its invention in the 2010s. Not only will the outcome be faster and larger capacity usage, but also, by virtually starting over with the security aspects in mind, the future Internet will be safer and more difficult to attack and disable.

Nanotechnology will increasingly impact cyberspace by the late 2010s, and as we try to gain the most advantage possible from new technologies, new security gaps will emerge that could turn into nightmares if not handled carefully. For example, as data nanobots are implanted in users' brains (later, organic bots will become an integral part of the individual), special attention will have to be paid to providing advanced firewalls to keep intruders from cracking into the bots and terrorizing the recipient. Could there be a more frightening crime than having your brain-stored knowledge erased or scrambled, or hearing voices threatening to destroy your memory unless you pay extravagant blackmail? Welcome to the prospects of mindstalking.

Designer nanobots may also be loosed on the World Wide Web to engender types of mischief and destruction not yet contemplated. All advanced technology has the capacity to be used for good or evil, depending on the developer/user; and nanotech would appear to be the ultimate example, as it literally can be used to develop either nanosize weapons that could destroy the world or nanosize defense systems that could protect the planet.

WHO'S IN CHARGE?

The exponentially improving capabilities of emergingWeb technologies spotlights the long-ignored issues of who owns the World Wide Web, who manages it, and who has jurisdiction over it. The answer now is: Nobody! Can the world's most powerful sociopolitico-economic network continue to operate almost at random, open to all, and thus excessively vulnerable to cybercriminals and terrorists alike? Yet any attempt to restrict or police the Web can be expected to be met by extreme resistance from a plethora of users for a variety of reasons, many contradictory.

Another reasonable prediction would be that the Internet will become not only the number-one means of communicating, conducting business, socializing, entertaining, and just living, but indeed will handle a huge majority of such interactions; thus, failure to establish and enforce some basic ground rules will likely lead to socioeconomic disaster.

If exchange of resources is to be accomplished almost exclusively over the Internet, anonymous surfing will be a potential threat. Moving funds without identification could not only perpetrate individual fraud, but also bankrupt the system itself. Biometrics and more-advanced systems of ID will need to be perfected to protect users and the network. In addition, multinational cybercrime units will be required to catch those preying on users worldwide, as Web surfers in Arlington, Virginia, and Victoria, British Columbia, may be victims of cyberscams perpetrated in Cairo or Budapest. Coordination and cooperation will be keys to making the Internet a safer place to travel and conduct business.

THE MATRIX MAY BE REAL

Kurzweil predicts that the equivalent of 4,000 years of technological advancement will occur during the first two decades of the twenty-first century, so it is extremely difficult to forecast what will happen. The concepts, theories, and formulas for many of these changes have yet to emerge from the plethora of ongoing research and development.

Still, some speculation is possible. For instance, every square meter of atmosphere hugging the earth may be filled with unseen nanodevices designed to provide seamless communication and surveillance among all people in all places. Humans will have nanoimplants, facilitating interaction in an omnipresent network. Everyone will have a unique Internet Protocol (IP) address.

Since nano-storage capacity is almost limitless, all activity and utterances by people everywhere will be recorded and recoverable. Transparency will become increasingly ubiquitous as word and deed—whether spoken or acted out in anger, frustration, or as a joke—can be almost instantly compared to "the record." Can human or even transhuman behavior evolve rapidly enough to withstand such scrutiny? If current laws were enforced with this level of supporting evidence, who could pay for the prison space required to carry out the mandated punishment?

Another possibility would be the perfection of The Matrix, as Gibson envisioned in a series of popular books and movies, where a powerful central force controls all activity in a seemingly free society. The reaction in individualistic societies such as the United States would likely be similar to that in these fictional portrayals—rebellion, with a goal of destroying the web of control.

A counterforce that could create a different type of harm for the individual would be continuance of the policy of no control of the Internet, allowing often destructive activity e.g., harassment, terrorism, and fraud—without jurisdiction and authority to curtail it. Which would be worse would depend on which value dominates—security (i.e., safety and order) or civil liberties (freedom and chaos). As always, the role of public safety in all this is to find the balancing point, where the degree of safety is enough to allow the pursuit of individual happiness.

CYBERCRIME PROGRESSION: PIGEON DROPS AND IDENTITY THEFT

As technology advances at a dizzying pace, so will the ways and means of those wishing to use the rapidly changing cyberspace as a tool/milieu for fun and profit, or worse. In the immediate future, the increasingly creative scams to bilk Internet users of their resources will continue, with literally scores of new schemes appearing daily on the Web. Sheiks, abandoned Russian women, and unclaimed lottery winnings will be joined by relatives seeking heirs and other electronic pigeon drops yet unimagined.

For those who burn with faith or passion for a cause, the Internet will continue to provide a means both to fleece infidels for funds to pursue their goals and to provide an avenue for recruiting others to their flock. The Internet presents opportunities to target one's enemies for economic and even physical destruction via cyberterrorism.

Identity theft—already the number-one crime in the United States and rapidly expanding throughout the Internet world—can be expected to increase at a faster pace and wreak havoc on the financial and social worlds of millions around the globe. It well may be that the only way to gain control over identity theft will be the suggested DARPA reconfiguration of the Web and its security apparatus.

These, however, are short-term crises, which may soon become out moded by the ubiquitous wireless communications network that should be fully evolved by the middle to late years of the 2010s.

With no computers, and only signals in the air to handle all social and economic activity, expect new cybercrimes yet to be invented. Unless a values revolution (whether spiritual, religious, or humanistic in origin) occurs and humans/transhumans choose to refrain from stealing, killing, and defiling one another, you can bet creative malcontents will develop new methods to manipulate the system for their own ends.

In the quest for speed and efficiency on the Web, networks will grow in size and scope. For example, a network including all branches of a large bank grows when several banks merge and becomes larger still when all banks in a region join to reduce costs and speed service delivery. Then a national banking net emerges and is soon replaced by a multinational and finally a worldwide net. While the network becomes more powerful as it grows, it also becomes more vulnerable to attack. A shutdown of a regional net would create havoc, but the slack could be picked up by other nets. If the worldwide net is closed, however, true chaos would ensue, leaving banks and their customers at the mercy of blackmailers, extortionists, or terrorists. Thus, the larger the networks (e.g., energy, medical, education; regional, international, worldwide), the more critical security becomes.

On the other hand, there may be a greater threat evolving from the powerful technology available to thwart cybercrime and, indeed, all criminal activity. Authorities have long said, "If you have nothing to hide, you have nothing to fear" when talking about police state surveillance capabilities. This theory may well be tested by the evolving technology of the next few years: All activity could be seen and recorded, ready for retrieval and prosecution. Next comes the development of preventive strategies. Do we really want to live in a society where law is supreme, without recourse, and where mistakes are not allowed, where "the record" is proof positive, and where there is no place for plea bargaining, mediation, or arbitration? Have we evolved to this level of "perfection"?

TAMING THE CYBERCRIMINAL

The future path through cyberspace is filled with threats and opportunities, most of which cannot even be imagined today. With the equivalent of 5,000 years of technological progress expected between 2000 and 2025, it's difficult to forecast the dilemmas that lie ahead, but thanks to the creativity and genius of William Gibson, Ray Kurzweil, and others like them, some predictions have been made and can be used as a basis for forecasting future cybercrime and crime fighting.

The Internet as we know it—computers, Web sites, e-mail, blogs, e-commerce, etc.—may be outdated as soon as the early years of the next decade (the "twenty-teens"). All communication will be handled by a seamless, wireless network of airborne signals moving between nanobots and individuals with transmitters implanted in them. At this point, cyberoffenses will become very personal, as an attack on the Web is a direct attack on the user—possibly even invading his brain and memory stored in neural networks.

As nanoscience advances to the point that bots in the atmosphere capture and record all spoken and physical activity, the choice for law enforcement—and society—will evolve: Do we tightly control all human interaction by holding individuals responsible for every deed and action (each of which is supported by permanently stored evidence) in an efficiently networked Web, or do we allow creativity and individualism to emerge by refusing to set boundaries and jurisdictions on the Internet, leaving it much as it is today—without management or enforcement?

Choosing a "total control" future might curtail cybercrime and make the Web a safe vehicle for communication, socializing, commerce, etc., but at a substantial cost to privacy, freedom of speech, and other civil liberties. Choosing a "nobody-in-charge" future might allow a free flow of information and exchange of goods and services without government interference, but with a substantial threat to the economic and social lives of individuals and society itself posed by cyberoffenders.

By 2025, the whole concept of the Internet and cybercrime may be dumped into the dustbin of history. The greatest threat then might be the extreme difficulty of separating virtual (cyber) reality from physical reality. Already, psychologists warn that perception can be more important than truth: If cyberreality is more convincing than physical reality, the virtual world might become the "real" world. Welcome to The Matrix.

2

A Social Learning Theory Analysis of Computer Crime among College Students

William F. Skinner and Anne M. Fream

Computer crime is a fairly new area of research in criminology and deviance. With the exception of Hollinger few studies have examined the occurrence of illegal computer acts and virtually none have tried to offer a theoretical explanation for the behavior. In this article, the authors provide data on the lifetime, past year and past month prevalence of five illegal computer activities from a multistage sample (N == 581) of students at a southern university. The authors also examine the etiology of computer crime by testing the ability of social learning theory to explain these behaviors. Using multiple regression procedures, they demonstrate that measures of differential association, differential reinforcement and punishment, definitions, and sources of imitation are significantly related to computer crime. Findings from this study are compared with Hollinger's data and discussed in terms of why social learning theory. is an appropriate and useful theoretical perspective for understanding why, college students commit illegal computer acts.

William F. Skinner and Anne M. Frearn, "A social learning theory analysis of computer crime among college students" *Journal of Research in Crime and Delinquency* 34 (4): 495-519,1997. Copyright © 1997 by Sage Publications. Reprinted by permission of Sage Publications.

Computer crime is a fairly new area of research in the field of criminology and deviance. Awareness of computer crime emerged in the early 1960s (Parker 1976), and since then, estimates of damage done by computer hackers or thieves have ranged between $145 million to $5 billion annually in the United States alone (American Bar Association 1984; McEwen, Fester, and Nugent 1989; Parker 1987). And there are estimates that "the average computer crime costs about $630,000" (Gottleber 1988:47).

Of the few studies conducted on computer crime, most have been directed toward identifying individual and corporate victims of computer crime, consequences of the crime, profiles of the perpetrators, and the criminalization of computer crime (American Bar Association 1984; Gottleber 1988; Parker 1976; Schwartz, Rothfeder, and Lewyn 1990; Wong and Farquhar 1986).

These studies tend to represent the most extreme (costly) instances of computer crime that were detected. To date, little is known about the majority who have managed to escape detection. Hollinger (1988, 1991, 1992) was one of the first criminologists to examine computer crime among college students. He found that during a 15-week semester, 10 percent of his college-based sample reported being involved in software piracy and 3.3 percent had gained unauthorized access to another computer account. Although his study is highly informative and provides the groundwork for the current analysis, Hollinger examined only two types of illegal computer activity and did not provide an organized theoretical analysis of why college students commit computer crime.

There are two main objectives to this study. First, using a multistage sample of students at a southern university, we examine the lifetime, past year, and past month occurrence of five illegal computer activities — software piracy, guessing passwords to gain unauthorized access, gaining unauthorized access solely for the purpose of browsing, gaining unauthorized access for the purpose of changing information, and writing or using a program like a virus that destroys computerized data. Second, because virtually no research has examined the etiology of computer crime, we examine the ability of social learning theory to explain these behaviors (Akers 1985). On the basis of multiple regression procedures, we demonstrate that measures of differential association, differential reinforcement and punishment, definitions, and sources of imitation are significantly related to computer crime.

PREVIOUS LITERATURE

Most studies on computer crime have been done on the victims of computer crime rather than the perpetrator. This literature has centered on documenting which businesses were being targeted as victims of computer crime and how much it cost them (O'Donoghue 1986; Schwartz et al. 1990; Wong and Farquhar 1986). For instance, the American Bar Association (1984) found in its survey of 283 businesses and organizations (banks, accounting or financial services, computer and electronic firms, and major federal government departments and agencies) that 25 percent had been victims of computer crime and that individually, average losses were between $2 to $10 million. And although 39 percent of the companies could not identify the perpetrators of specific crimes, in 77 percent of the cases where the companies actually caught a computer criminal, the offender was a company employee.

One of the first statistical studies on unknown perpetrators of computer crime was done by Hollinger (1992) at the University of Florida. The computer-related crimes that 1,766 students responded to dealt with giving or receiving "pirated" computer software and accessing another person's computer account or files without the owner's knowledge or permission. The findings showed that during a 15-week semester, 10 percent of the respondents had broken copyright laws on computer software and 3.3 percent had unauthorized access to someone else's computer account or files. Although these figures may not seem to pose a real threat to computer security, Hollinger extrapolated this information to the rest of the student body to show that there would be more than 3,500 instances of felony piracy on campus and over 1,000 instances of illegal intrusions per semester.

Hollinger's examination of correlates of computer crime indicated that those students most likely to be involved in piracy were male, 22 years of age and older, seniors and graduate students, Asian or Hispanic, cohabitating with someone of the opposite sex, and enrolled in majors dealing with forestry, engineering, business, liberal arts, and science. For involvement in unauthorized computer accounts access, the only significant difference occurred for gender, with male students significantly more likely than female students to engage in this type of computer crime. All other variables, although showing some trends, were not significantly correlated with unauthorized access.

Hollinger did find two variables that were strongly correlated with computer crime — friends' involvement and perceived certainty of being caught. When students in Hollinger's study reported that none of their best friends had been occasionally involved in piracy, less than 2 percent had committed the act. On the other hand, when more than half of the students' best friends had occasionally committed piracy, almost 40 percent had committed the act themselves. Similarly, about one-third of the students who had more than half their best friends involved in illegal computer account access had engaged in the same activity. Hollinger also found that when the source of social control was university officials, there was a moderately strong, negative relationship between perceived certainty of being caught and frequency of piracy. A similar negative relationship was found between perceived certainty of being caught by fellow students and self-reported piracy. These two deterrence variables did not, however, significantly relate to unauthorized access to computer accounts.

We are in the very beginning stages of understanding and explaining computer crime. Most information to date has been anecdotal, based on face-to-face interviews with a few known computer criminals, or gleaned from victim surveys that were more interested in whether the perpetrators were employees. Although Hollinger's (1992) study was highly informative and lays the groundwork for future research, it was limited: Only two acts of computer crime were included in the questionnaire, the prevalence and incidence of computer crime were restricted to the previous four months, the analysis did not examine a theoretical model explaining computer crime, and no multivariate analysis was done.

This study attempts to overcome these limitations by first providing additional epidemiological information about computer crime. This includes the lifetime, past month, and past year prevalence of five types of illegal computer activity. Second, we test hypotheses that relate social learning theory variables (Akers 1985) to the past year frequency of three types of computer crime and a computer crime index using multivariate procedures.

SOCIAL LEARNING THEORY AND COMPUTER CRIME

As one of the major theories of deviance and crime, social learning theory provides an ideal context in which to understand computer crime. First, it has been empirically verified across numerous studies. Furthermore, it claims to be a general theory that applies to all types of deviant behavior (see Akers 1985 for a discussion). Thus, it should be applicable to illegal computer activities. Second, the very nature of computer crime requires that individuals learn not only how to operate a highly technical piece of equipment but also specific procedures, programming, and techniques for using the computer illegally. And third, as Sutherland and Cressey (1974) state, "An individual learns not only the techniques of committing the crime, no matter how complex or simple, but he/she learns specific motives, drives, rationalizations, and attitudes" (p. 75). Akers's (1985) theoretical synthesis of differential association and operant behavioral principles (Bandura 1986; Skinner 1953) elaborates on this theme.

Social learning theory is organized around four major concepts: differential association, differential reinforcement/punishment, definitions, and imitation. Differential association refers to the process by which individuals, operating in different social contexts, become exposed to, and ultimately learn, normative definitions favorable and unfavorable to criminal and legal behavior (Akers 1994). Although the family and peer groups tend to be the most important social groups in which differential association occurs, other contexts such as schools can be equally important to learning normative definitions. Research has clearly demonstrated a moderate to strong relationship between association with conforming and deviant others and deviant behavior (Burkett and Jensen 1975; Kandel et al. 1976, Krohn et al. 1985).

Definitions are attitudes about certain behavior learned through the process of differential association, imitation, and general interaction or exposure to various sources of learning located in one's social environment. In essence, they are "orientations, rationalizations, definitions of situations, and other evaluative and moral attitudes that define the commission of an act as right or wrong, good or bad, desirable or undesirable, justified or unjustified" (Akers 1994:97). Definitions can be of a general nature (e.g., moral or religious norms that guide general behavior) or specific to particular conforming and nonconforming behavior. Moreover, social learning distinguishes between positive, negative, and neutralizing definitions. Positive definitions define illegal behavior as desirable, acceptable, and permissible. Negative definitions define illegal behavior as undesirable, unacceptable, and wrong. And neutralizing definitions define illegal behavior as excusable, justifiable, and tolerable.

Differential reinforcement/punishment is a concept that captures the diversity of anticipated and actual consequences of engaging in certain behavior. It refers to the balance of social and nonsocial (i.e., physical) rewards and punishments associated with behavior. As Akers (1997) contends, positive reinforcers (e.g., approval from friends, family, teachers) and negative reinforcers (e.g., the avoidance of unpleasant experiences) tend to increase the likelihood that a certain act will occur. On the other hand, positive punishers such as reprimands or more punitive reactions to behavior and negative punishers such as the removal or retraction of rewards, praise, or affection tend to decrease the likelihood that a certain act will occur. Both reinforcers and punishers can, and most of the time do, exist for any behavior. Therefore, it is the balance between these two exigencies that predicts behavior: "Whether individuals will refrain from or commit a crime at any given time (and whether they will continue or desist from doing it in the future) depends on the past, present, and anticipated future rewards and punishment for their actions" (Akers 1994:98).

Finally, imitation refers to the modeling of certain behavior through the observation of others. Sources of imitation or modeling come primarily from salient social groups (parents, peers, teachers) and other sources such as the media. Imitation tends to be more important in the initial stages of learning deviant behavior and less important, although still having some effect, in the maintenance and cessation of behavior.

Because of its complexity, any full test of social learning theory requires operationalizing and measuring numerous variables (Akers et al. 1979; Akers and La Greca 1991; Krohn et al. 1985). We do not claim in this study to completely test social learning theory and, in some instances, do not operationalize the concepts as directly as more extensive studies. However, learning theory does provide a theoretical basis for hypothesizing relationships among selected learning variables and computer crime. Therefore, findings of hypothesized relationships provide support for the theory, and findings counter to the hypothesized relationships detract from the theory.

Because peer groups are undoubtedly the major social context in which college students interact, they will undoubtedly have a great impact on learning computer crime. Friends can be a source for learning the "technical" component of computer crime (e.g., how to bypass a security system or program a virus). They also can provide access to software for the purposes of pirating. Most important, it is in the peer group where an individual is exposed to the various norms and values relating to legal and illegal computer activities. This interaction can be face-to-face or through a "virtual" peer group, where interaction occurs electronically. Thus, we would expect that the more college students associate with peers who are engaging in illegal computer activity, the greater the frequency of the behavior.

Legal statutes provide a source for negative definitions of computer crime. Virtually every state has enacted legislation making a variety of computer activities illegal (Hollinger and Lanza-Kaduce 1988; Soma, Smith, and Sprague 1985). And in our sample, close to 90 percent of college students know that pirating software, guessing passwords, and unauthorized accessing of computer accounts are illegal (Fream 1993). Thus, we would expect that greater endorsement of the laws against computer crime would reduce the frequency of the behavior. Although students may approach the computer world with their moral and ethical beliefs intact, social groups such as friends or older students can influence illegal computer activity under the guise that "everybody does it." That is, students begin to adopt attitudes or neutralizing definitions that rationalize these unethical and illegal computer practices. These rationalizations, learned from friends, movies, printed media, and other sources temper the illegality of the act. In this study, we operationalize a number of neutralizing definitions and hypothesize them to be positively related to computer crime.

Hollinger (1992) found a fairly strong negative relationship between perceived certainty of apprehension and software piracy. On one hand, this could be a surprising finding because judicial leniency has been a problem that the federal war on computer crime has recently experienced. The biggest computer crime cases in history have resulted in dismissals or relatively light punishments (Hafner and Markoff 1991; Hanson 1991: Lewyn and Schwartz 1991). Consequently, young computer criminals may realize from reading articles and from experiences they or their friends have had that they are very unlikely to get caught and if they do, very little will be done to punish them.

On the other hand, with the increase in computer literacy, a heightened awareness primarily ascribable to the media of how computer crime affects individuals, and slightly stiffer penalties given to perpetrators. the perceived threat of legal apprehension and punishment may, as Hollinger's data suggest, serve as a source of differential reinforcement/punishment that deters individuals from committing computer crime. Two aspects of deterrence — perceived certainty of apprehension and severity of punishment — are used in this study to test the hypothesis that the greater the perceived deterrent effect of being caught and severely punished, the less likely college students will engage in illegal computer activities.

Finally, certain role models can serve as a source of imitation for computer crime. Besides family and friends, one of the major sources of imitation for college students is college teachers. Teachers' behavior can impart moral and legal standards. However, if a teacher advocates or engages in any form of computer crime, it can have the damaging effect of condoning and reinforcing (either directly or vicariously) illegal computer activities. For example, a university faculty member, in his letter to the editor of the New York Times, recommended that "bright youngsters who breach computer security should receive commendation, not condemnation" (Pfuh), 1987:121). And Parker (1987) notes that at the California Institute of Technology, students reportedly received course credit for taking control of the computerized scoreboard during the 1984 Rose Bowl game. Thus, we hypothesize that the more students learn about computer crime from family and teachers, the more they will engage in the behavior. In addition, to the extent that college students hear about or observe teachers engaging in or encouraging students to become involved in computer crime, they may begin to imitate this behavior.

Another very influential area where role models abound is the media. As Hollinger and Lanza-Kaduce (1988) convincingly demonstrate in their study of the criminalization process of computer laws, "there are several ways in which the media influence perceptions about crime and criminal enactment" (pp. 114-15). They argue that the media provide the public with a "sense of frequency" about computer crime and help to symbolically "influence the social definition of the phenomenon," both of which fuel the criminalization process. Paradoxically, the media cannot only be viewed as a mechanism for communicating the social threat of computer crime but also contain numerous examples of negative role models that are imitated by would-be computer criminals. Such images serve as teaching roles by giving their audience new or creative methods of hacking into systems or writing sophisticated programs. Because computer-literate people with an affinity toward improving and challenging their technical abilities are always looking for new information, one can expect that the frequency of computer crime will increase as individuals are exposed to various media sources — books/magazines. TV/movies, and computer bulletin boards - -where they an learn about computer crime and where the illegal activity is portrayed in a favorable, glamorous, and appealing light.

METHODOLOGY
SAMPLE AND PROCEDURES

A multistage sampling procedure was used to administer a confidential, self-administered questionnaire to a sample of 581 undergraduate students at a major university in a southern state. The aim was to survey students enrolled in three colleges within the university that have academic departments with the highest levels of computer usage and students who have a broad knowledge of computer applications and are more likely to know how to commit a computer crime. As such, we do not have a representative sample of all students attending the university. Rather, we purposively sample students to maximize variation on our dependent variable — computer crime.

The first stage involved a selection of colleges from among the 17 within the university that had the highest levels of computer usage by students. The three colleges chosen were Arts and Sciences, Business and Economics, and Engineering. These particular colleges were specifically selected on the basis of the findings from Hollinger's (1992) study, which indicated that the highest rates of computer crime would come from the departments that belonged to those three colleges. Also, the university's computer security and contingency planning officer suggested that illegal computer activity, if it has occurred would most likely be committed by students within those three colleges more so than any of the other 14 colleges.

In the second stage, departments were selected from the three colleges. The 13 departments chosen within the College of Arts and Sciences were limited to the social sciences and natural sciences. These departments have typically required some degree of computer expertise other than basic word processing skills to be applied to course work and assignments. All five departments within the College of Business and Economics and all eight departments from the College of Engineering were incorporated into the sampling frame.

In the third stage, undergraduate classes were randomly selected from those departments. The list of undergraduate classes offered in the spring of 1993 was reduced to include only those classes that were required or considered as departmental electives by the university for degree status. This excludes internships, independent studies, fieldwork, or self-directed reading courses. A random selection of 45 classes was taken from the edited sampling frame until about 950 students had been chosen, based on the maximum enrollment figures given for each class. Of those 45 classes, 30 were scheduled to be surveyed. A total of 581 students participated in the study. which represented a 60.2 percent response rate of the 965 students enrolled in the classes.

Table 1 shows the demographics of the sample as compared to the university's 1992 fall enrollment figures. Most participants are male (60.8 percent). However, it should be noted that the college with the largest number of participants, Engineering, is 84 percent male and has the lowest number of female students (276) enrolled than any other college within the university (Kentucky Council on Higher Education 1992). There was also a larger percentage of White students completing. surveys (87.6 percent) than any other race or ethnic group, but that number is equivalent to the university's enrollment figures. Because the principle sampling unit was undergraduate classes, it was not unexpected that close to 90 percent of the sample contains 18-to 25-year-olds.

TABLE 1: Demographics of Sample

University Demographics Enrollment	Sample	1992
Gender		
Female (12,190)	37.9 (220)	50.4
Male (12,007)	60.8 (353)	49.6
Race		
White (21,315)	87.6 (509)	88.1
African American (998)	4.3 (25)	4.1
Asian (327)	5.9 (34)	1.4
Other (1,557)	1.5 (9)	6.4
Age		
18-19 (4,715)	22.4 (130)	19.5
20-21 (5,564)	35.3 (205)	23.0

22–25 (6,463)	29.6 (172)	26.7
26 and over (7,407)	11.3 (66)	30.6
College		
Agriculture (1,078)	4.1 (24)	4.5
Arts and Sciences, Natural Sciences (1,646)	9.5 (55)	6.8
Arts and Sciences, Social Sciences (1,944)	16.7 (97)	8.0
Arts and Sciences, other (4,220)	6.4 (37)	17.4
Arts and Sciences, total (7,810)	32.5 (189)	32.3
Business & Economics (2,746)	23.1 (143)	11.3
Engineering (2,107)	29.4 (171)	8.7
Other (10,456)	10.5 (61)	43.2
[Year.sup.a]		
Freshman (4,027)	10.7 (62)	16.6
Sophomore (3,550)	19.8 (115)	14.7
Junior (3,685)	29.3 (170)	15.2
Senior (5,200)	33.2 (193)	21.5
Graduate (4,980)	5.0 (29)	20.6
Total (24,197)	100.0 (581)	100.0

a. High school and fifth-year students were not included.

MEASUREMENT OF VARIABLES

To estimate the prevalence and frequency of computer crime, five types of activities were measured: knowingly used, made, or gave to another person a "pirated" copy of commercially sold computer software; tried to guess another's password to get into his or her computer account or files; accessed another's computer account or files without his or her knowledge or permission just to look at the information or files; added, deleted. changed, or printed any information in another's computer files without the owner's knowledge or permission; and wrote or used a program that would destroy someone's computerized data (e.g., a virus, logic bomb, or trojan horse). Prevalence rates were computed from responses (never, within the past month, within the past year, one to four years ago, and five or more years ago) to questions on the lifetime, past year, and past month occurrence of each type of offense. Frequency was measured by asking students how often in the past year they had committed each of the five types of computer crimes. The response categories were the following: never, 1 to 2 times, 3 to 5 times, 6 to 9 times, and 10 times or more, Finally, a computer crime index was created that summed the responses to the frequency measure (Cronbach's alpha = .60).

Differential association was measured using the following question: "How many of your best friends have done one or more of the five computer acts?" The possible responses were none, just a few, about half, more than half, and all or almost all. To measure negative definitions, respondents were asked to indicate their agreement or disagreement with the statement, "Because it is against the law, I would never do anything, illegal using a computer." The responses range from strongly disagree to strongly agree. Neutralizing definitions were assessed on the same 4-point scale using the following statements: If people do not want me to get access to their computer or computer systems, they should have better computer security; I should be able to look at any computer information that the government, a school, a business, or an individual has on me even if they do not give me access; I would never turn in a friend who used, made, or gave to another person a "pirated" copy of software; I would never turn in a friend who accessed another's computer account or files without the owner's knowledge or permission; and it is OK for me to pirate commercial software because it costs too much for me to buy.

We asked respondents to respond to a series of deterrence questions as our measure of differential reinforcement/punishment. In earlier work, Akers (1973, 1977) has shown how deterrence variables can be subsumed under social learning theory. The certainty of apprehension dimension of deterrence was measured using the following questions: How likely is it that you would be caught using, making, or giving to another person a "pirated" copy of software? and How likely is it that you would be caught accessing or trying to access another's computer account or files without his or her knowledge or permission? Possible answers ranged from never to very likely. The severity of punishment aspect to deterrence was measured by the following questions: How severe do you think the punishment would be if you got caught using, making, or giving to another person a "pirated" copy of software? And How severe do you think the punishment would be if you got caught accessing or trying to access another's computer account or files without his or her knowledge or permission? Possible answers ranged from not severe at all to very severe.

To assess the sources of imitation, students were asked the following question: How much have you learned about ... [the five computer crimes listed for the dependent variables] from each of the following: family, teachers, books or magazines, television and movies, and computer bulletin boards. These variables do not directly measure observation of the behavior as Akers conceptualized imitation but rather assume that by observing the behavior or reading about it, students imitate and learn computer crime from different sources. For each source of imitation, the students had a 5-point measure ranging from learned nothing to learned everything. Two additional measures of imitation from teachers were how many times the student had seen or heard any of their college or high school teachers offer students the chance to "pirate" a copy of commercially sold computer software and praise or encourage students who have done computer activities you thought they should not be doing. The possible responses ranged from never to 10 times or more. The former measure referencing teachers could be seen as tapping opportunity and the latter tapping vicarious reinforcement, but both still reflect the extent to which teachers are sources of imitation for students.

RESULTS

EXTENT OF COMPUTER CRIME

The percentage of college students engaging in computer crime is reported in Table 2. In general, the lifetime, past year, and past month rates tend to decrease as the seriousness of the activity increases. For instance, the most common form of illegal activity reported was pirating software. At least once in their lives, 41.3 percent of the students surveyed had knowingly used, copied, or given to another person a copy of pirated software; 33.9 percent had pirated software in the past year; 12.4 percent had done so within the past month. On the other end of the seriousness continuum, 2.1 percent had written or used a program like a virus or logic bomb to destroy someone's computerized data at least once in their life; 1.7 percent had done so in the past year; only 0.3 percent (less than five cases) had done so in the past month. In total, 49.7 percent of the students surveyed had at some point during their lives committed at least one of the five computer crimes examined in this study.

TABLE 2: Prevalence of Software Piracy, Guessing Passwords to Gain Unauthorized Access, Unauthorized Access Just to Browse, Unauthorized Access to Change Files, and Writing or Using a Virus by Demographics[a]

	Piracy			Guessing Passwords			Browse			Change Files			Virus		
	Lifetime	Past Year	Past Month	Lifetime	Past Year	Past Month	Lifetime	Past Year	Past Month	Lifetime	Past Year	Past Month	Lifetime	Past Year	Past Month
Gender															
Female (220)	19.5	15.0	3.2	13.6	10.5	3.2	9.5	5.9	1.8	2.3	2.3	0.9	0.0	0.0	0.0
Male (353)	55.5	46.5	18.4	25.2	20.1	6.2	22.7	17.8	4.2	10.5	6.8	2.0	3.4	2.5	0.6
Race															
White (509)	43.4	35.6	13.6	20.6	16.3	4.9	18.5	13.9	5.5	7.6	5.1	1.6	2.2	1.8	0.4
African American (25)	4.0	4.0	0.0	24.0	16.0	4.0	12.0	8.0	0.0	0.0	0.0	0.0	0.0	0.0	0.0
Asian (34)	38.2	29.4	5.9	14.7	14.7	8.8	8.8	8.8	0.0	8.8	8.8	2.9	0.0	0.0	0.0
Other (9)	33.3	33.3	0.0	22.2	11.1	0.0	11.1	0.0	0.0	0.0	0.0	0.0	0.0	0.0	0.0
Age															
18-19 (130)	33.1	25.4	6.2	23.1	22.3	8.5	16.2	13.8	4.6	5.4	4.6	1.5	1.5	1.5	1.5
20-21 (205)	40.5	36.1	13.2	23.9	18.5	6.3	18.0	13.7	4.9	7.8	4.4	0.5	2.4	2.0	0.0
22-25 (172)	47.1	37.2	16.3	16.3	12.8	1.7	16.3	11.6	3.5	6.4	4.1	1.2	1.7	1.2	0.0
26 and over (66)	47.6	37.3	13.4	16.4	6.0	3.0	22.4	14.9	9.0	11.9	9.0	4.5	1.5	1.5	0.0
College															
Agriculture (24)	45.8	37.5	8.3	33.3	20.8	12.5	20.8	8.3	8.3	12.5	8.3	4.2	4.2	4.2	0.0
Arts and Sciences, Natural Sciences (55)	29.1	21.8	9.1	16.4	20.9	3.6	18.2	12.7	5.5	3.6	3.6	1.8	1.8	1.8	0.0
Arts and Sciences, Social Sciences (97)	43.3	35.1	14.4	20.6	14.4	2.1	18.6	12.4	3.1	7.2	6.2	1.0	3.1	3.1	1.0
Arts and Sciences, other (37)	21.6	18.9	2.7	16.2	16.2	2.7	24.3	24.3	5.4	8.1	5.4	0.0	0.0	0.0	0.0
Business and Economics (134)	32.8	29.1	9.7	20.1	17.2	6.0	14.2	11.2	3.7	6.0	4.5	3.0	0.7	0.7	0.0
Engineering (171)	57.3	47.4	19.9	23.4	18.7	6.4	16.4	12.9	4.7	10.5	5.8	1.2	3.5	2.9	0.6
Other (61)	32.8	23.0	3.3	14.8	13.1	3.3	19.7	13.1	8.2	1.6	0.0	0.0	0.0	0.0	0.0

TABLE 2: Continued

	Piracy			Guessing Passwords			Browse			Change Files			Virus		
	Lifetime	Past Year	Past Month	Lifetime	Past Year	Past Month	Lifetime	Past Year	Past Month	Lifetime	Past Year	Past Month	Lifetime	Past Year	Past Month
Year															
Freshman (52)	32.3	24.2	8.1	22.6	22.6	4.8	14.5	12.9	3.2	6.5	4.8	1.6	0.0	0.0	0.0
Sophomore (115)	35.7	29.5	7.8	22.6	20.9	10.4	13.9	12.2	7.0	7.8	7.8	1.7	2.6	2.6	1.7
Junior (170)	41.2	35.9	13.5	22.4	15.3	5.3	20.6	14.1	4.1	8.8	4.7	0.8	2.4	2.4	0.0
Senior (193)	43.5	33.7	14.0	18.1	13.0	2.1	16.2	14.0	5.2	3.6	2.1	2.1	1.0	1.0	0.0
Graduate (29)	72.4	65.5	24.1	17.2	13.8	3.4	13.8	10.3	3.4	3.4	3.4	0.0	0.0	0.0	0.0
Total (561)	41.3	33.9	12.4	20.7	16.4	5.0	17.6	13.1	4.6	7.4	5.0	1.6	2.1	1.7	0.3

a. Number of cases in parentheses.

In general, there is a 3:1 to 2:1 ratio of male students to female students among those who admitted committing the activities. And as the far right columns in Table 2 indicate, writing or using a virus is strictly the province of male college students. With the exception of lifetime and past year prevalence of guessing passwords, White and Asian students are more likely to engage in illegal computer acts than other racial groups (Swinyard, Heikki, and Ah 1990). There does not seem to be a consistent relationship between the prevalence of illegal computer activity and the student's college. For instance, engineering students report the highest involvement in pirating software, whereas agricultural students tend to have the highest prevalence for guessing passwords, gaining access to accounts to change files, and writing or using a virus. Finally, except for the unusually high percentage of graduate students who pirate software, there does not appear to be any substantial relationship of computer crime to age and year in school. Indeed, subsequent correlational analysis indicated that age had a small, negative relationship with only frequency of guessing a password ($r = -.07$).

Table 3 shows both how often those involved in computer crime committed the act and an estimated minimum and maximum incidence figure. Most of the students who had admitted to committing a computer crime had done so fairly infrequently. For instance, most password guessers (73.4 percent), browsers (63.1 percent), and virus writers/users (85.7 percent) had done this act one to two times in the past year. However, it is interesting to note that whereas about 44 percent of students who pirate software did so only 1 to 2 times in the past year, about one-third (31.8 percent) had committed this crime 10 times or more. By taking the minimum number for each of the following categories (1-2 times, 3-5 times, 6-9 times, and 10 times or more), we calculated the minimum and maximum number of occurrences for each of the five crimes in the past year. These figures indicate that 198 students pirated software at least 906 times and possibly more than 1,167 times. Assuming that the pirated software was priced between $100 and $500, these students cost software companies and distributors between about $90,600 and $453,000 in lost revenues. Also, in the past year, there were between 223 and 335 occurrences of students who tried to guess passwords to gain unauthorized access to computer accounts or files. Illegally gained access, whether the purpose was to just browse the files or to change information, occurred between 312 and 451 times in the past year. And although an extremely small number of students were involved in writing or using viruses, they did so at the very least 9 times and possibly more than 17 times in the past year.

26

TABLE 3: Frequency and Incidence of Computer Crime in the Past Year

Frequency	Pirated Software	Guessed Passwords	Unauthorized Access Just to Browse	Unauthorized Access to Change Files	Wrote or Used a Virus
1-2 times	43.9 (87)	73.4 (69)	63.1 (48)	40.0 (10)	85.7 (6)
3-5 times	16.7 (33)	12.8 (12)	13.2 (10)	40.0 (10)	14.3 (<5)
6-9 times	7.6 (15)	3.2 (<5)	9.2 (7)	8.0 (<5)	— —
10 times or more	31.8 (63)	10.6 (10)	14.5 (11)	12.0 (<5)	— —
Total number of students	100.0 (198)	100.0 (94)	100.0 (76)	100.0 (25)	100.0 (7)
Minimum Incidents	906	223	230	82	9
Maximum incidents[a]	1,167+	335+	330+	121+	17+

a. The maximum number of incidents is based on the highest number of each of the given ranges. For the category of "10 times or more," estimates were based on 11 occurrences, so the actual maximum number may be higher.

These findings add to a small store of knowledge on the extent and seriousness of computer-related violations. They do not help, however, in explaining individual differences in committing computer crimes. We have argued that the explanation lies at least, in part, in differences in exposure to models of association with other offenders, taking on definitions favorable to engaging in unlawful computer uses, and failing to be deterred by fear of being caught and punished for such acts. We turn now to examining these social learning hypotheses.

SOCIAL LEARNING THEORY ANALYSIS

The regression analysis for determining the predictive value of the social learning variables included in this study appears in Table 4. The responses on two of the illegal computer acts examined in this study — gaining access to change files and writing/using a virus — were so limited that the acts were not included in this analysis. An index including all individual acts was used in the regression analysis as a global measure of computer crime.

TABLE 4: Standardized (Unstandardized) Regression Coefficients for Social Learning Predictor Variables (*N* = 545)

	Piracy	Guess Password	Illegal Access to Browse	Computer Crime Index
Sources of imitation				
Family	.12 (.18)*	−.06 (−.05)	−.02 (−.01)	.04 (.10)
Teachers	−.05 (−.07)	.05 (.04)	.03 (.02)	.01 (.01)
Books/magazines	.03 (.04)	−.07 (−.05)	.03 (.02)	.02 (.05)
TV/movies	−.07 (−.11)	.01 (.01)	−.07 (−.06)	−.08 (−.20)
Bulletin boards	.04 (.08)	.12 (.13)*	.07 (.08)	.10 (.37)*
Teacher pirated	.12 (.20)*			.14 (.45)*
Teacher encouraged	−.01 (−.03)	.10 (.13)*	−.01 (−.01)	.02 (.09)
Differential association				
Friends	.28 (.38)*	.18 (.13)*	.12 (.09)*	.26 (.62)*
Reinforce-punish				
Certainty-piracy	.03 (.05)			.03 (.10)
Severity-piracy	−.01 (−.02)			.06 (.16)
Certainty-access		.07 (.05)	.02 (.01)	.02 (.04)
Severity-access		−.07 (−.05)	−.13 (−.10)*	−.08 (−.22)*
Definitions				
Against the law	−.15 (−.22)*	−.18 (−.14)*	−.18 (−.15)*	−.23 (−.62)*
Better security		.17 (.13)*	.12 (.09)*	.06 (.15)
Any access		.01 (.01)	.00 (.00)	−.04 (−.09)
Never report friend piracy	.12 (.21)*			.13 (.40)*
Never report friend access		.04 (.04)	.07 (.07)	−.04 (−.11)
Software too costly	.11 (.17)*			.07 (.20)
Control variable				
Gender	−.12 (−.33)*	.01 (.02)	−.04 (−.07)	−.08 (−.39)*
R^2	.37*	.20*	.16*	.40*
M	1.78	1.24	1.23	6.35
SD	1.32	0.68	0.72	2.35

*$p < .05$.

The results of the regression analysis show significant support for the application of social learning theory to illegal computer behavior by college students. When all the relevant variables were incorporated into the full regression model for each of the four dependent variables, 37 percent of the variance was explained in software piracy, 20 percent for guessing passwords to gain unauthorized access, 16 percent for unauthorized access for the purpose of browsing, and 40 percent for the computer crime index. If gender is entered first into the regression equation and all the learning variables second, the learning variables by themselves account for about 75 percent of the reported explained variance when gender does have a significant effect and 90 percent when gender does not have a significant effect.

Table 4 shows that the sources of imitation variables operate differently depending on the type of computer crime. Learning about illegal computer activities from family members has a significant positive relationship with piracy. A similar positive effect is evidence when students frequently observe or hear about teachers pirating software. Teachers also significantly affect guessing passwords if students frequently observe or hear them encourage students to engage in illegal computer activity. It is also interesting to note that the more students learn about illegal computer activity from computer bulletin boards, the more likely they are to guess passwords and be frequently involved in all types of computer crime examined in this study. This points to the viability of the virtual" peer group as a source of learning computer crime.

The two main social learning variables in this study, differential association and definitions, consistently influence all types of reported computer offenses. Differentially associating with friends who participate in computer crime is the strongest predictor of piracy and the computer crime index. Definitions associated with adherence to the laws against these acts are significantly and negatively related to all types of computer crime and are the most important predictor of illegal access to browse.

Whereas our findings on friends' effects concur with those reported by Hollinger (1992), the findings on certainty of apprehension are at odds with his findings. That is, we did not find that the certainty of apprehension was negatively related to piracy. Also, the severity of punishment for piracy did not predict this type of behavior. However, our findings do concur with Hollinger's in that certainty of apprehension for illegal access to computer accounts does not deter college students from committing the act. Indeed, the only deterrence variable that significantly predicted computer crime (e.g, illegal access to browse) was the severity of punishment associated with illegal access. The hypothesis that differences in perceived punishment account for differences in violative behavior, therefore, was not supported. As we noted earlier, this variable did not incorporate perceived differences in social and nonsocial reinforcement for committing the acts. By leaving out that side of the balance, we have most likely underestimated the effects of the differential reinforcement process.

Our analysis of neutralizing definitions showed modest support for our hypotheses. College students who feel that companies and institutions should provide better security were more likely to guess passwords and browse accounts illegally than students not feeling this way. Also, when students felt that software companies overpriced their product and they would not report a friend who pirated software, they were more likely to pirate software and commit different types of computer crime than those not holding these attitudes. The other neutralizing definitions had no effect on any of the illegal acts.

Finally, gender plays an important role in explaining at least one type of illegal computer activity and computer crime in general. Controlling for the social learning variables in the equations, female students were significantly less likely to pirate software and be involved, overall, in computer crime than were male students.

DISCUSSION AND CONCLUSION

We looked at a segment of the population who are in an educational environment that not only offers access to the tools and techniques necessary to compete in a computer-literate society but also may provide conditions favorable to learning and committing computer crime. The prevalence analysis indicated that these activities may be higher and more widespread than was previously indicated by other studies. Hollinger (1992) found that during a 15-week semester, 10 percent of his sample had pirated software and 3.3 percent had gained illegal access to computer accounts without the owner's knowledge or permission. This study found that 34 percent of the sample had pirated software in the past year (12.4 percent in the past month) and 16 percent had gained illegal access, whether to browse or to change information (5 percent in the past month). Just by comparing the past month's rates of this study to Hollinger's 15-week rate, it is obvious that there is a higher prevalence of computer crime in our sample. However, this could be due to the fact that our sample was purposively selected from students in academic disciplines where computer crime was thought to be more concentrated, whereas Hollinger's sample was a random selection of the entire study body at his university. Also, this study was conducted one year later than the Hollinger study. Consequently, students in 1993 may be more exposed to, and involved with, computers than students in 1992. In essence, taken together, these two studies could be viewed as establishing high and low estimates of computer crime among college students. And although slightly higher levels of computer crime were reported by males, Whites, Asians, and engineering students, computer crime reaches across gender, race, age. year, and college categories.

The multivariate analysis showed strong support for social learning theory as a conceptual framework for understanding computer crime in general. It showed modest support for the theory as an explanation of some particular forms of computer crime such as gaining illegal access to browse other accounts and files. As with other types of deviance, one of the major predictors of computer crime is associating with friends who engage in the activity. Friends who are successful at certain activities or in scholastic areas are generally the ones whom other students seek out for help and advice. Also, friends are usually more willing to share such information or challenge others to best them at their new found games, programs, or techniques. Thus, it comes as no surprise that learning computer crime is primarily peer driven.

Our analysis of other sources of imitation indicated that computer crime is learned from a variety of conventional sources. Students learn about pirating from family members undoubtedly because they are the sources of pirated software, Siblings and even parents may have copies of new programs and games they illegally acquired from other sources and make them available to others in the family. Similarly, our analysis indicated that teachers who not only condoned piracy but who strongly advocated it by words and actions increased the frequency of piracy and commission of any type of computer crime among students.

However, one of the most interesting findings regarding sources of imitation concerns computer bulletin boards. Our analysis indicated that using computer bulletin boards increased the frequency of trying to guess passwords to gain illegal access and the number of illegal acts as measured by the computer crime index. This could be explained by the fact that computer bulletin boards are notorious for underground networks that post passwords to various corporate, governmental, and institutional computer systems. Because many government bulletin boards and various other systems use the generic password "anonymous," some students may have tried to gain access with this method only to find out that the system is open only to specific authorized users. Also, with electronic bulletin boards and the Internet, students can now see what computer systems throughout the world have to offer in the way of interesting applications, games, or information. However, because some of these offerings are view-only or have noninteractive access, students may try to find illegal ways of accessing this information.

Although most students were aware that computer crime is illegal, the possibility of suffering penalties seemed to have little effect on their behavior. Contrary to the Hollinger study, we did not find that the perceived certainty of apprehension and severity of punishment decreased the frequency of piracy. In fact, the only significant deterrent effect was associated with severity of punishment for illegally accessing accounts. One possible reason for this difference is that Hollinger specified the agents of social control — other students and administrative officials — and we did not. A more substantive interpretation is that there is neither a general nor specific deterrent effect that serves as a differential reinforcement/punishment for computer crime. Subsequent analysis of our data indicated that of the total number of students who participated in the survey, only 42 students (7.3 percent) have been caught and only 75 (13.3 percent) of those who responded had friends who were caught during or after illegal computer activity. If this is coupled with the more general recognition that "notorious" computer criminals are rarely apprehended or punished, there appears to be little incentive from a deterrence perspective for students to quit engaging in illegal computer activity. Also, as we have noted, the general concept of differential reinforcement that includes both rewards and punishment was underspecified in this study.

Where the law does affect the frequency of computer crime is in its educative effect. Our analysis indicated that in addition to differential association, the other most consistent predictor of computer crime was the negative definition that "because it is against the law, I would never do anything illegal using a computer." As Hollinger and Lanza-Kaduce (1988) indicate, "Computer crime laws are symbolic in that they `educate,' `moralize,' and `socialize' computer users" (p. 114). They point out, as we do above, that "if the primary function of the new computer statutes was to deter rampant abuse, one would expect the new laws to result in vigorous prosecution" (p. 117). However, vigorous prosecution has not been forthcoming. Indeed, Kevin Mitnick, the most recent hacker to receive nationwide publicity, was charged with 23 counts of breaking into a San Francisco area computer network. He plea-bargained and admitted to illegally possessing 15 telephone numbers to gain access to computer systems. For that crime, he received eight months in jail and had the other 22 counts dropped ("Hacker Is Said" 1995). If harsher punishments were levied against computer criminals, we would have expected a stronger effect from the deterrent variables. Thus, our data support Hollinger and Lanza-Kaduce's contention that computer laws serve more of a symbolic than a deterrent function.

We have not conducted a full test of social learning, and one could argue that if we had conducted such an analysis, we would have explained even more variance in computer crime. However, this study has demonstrated the utility of social learning in understanding a variety of illegal computer activities among college students. Future research should expand on these measures and test more complete social learning models. Moreover, because gender was found to influence some types of computer crime, additional research could focus on possible interaction effects between gender and the learning variables. Other types of samples should also be used to further investigate computer crime. Systematic studies of business employees, Internet companies, and Internet users could offer some valuable insights for understanding the breadth and depth of computer crime, its threat to the security of private information, and its monetary cost to society. Clearly, widespread illegal computer acts are being committed every day. Because educational institutions are teaching students how to use computers and provide access to computer technology, the best place to start teaching them computer ethics and laws should be in the classrooms.

NOTES

(1.) The Penal Code of the Kentucky Revised Statutes Sections 434.845, 434.850, and 434.855 relating to unlawful access to a computer and misuse of computer information became effective on July 13, 1984. Section 434.845 entitled "Unlawful Access to a Computer in the First Degree" states the following: (1) A person is guilty of unlawful access to a computer in the first degree when he knowingly and willfully, directly or indirectly accesses, causes to be accessed, or attempts to access any computer software, computer program, data, computer, computer system, computer network, or any part thereof, for the purpose of: (a) Devising or executing any scheme or artifice to defraud; or (b) Obtaining money, property, or services for themselves or another by means of false or fraudulent pretenses, representations, or promises; or (c) Altering, damaging, destroying or attempting to alter, damage, destroy any computer, computer system, or computer network, or any computer software, program, or data; (2) Accessing, attempting to access, or causing to be accessed any computer software, computer program, data, computer, computer system, computer network, or any part thereof, even though fraud, false or fraudulent pretenses, representations, or promises may have been involved in the access or attempt to access shall not constitute a violation of this section, if the sole purpose of the access was to obtain information and not to commit any other act proscribed by this section; and (3) Unlawful access to a computer in the first degree is a Class C felony. Section 434.850 entitled

"Unlawful Access to a Computer in the Second Degree" states the following: A person is guilty of unlawful access in the second degree when he without authorization knowingly and willfully, directly or indirectly accesses, causes to be accessed, or attempts to access any computer software, computer program, data, computer, computer system, computer network, or any part thereof and Unlawful access to a computer in the second degree is a Class A misdemeanor. Section 434.855 entitled "Misuse of Computer Information" states the following: A person is guilty of misuse of information when he: (a) Receives, conceals, or uses, or aids another in doing so, any proceeds of a violation of KRS 434.845; or (b) Receives, conceals, or uses or aids another in doing so, any books, records, documents, property, financial instrument, computer software, computer program, or other material, property, or objects, knowing the same to have been used in or obtained from a violation of KRS 434.845 and Misuse of computer information is a Class C felony. According to Section 532.020 of the Penal Code of the Kentucky Revised Statues, a class C felony has a prison term of at least 5 years but not more than 10 years. A person convicted of a class A misdemeanor can be sentenced to prison at least 90 days but not more than 12 months and could be fined up to a maximum of $500.

(2.) The social science departments chosen from the College of Arts and Science were composed of Anthropology, History, Economics, Geography, Political Science, Psychology, and Sociology, The natural sciences contained the following departments from the College of Arts and Sciences: Biology, Chemistry, Computer Science, Mathematics, Physics and Astronomy, and Statistics. This excludes a total of 12 departments in the College of Arts and Sciences: Classical Languages, English, French, German, Latin American Studies, Linguistics, Military Science, Philosophy, Russian and Eastern Studies, and Spanish and Italian. The following Interdisciplinary Minors were also excluded: African American Studies, Appalachian Studies, Religious Studies, and Women's Studies.

(3.) For the College of Business and Economics, these included Accounting, Decision Sciences, Economics, Finance, Management, and Marketing. For the College of Engineering, these included Agricultural Engineering, Chemical Engineering, Civil Engineering, Electrical Engineering, Engineering Mechanics, Geological Sciences, Material Science Engineering, Mechanical Engineering, and Mining Engineering.

(4.) Additional classes whose combined enrollments were in excess of the needed 500 to 600 students were chosen for several reasons. It was reasonable to assume that some faculty members would prefer that their classes not be surveyed or that the time period of data collection may conflict with class curriculums that would not be able to be adjusted to include the administration of the survey. Also, the number given on the database was the maximum number of available openings for each class. However, fewer students may actually have enrolled in any of the classes that were chosen or they may have dropped the class during the drop/add process at the beginning of the semester. The reverse was also a possibility if the faculty member allowed more than the stated number of students in his or her classroom. In addition, those students who attended more than one class where the survey was conducted were asked not to complete the survey for a second time. Also. students who were enrolled in one of the randomly selected classes and were minors (under the age of 18) were asked not to complete a questionnaire because of the necessity and difficulty associated with acquiring written parental consent and any breaches to confidentiality that could occur.

(5.) A total of 15 classes in the sample were not surveyed because a faculty member did not want his or her class included in the study, the timing of the data collection could not be scheduled into his or her curriculum, the students had been over-surveyed in a particular class, or the class chosen was a lab where the students would have been conducting experiments that would he difficult to interrupt.

(6.) We recognize that these measures do not capture important sources of rewards and punishments from family and friends that may be attached to successful pirating or other acts. The measures used in this study include only the punishment component of differential reinforcement emanating from formal social control. As such, these measures offer an incomplete test of the differential reinforcement/punishment process.

(7.) Multicollinearity is a concern in any multivariate analysis. In checking for this problem in the regression analysis, we found no variance inflation factor (VIF) over 2.00. Also, the threat of multicollinearity is reduced because we have not operationalized all the dimensions of the core concepts of social learning theory, in particular, differential reinforcement/punishment for family and friends and other moral or nonnative definitions.

Footnotes deleted.

2

Internet Pornography

3

Internet Providers to Cut off Child Porn

Three Companies Settle after Probe by Cuomo

Susan Schulman

Jun. 11 – Under pressure from the state attorney general, Internet providers Verizon, Time Warner Cable and Sprint are taking steps to block computer access to news groups that disseminate child pornography and to knock down Web sites hosting the illegal material.

The moves, long sought by the National Center for Missing & Exploited Children, are considered a significant effort to deal with the child pornography explosion on the Internet around the world.

"This is a major step forward. We hope this will become a model for the rest of the industry," said Ernie Allen, head of the center based in Alexandria, Va.

State Attorney General Andrew M. Cuomo announced the settlement Tuesday after an eight-month investigation by his office into the proliferation of online child pornography.

S. Schulman. Internet providers to cut off child porn: Three companies settle after probe by Cuomo. *The Buffalo News*, June 11, 2008. Copyright © 2008 The Buffalo News. Reprinted by permission.

Under the settlement, the three major Internet providers, which did not admit any wrongdoing, not only will take steps to rid their own networks of child pornography but also will contribute $1.12 million to fund additional efforts by the attorney general's office and the national center to remove child pornography from the Internet.

In "The Child Porn Pipeline," a series published last June, The Buffalo News revealed that most of the commercial child pornography disseminated worldwide — one study put the figure at 62 percent — is posted through Internet service providers in the United States.

The series described the national center's efforts to persuade service providers to shut down and block access to child pornography sites.

But many providers resisted, saying that policing the Internet was not their job.

A decade ago, service providers in Great Britain began closing sites and cutting off access to Internet child pornography.

British computer servers and Web sites, which once provided 18 percent of commercial child pornography produced in the world, now account for 1 percent.

While U. S. law enforcement focused much of its attention on arresting the people viewing, and to a lesser extent making and distributing, child pornography, Cuomo's investigation went after the Internet companies whose servers and networks host and disseminate the material.

Allen has supported that approach, saying so many people view child pornography that "unless you turn off the spigot, you are not really going to address the enormity of the problem."

The undercover probe by the attorney general's office found 88 different news groups — online bulletin boards where users can upload and download files — with a total of 11,390 lewd photos of young children, including some being raped.

Posing as subscribers, investigators then complained to the Internet providers about the availability of child pornography.

But the material remained available, and the service providers contended they were not responsible for the material that others share on news groups or post on Web sites, Cuomo said.

But he rejected that argument and threatened to bring charges against the companies, which led to the settlement announced Tuesday.

Two of the three service providers agreed to block access to news groups linked to child pornography, while Time Warner said it will eliminate news groups from its services.

"It's a small percentage of our users," said Alex Dudley, Time Warner spokesman.

"We are not comfortable with them," he continued. "Our best recourse is to take them down. Time Warner is discontinuing news groups."

The three Internet companies also agreed to work with the national center to remove Web sites hosting child pornography.

The center maintains a list of 39,000 Web addresses that contained child pornography, Allen said.

A few of the larger Internet companies use the list to identify and remove child pornography, but thousands of smaller Internet companies do not, the center has said.

Time Warner said that, upon learning that no action had been taken on a child pornography report, the company, under its established policy, immediately submitted the report to the national center.

Once it received confirmation of child pornography, the company took down the news groups, Dudley said.

At Verizon, any child pornography news group reported to the company was taken down promptly, said Eric Rabe, vice president for communications.

Verizon and Time Warner also are working with the national center to take down any confirmed child pornography sites, their spokesmen said.

Sprint spokesman Matthew Sullivan said getting child pornography off the Internet is one of the company's priorities.

"Battling this scourge requires close collaboration of many parties," he said at Tuesday's news conference in Cuomo's New York City office.

Verizon, with 8.2 million subscribers, and Time Warner's Road Runner, with 7.9 million, are two of the five largest Internet service providers in the world, while Sprint is one of the three largest wireless companies in the United States.

While the five largest companies control a major share of the Internet market, thousands of smaller servers are also involved in Internet operations.

Cuomo said his investigation is continuing.

4

Pedophiles in Wonderland

Censoring the Sinful in Cyberspace

Gabrielle Russell

The primary allure of virtual worlds, and no doubt a large part of their success, derives from the anonymity they afford their denizens. In the real world, people often tailor their behavior according to what they perceive as their society's norms of what is appropriate for people of their age, appearance, job, social skills, or social status. The physical remove of virtual worlds inspires people to speak and move about freely, uninhibited by a fear of real-world repercussions. Recent developments at the intersection of cyberspace and terrestrial law, however, suggest that not all actions in virtual worlds are consequence-free.

This Comment analyzes the widely publicized issue of ageplay in virtual worlds, and discusses the merits of past and present regulations criminalizing such behavior. Congress has made numerous attempts to prevent the possession and distribution of sexually explicit renderings of minors which involved no actual minors in their production.

G. Russell, Pedophiles in wonderland: censoring the sinful in cyberspace. *The Journal of Criminal Law and Criminology*, Summer 2008, 98(4): 1467-1500. Reprinted by special permission of Northwestern University School of Law, The Journal of Criminal Law and Criminology.

This Comment points out the logical and constitutional problems with Congress's efforts to render this victimless activity criminal under both child pornography law and obscenity law, and concludes that so far as online ageplay is concerned, adults should be allowed to explore their fantasies with other consenting adults without the interference of terrestrial law.

No one needs a First Amendment to write about how cute newborn babies are or to publish a recipe for strawberry shortcake. Nobody needs a First Amendment for innocuous or popular points of view. That's point one.

Point two is that the majority—you and I—must always protect the right of a minority—even a minority of one—to express the most outrageous and offensive ideas. Only then is total freedom of expression guaranteed.

—Lyle Stuart in his introduction to The Turner Diaries

INTRODUCTION

In September of 1998, police forces across the world banded together to bring down the Wonderland Club, an online child pornography ring spanning twelve countries. Club membership was contingent on possession of a digital library containing no less than 10,000 indecent images of minors. Members would circulate these photographs throughout the network by sending them from computer to computer as encrypted image files. The network eventually collapsed as the result of a worldwide criminal investigation, code-named Operation Cathedral, when over a hundred men suspected of being members were arrested. Nearly a decade later, in 2007, two undercover reporters, one German and the other British, independently investigated rumors that Wonderland had reemerged and was flourishing as an adult theme park. The reporters confirmed these rumors when they returned with graphic footage of the unsavory activities they had witnessed while undercover.

The new Wonderland, while dedicated to the same cause as the first, was an entirely different beast, it was not a file exchange, but rather a place, with slides and swing sets, schoolrooms and rose-colored bedrooms, and children that moved, spoke, and had sexual relations with adults in real time. Report Mainz, a German television news program, aired a segment featuring scenes from journalist Nick

Schader's investigative report. At one point, the camera captures Schader entering a playground, zooming in as he approaches a circle of young children seated calmly on the grass. Moments later, he is propositioned by a small girl.

The taboo nature of the graphically sexual scenes that follow is paralleled only by those featured in Jason Farrell's Wonderland report for British television channel Sky News. During the course of their undercover investigations, Farrell and Schader discovered a dungeon located in a high school basement where children were bound and tortured, came across a club where children spoke of being held against their will and raped repeatedly, and were permitted to enter a room where adults met to watch and participate in the brutal rape of a teenage girl. Though this new Wonderland disappeared shortly after the German and American footage was aired, a new clone has already taken its place.

It is a relief to know that the bleak underworld exposed by Schader and Farrell exists only on the Internet. No real minors were subjected to the violence described above—the sexual partners were little more than high-tech puppets manipulated by adults in an entirely computer-generated environment called Second Life. (These online personae, called "avatars," are three-dimensional characters that computer users create to represent themselves in online environments. While some adults design avatars that look like monsters or celebrities, others prefer to adopt a childlike appearance. And while some adults make innocent use of their youthful avatars, others favor less socially acceptable activities and use their young counterparts accordingly. Indeed, "virtual ageplay" —sexual role-play occurring in a virtual world like Second Life, where one avatar appears to be a child and the other an adult—has become a very popular and newsworthy online pastime.

This Comment describes the constitutional problems with legally proscribing "virtual ageplay" under either child pornography or obscenity law. It will begin with an explanation of virtual ageplay and an overview of the laws that bear on its legal standing, followed by a discussion of why regulation of such activity under child pornography law is inappropriate. The Comment concludes by exploring the potential regulation of virtual ageplay under obscenity law, ultimately rejecting that strategy as an unconstitutional restriction on free speech and individual liberty.

BACKGROUND

WHAT IS SECOND LIFE?

Second Life is a popular virtual world created by Linden Research, Incorporated (Linden). While there are many kinds of virtual environments, many of which are text-based, massively multiplayer online game (MMOG) environments are the most like real-world environments, in appearance and in the way that users can interact with their surroundings and with each other. A user navigates through these virtual worlds as an avatar that, depending on the MMOG, a user can design to look like anything from a wizard, to Bono from U2, to a dominatrix rabbit.

Unlike some online environments that are themed or are specifically tailored to accommodate certain types of roleplay, such as the popular roleplaying games World of Warcraft and Everquest, Second Life has no prefabricated motif, and users are not encouraged to perform set tasks or achieve specific goals. In Second Life, avatars are free to do whatever their creators please: talk, dance, shop, give and attend rock concerts, trade currency, interview for real-world jobs, fly, smoke, and have sex—anything a real person can do, and more. What makes Second Life truly unique, however, is the degree to which users themselves are responsible for creating the environment. At the outset, Linden created the basic software code for Second Life, which laid down the environment's geographical foundations and set the outermost boundaries for what could and could not occur there. Beyond that, individual users are left to create their own content. In Second Life, empty cyberspace can be turned into night clubs, shopping malls, breathtaking natural landscapes, reproductions of real-world places, scenes from dreams, and everything in between. Anyone with enough time and the ability to write new pieces of code can make her fantasy a reality, and those without sufficient time or technological skill can purchase developed land, property, objects, and even complex gestures, such as the ability to French kiss or moonwalk, from someone else.

Although the future of Second Life and similar virtual worlds is uncertain, membership increases daily, and it seems likely that the popularity of the social medium of virtual worlds will only increase as technology advances. In fact, Second Life's economy is growing steadily, and the prospects for investment and development have attracted many new users as well as the attention of many successful real-world companies. Moreover, society is just starting to explore the potential of these forums. For instance, Seventh Circuit federal judge Richard Posner gave an in-world lecture on intellectual property rights to a group of avatars in 2006, and leaders in fields as diverse as architecture and neurology have discussed the use of Second Life as a powerful educational and research tool. For example, John Lester, a research associate at Harvard Medical School, created an island in Second Life for people with Asperger syndrome and their caregivers. The private island provides a safe place for Asperger patients to develop social skills without the pressure of having to face the real-world consequences of failed interactions.

Increasing interest and active participation in virtual worlds are good indications that the popularity of online communities like Second Life will continue to grow, attracting a more diverse user base and impacting the lives of active users ever more significantly. But just as there is great potential for these worlds to have a positive influence on the lives of individuals and on society at large, this social experiment also carries with it potential dangers. Users have already begun to complain about the presence of crime in Second Life, and both the academic and practicing legal communities have started to take these concerns more seriously, writing various papers (cited throughout this Comment) and even in some cases filing lawsuits based on incidents that have occurred in-world.

If the harms arising from participation in virtual worlds only affected people's in-world status, there would be less cause for involvement by real-world legal authorities. However, in-world actions can have real world consequences. For example, the in-world currency of Second Life, called Linden, attained real-world value when users became willing to pay real-world money for virtual property, goods, and services or, indirectly, to pay real-world money for virtual money to buy virtual goods. To facilitate these transactions, Linden Labs set up an online exchange where users can buy or sell Linden dollars. When the LindeX Dollar Exchange closed on February 5, 2008, the Linden traded at 267.7 per U.S. Dollar, and users had spent approximately 1.35 million U.S. Dollars buying virtual goods for use in Second Life since the previous day's closing. Naturally, a number of enterprising Second Life salesmen have already achieved significant real-world success. Virtual real estate developer Ansche Chung, known in-world as Ailin Graef, made a million dollars (and the cover of Business Week) by selling real estate in Second Life. Kevin Alderman, known in world as Stroker Serpentine, in 2007 sold his virtual reproduction of Amsterdam on eBay to a Dutch media firm for $50,000.

The backing of the virtual goods market by real-world currency enables users to violate real-world criminal laws without ever leaving the virtual world. On July 3, 2007, Kevin Alderman brought suit against Second Life resident Volkov Catteneo, whose real-world identity was unknown at the time, for copyright infringement. Alderman, the creator of the SexGen bed, a piece of virtual furniture that enables avatars to engage in a wide range of sexual activities, alleged that Catteneo copied the bed and sold copies of it for one-third of Alderman's asking price of 12,000 Linden (roughly $45). Concluding that the in-world "abuse reporting" system would prove inadequate, Alderman turned to the federal court system for assistance.

VIRTUAL SEX

Online sexual expression has taken many forms, and continues to evolve in response to technological innovation. During the Internet's early years, the presence of sexual content was necessarily less overt. There were no websites as we now know them, no streaming videos or chat rooms, and avatars were still a thing of science fiction. In the 1990s, one of the most technologically advanced methods available to groups of Internet users interested in sharing sexually explicit materials was to set up a Bulletin Board System (BBS). A BBS allowed users to share sexually explicit pictures by posting materials to, and retrieving materials from, a centralized location, accessible by dial-up modem. Currently, while the content of messages and nature of materials transmitted may not be fundamentally different than they were ten years ago, the manner in which information, including sexually explicit information, is disseminated has evolved dramatically. With the creation of email, people can now exchange long, complex messages almost instantaneously. Chat rooms allow users to respond to the comments of others, who are potentially seated in front of computers halfway around the world, within seconds. Individuals can now reach a global audience simply by creating a website. And the existence of virtual worlds allows people to interact as avatars, not only through language, but through graphical displays, gestures, and pseudophysical contact.

The fact that all of this can be done anonymously, or pseudonymously, allows people to voice thoughts and feelings, and explore parts of themselves, that real-world norms compel them to suppress. Because the Internet offers a forum for every viewpoint and a safe corner for every fantasy, it is easy to see why sex has such a major presence there. The advent of chat rooms and instant messaging created a means for people to use explicit language to experiment sexually. Once the technology became available, some bold users, comfortable shedding a layer of anonymity, began to incorporate Internet-linked cameras, or webcams, into their online sex lives. Those more comfortable off camera, or just interested in a different type of interaction, explored their fantasies with the help of avatars in MMOGs.

That sex is at least as popular a pastime in virtual environments as it is in the real world makes sense, given the unique opportunity for consequence-free experimentation that virtual environments provide. Worlds like Second Life afford even the most inhibited, risk-averse individuals the chance to explore their sexuality and toy with taboos like sadomasochism, prostitution, ageplay, and group sex. However, despite the spirit of freedom that reigns in places like Second Life, there are certain behaviors governments will not tolerate in any space, real or virtual. Thus, while heated debates rage over how the Internet should be regulated, governments continue to extend the long arm of terrestrial law into cyberspace, as they have done since its inception. While the branches of the United States government are still laboring to articulate the constitutionally permissible scope of legislative control over the availability of sexual content on the Internet, Congress's actions over the past ten years suggest that virtual worlds may not remain free-love zones for much longer.

In the past, Congress has created laws to curtail the distribution of child pornography and to prevent minors from accessing age-inappropriate content. More recently, Congress has expressed an interest in regulating sexually explicit communication between consenting adults that involves the mere idea of minors, namely, virtual ageplay. Regulations of this variety grew out of child pornography jurisprudence, with Congress attempting to expand the scope of child pornography law to cover images of "virtual children" (61) as well.

C. OBSCENITY

Although child pornography law grew out of obscenity law precedents, the two areas of law are distinct. Obscenity law deals with sexual content featuring adults, whereas child pornography law deals with content featuring minors. Because the government has claimed a special interest in protecting minors from the harms incident to their involvement in pornography, a separate jurisprudence has evolved to regulate child pornography. Child pornography law imposes stricter controls on sexual materials which involve children, and operates according to a different standard.

Obscenity law plays a strange and contentious regulatory role in the United States. While the Supreme Court has interpreted the First Amendment to deny the federal government the "power to restrict expression because of its message, its ideas, its subject matter, or its content," it has also acknowledged a number of exceptions to this rule. For example, speech which is used to commit fraud, incite unlawful conduct, or otherwise seriously threaten or harm third parties, falls outside the First Amendment's scope. As a category of unprotected speech, obscenity is unique because it is excluded from First Amendment protection despite the lack of a definite link between it and any unlawful conduct or specific harm. It is also anomalous in that its roots are grounded less firmly in the soil tread upon by our nation's Founders than in that of Victorian England.

Obscenity laws are aimed at completely suppressing any speech deemed offensive by a particular majority. The first obscenity regulations were developed in response to concerns about the corruption of individual morals and the maintenance of decency norms. Despite modern justifications offered to the contrary, obscenity laws were actually created to prevent the formation of certain thoughts by banning the materials that were thought to inspire them. However, no single, coherent rationale for the continued existence of obscenity law dominates pro-obscenity scholarship or relevant case law. Some scholars subscribe to the view that speech banned as obscene contributes so little to society politically or otherwise on account of its purely sexual content that it does not embody any of the values the First Amendment was adopted to protect, and is thus unprotected and suppressible by the government at will. This seems to be the view taken by the Supreme Court, though it has never explicitly settled on any one theory.

Courts nationwide currently use the three-part test introduced by the Supreme Court in the 1973 case of Miller v. California to determine whether contentious materials qualify as obscene. In Miller, the Court declared that federal and state courts may find a particular work obscene if it satisfies each of the following three elements:

(a) [W]hether "the average person, applying contemporary community standards" would find that the work, taken as a whole, appeals to the prurient interest, ... (b) whether the work depicts or describes, in a patently offensive way, sexual conduct specifically defined by the applicable state law; and (c) whether the work, taken as a whole, lacks serious literary, artistic, political, orscientific value.

The Miller court also reaffirmed the validity of obscenity prohibitions in general, announcing that "the States have a legitimate interest in prohibiting dissemination or exhibition of obscene material when the mode of dissemination carries with it a significant danger of offending the sensibilities of unwilling recipients or of exposure to juveniles."

B. CHILD PORNOGRAPHY

While all pornography was originally regulated under obscenity law, in New York v. Ferber, the Supreme Court recognized a new, distinct category of speech not subject to First Amendment protection: child pornography. In Ferber, the Court held that the state interest in protecting minors from physical and psychological harm warranted the creation of a set of laws specifically tailored to address the use of minors in the production of sexually explicit materials. Since the Court found there was no viable way to attack the problem at its source, the "industry of pornography production" being prohibitively "low-profile" and "clandestine," it approved state legislation aimed at bringing down the market for child pornography. The Court reasoned that "dry[ing] up the market" for the material by imposing sanctions on consumers might be the only way to stop the abuse of children by pornographers.

Motivated by this mission and rationale, the Supreme Court decided that even pornographic materials that did not satisfy the Miller test could be regulated if those materials featured minors. In particular, the Supreme Court saw no need to include the third prong of Miller in its new test on the grounds that the question of whether a form of speech has value "bears no connection to the issue of whether or not a child has been physically or psychologically harmed in the production of the work." At this prompting, Congress passed the Child Protection Act of 1984, which expanded the definition of child pornography to include sexually suggestive, non-obscene images; raised the age of protection to eighteen; increased penalties; and removed the requirement that for images to be criminalized, there must be proof that they were created for commercial purposes.

In 1988, Congress made its first attempt to neutralize the Internet's influence on the child pornography market by passing the Child Protection and Obscenity Enforcement Act, which prohibited the use of computers as vehicles for the transportation, distribution, and receipt of child pornography. Two years later, the Supreme Court added another weapon to the government's arsenal for the war against child pornography with its holding in Osborne v. Ohio that mere possession of child pornography could be criminalized. Earlier the Court had declared in Stanley v. Georgia that in the absence of a proven intent to sell or distribute obscene materials, the right to privacy protects a person from being convicted for simple possession. In Osborne, however, the Court made it clear that in the case of child pornography personal privacy rights are outweighed by the state's interest in preventing harm to children. In other words, a person found to possess a sexually explicit image of a minor may be subject to criminal charges because the severity of the inherent third party harm—that is, the abuse of the child photographed—outweighs any right the possessor may have to privacy.

In sum, the government has justified the First Amendment liberties taken by child pornography law as necessary to protect a particular class of victims, while obscenity law suppresses a category of speech without any clearly identified victim or rational interest. The Court sanctioned a relaxation of the Miller standard for materials depicting minors because it feared that the traditional obscenity standard was incapable of preventing the sexual abuse of children by pornographers. Thus, while the Court's justification for suppressing "obscenity" is questionable at best, it has more plainly laid out its reasons for enforcing child pornography laws; its method of regulating that area is backed by reasonable concerns regarding third-party harm.

C. VIRTUAL CHILD PORNOGRAPHY

Just as pornographers and pedophiles quickly discovered the benefits of using the Internet as a vehicle for distribution and acquisition, they also incorporated computers into the child pornography production process. As digital imaging and editing technologies became more readily accessible, technologically savvy individuals interested in child pornography discovered a way around child pornography laws. Adults in photographs could be digitally modified to look like children, making it possible to create what appeared to be sexually explicit images of children without involving actual minors.

In an attempt to counteract the threats posed by "virtual" child pornography, Congress passed the Child Pornography Prevention Act (CPPA) in 1996. Though the rationales proffered in support of prior child pornography regulations had focused on harms to actual minors, Congress now reasoned that sufficient harms existed to justify expanding the ban on child pornography to include virtual images of child pornography as well. The definition of child pornography was thus broadened to include any image that "is, or appears to be, of a minor engaging in sexually explicit conduct" or has been promoted in a way that "conveys the impression" that it depicts minors engaging in sexually explicit conduct.

Once CPPA's expanded definition of child pornography took effect, courts began to issue opinions in support of Congress's rationale for passing it. For example, in United States v. Fox, the Fifth Circuit Court of Appeals defended the government's interest as sufficient to sustain a ban on visual depictions that merely "appear to be" or "convey the impression of" minors engaging in sexually explicit conduct in the face of First Amendment challenges. Citing the Supreme Court's opinion in Osborne v. Ohio and congressional findings collected in support of CPPA, the Fifth Circuit upheld the ban at issue on the grounds that virtual child pornography contributed to the creation of an "unwholesome environment," and that "the danger to actual children who are seduced and molested with the aid of child sex pictures is just as great when the child pornographer or child molester uses [computer simulations] as when the material consists of unretouched images of actual children." Evidently, the Fifth Circuit shared Congress's concern that child molesters might use real or virtual images of child pornography to convince actual children that performing the depicted acts would be acceptable or even enjoyable, and agreed that this possibility justified banning materials that could be used in this way.

In 2002, the Supreme Court in Ashcroft v. Free Speech Coalition struck down two provisions of CPPA dealing with virtual child pornography. The CPPA section that broadened the definition of child pornography to include virtual images was deemed overbroad because it would have suppressed speech—including valuable artistic works such as productions of Romeo and Juliet, Renaissance paintings, and mainstream movies like Traffic and American Beauty—that was neither obscene nor injured any minor in its production or dissemination. The second section of CPPA, which dealt with "pandering," was declared overbroad as it criminalized materials if they had once been advertised as involving minors, regardless of whether they actually did so.

The Court found the government's arguments for upholding CPPA's new definition of child pornography inadequate. The Court determined that the harms the government claimed grew from virtual child pornography were "not 'intrinsically related' to the sexual abuse of children," and, therefore, could not serve as a sufficient basis for suppression. The government's first argument, that virtual child pornography could be used just as effectively as real child pornography by pedophiles to seduce children, was rejected because things innocent in themselves cannot be outlawed simply because they are sometimes used to achieve an "immoral" goal. The second argument, that virtual images were just as good at "whet[ing] the appetites" of pedophiles and thereby encouraging them to abuse actual children, was dismissed because the First Amendment forbids the government to suppress speech that might encourage illegal acts unless it is "directed to inciting or advocating imminent lawless action and is likely to incite or produce such action."

The government also offered a market deterrence theory in support of the contested CPPA provisions, claiming that keeping virtual child pornography on the market sustains the market for "real" child pornography, since the two types of material can be indistinguishable. The Court responded that eliminating the child pornography market was only a valid goal insofar as the images themselves reflected underlying crimes, such as statutory rape or child abuse. Preexisting regulations targeting the market were valid for preventing actual injury to minors, but no corresponding harm results from the market for virtual child pornography.

In its final argument, the government argued that advances in technology would eventually render the task of distinguishing between virtual and real child pornography impossible, making prosecution of individuals likewise impossible if the burden were on the government to prove the involvement of actual minors in the production of suspect materials. The Court rejected this argument because the idea that "protected speech may be banned as a means to ban unprotected speech ... turns the First Amendment upside down." As the Court had warned nearly fifty years before, speech regulations which would "bum the house to roast the pig" must be invalidated.

Ashcroft v. Free Speech Coalition emphasized the boundaries of child pornography law by underscoring the importance of the rationale behind it. The Ferber Court was justified in truncating the Miller standard for materials containing minors because the state has a special interest in preventing child abuse, and sexually explicit photographs of minors are part and parcel of that abuse. Such photographs document the abuse; contribute to the abuse; and are the purpose of the abuse. The fact that child pornography causes irrevocable harm to minors justifies a stricter law. When an actual child is depicted, there is a crime. However, in the case of virtual child pornography, where no actual child is depicted, there is no underlying crime, and, therefore, no justification for the application of a standard stricter than that which governs obscenity in general.

Shortly after the Supreme Court's decision regarding CPPA in Free Speech Coalition, Congress passed the Prosecutorial Remedies and Other Tools to End the Exploitation of Children Today (PROTECT) Act. The PROTECT Act, which was signed into law by

President George W. Bush in 2003 and remains in effect today, modifies both child pornography law and obscenity law in important ways. The new act contains revised versions of provisions which failed under CPPA, modified to withstand the challenges to constitutionality raised in Free Speech Coalition. For example, instead of permanently attaching criminal liability to materials advertised as child pornography further up the distribution chain, the new pandering provision criminalizes the speech used in pandering alone, without permanently marking the materials. Congress's hope was that by tailoring the language of the pandering provision in this manner, the law would resist attacks to its constitutionality while allowing the government to successfully prosecute defendants who had pandered materials in a way that sustained the child pornography market.

This particular provision did not prove impervious to First Amendment criticism, and was declared overbroad by the Eleventh Circuit in United States v. Williams. Williams was charged with possessing and pandering child pornography, and while he pleaded guilty to possession, he challenged the pandering provision as overbroad and vague. The Eleventh Circuit found the market deterrence rationale that Congress had offered in support of the PROTECT Act's pandering provision unconvincing, since Congress failed to show how simply permitting people to advertise that certain materials are child pornography sustains the market for actual child pornography. However, a majority of the Supreme Court disagreed with the Eleventh Circuit. In May 2008, the Court overturned Williams and declared the pandering provision of the PROTECT Act constitutional under the First and Fifth Amendments. Writing for the majority, Justice Scalia distinguished the Act's pandering provision from that declared overbroad in Free Speech Coalition, arguing that the key difference is that the PROTECT Act does not criminalize materials which themselves could not be constitutionally proscribed merely because they had once been pandered as child pornography, but rather criminalizes the act of pandering itself.

Another provision of the PROTECT Act with roots in CPPA modifies child pornography law by expanding the definition of child pornography. This new definition brings into its purview any digital or computer generated image that is "indistinguishable from ... that of a minor engaging in sexually explicit conduct" or any image that has been created or modified to make it appear that an "identifiable minor is engaging in sexually explicit conduct."

Finally, in addition to modifying the pandering provision and the preexisting definition of child pornography, the PROTECT

Act also substantively revised the general obscenity statute. As a result of this revision, the law now prohibits possession, production, distribution, or receipt of "a visual depiction of any kind, including a drawing, cartoon, sculpture, or painting," that depicts sexually explicit conduct by a minor and which is either obscene or "hard-core," and that "lacks serious literary, artistic, political, or scientific value." This component of the PROTECT Act has basically reinstated the ban on virtual child pornography struck down under the child pornography provision of CPPA, but has refashioned it as an obscenity law to avoid having to prove actual harm to minors. Though written as an obscenity law rather than a child pornography law, this standard allows materials containing images of virtual minors to be banned without passing Miller's standard test for obscenity. No official justification has been offered for why images do not need to pass the full three-prong Miller test to qualify as obscene when only virtual children are depicted. The Supreme Court has yet to test the constitutionality of this new obscenity provision, but some legal scholars predict that it would fail under challenges similar to those which prevailed in Free Speech Coalition.

ARGUMENT

COULD VIRTUAL AGEPLAY BE BANNED UNDER CHILD PORNOGRAPHY LAW?

What types of behavior should the government regulate in a fantasy world? Various scientists, artists, and programmers are involved in efforts to make the virtual reality experience more interactive— consider the Holodeck from Star Trek or the training sequence from The Matrix. Virtual worlds will eventually be fully immersive, with cliffs so realistic one would not dare step off the side, and people so realistic they may be indistinguishable from real human beings. Yet, no matter how immersed one becomes in a virtual world, how emotionally affected one is by the events that occur there, or how real the virtual world starts to feel, the entire realm is only computer-generated. If one did step off a virtual cliff or stick a virtual knife through the heart of a computer-generated person, no one would suffer actual injury.

Though real and virtual goods may, on a monetary level, be valued similarly, the non-monetary values of things virtual and real are not neatly aligned. The way some interactions impact one's bank account may be the same whether they occur in the real world or a virtual one, but other interactions have fundamentally different effects and consequences depending on the world in which they are conducted. It follows, then, that consequences for criminal actions in virtual worlds should often be different from those attaching to the same type of action in the real world.

How should the law deal with this disconnect? Determining how virtual events affect people's real lives is the first step. For example, rape committed in a virtual world cannot be prosecuted as the crime of rape in terrestrial courts, for there was no physical assault. Some legal scholars have argued that an act like rape, when carried out in a virtual setting, may be more sensibly viewed as a tort akin to intentional infliction of emotional distress or even as a crime akin to theft. They argue that, while it may make sense for a woman to sue a man who forced her avatar to have sex with his avatar against her will for harassment or intentional infliction of emotional distress, this fact scenario would not support a claim of rape. The real-world individual may be distressed by the in-world event, conceivably to an actionable extent, but she has not been physically violated. Conversely, if an adult avatar were using the virtual medium as a means of connecting with minors and inducing them into real-world meetings, a child or a child's guardian may have a viable cause of action under a state child luring statute. In that case, the in-world event—solicitation of a minor—more closely mirrors its real-world instantiation, as this act is fundamentally the same in substance and result whether conducted online or on terra firma.

Virtual sex between two consenting adults, however, whether those adults choose to represent themselves virtually as fairies, cows, pulsating orbs, or child and adult, is not a crime committed on either of the consensual participants. What may be a crime, however, is the image produced on the computer screen as a result of the participants' actions. The graphic that appears on the monitor—of a child avatar having sex with an adult avatar—is viewed by the participants themselves, and also may appear on the screens of other participants in the vicinity should their avatar encounter the copulating couple, and can even be saved as a screenshot and distributed to others.

Surely, while the graphics in virtual worlds like Second Life are still far from realistic, avatar sex is often stimulating for the participants, and quite possibly for spectators as well. Japanese manga, sexually explicit cartoons sometimes referred to as hentai, are wildly popular both there and here, and have excited viewers since at least the nineteenth century. And as some indication that there is a more mainstream following for virtual pornography than one might think, Playboy's October 2004 issue featured several computer illustrations of popular video game characters in various states of undress. Further, the popularity of virtual sex has spawned an entire

56

industry focused on making virtual sexual experiences more realistic. "Teledildonics" designers and engineers are in the process of developing a wide range of computer attachments that, when strapped to the customer and connected to a printer port, allow a virtual accomplice to control the sexual pleasure of the user.

Still, just because some might find sex between avatars involving a childlike character arousing does not make it "child pornography." Though the actions portrayed are overtly sexual, they do not involve actual children. The Supreme Court justified creating a new, stricter standard for child pornography law on the grounds that it would protect children from being harmed in the production of those materials. Because the government's interest in preventing the harms inherent in child pornography outweighs any interest the public might have in that speech, the test for suppressing it is less rigorous than when there is no similarly compelling governmental interest. Thus, it stands to reason that materials that do not directly harm children should not be held to this heightened standard and should instead be subject only to the Miller test.

If the CPPA standard were still operable, avatar ageplay could be outlawed on the theory that an image of an avatar could "appear[] to be[] of a minor engaging in sexually explicit conduct" (144) even though it "records no crime and creates no victims." But CPPA was overturned shortly after its inception because it would have suppressed speech that was not inherently harmful and, therefore, not subject to the strict controls placed on real child pornography. However, the fact that CPPA was overturned does not mean ageplay is immune from legal attack under child pornography law.

Like CPPA before it, the PROTECT Act criminalizes pandering materials as child pornography and modifies the definition of child pornography. Ageplayers are probably safe under the pandering provision, as long as no one involved holds the "belief, or intend[s] to cause another to believe" that images of real children are used in the roleplay. The new definition of child pornography created by the PROTECT Act also does not immediately threaten the activities of ageplayers, as it now encompasses only computer-generated images that are "indistinguishable from that of a minor engaging in sexually explicit conduct," or images that have been created or modified to look like an "identifiable" minor. This definition does not currently apply to ageplaying avatars, as avatars are still more cartoonish than realistic, and therefore, far from being "indistinguishable" from a photo of a minor. There have also been no reported cases of anyone modeling their child avatar after a real-world, "identifiable" minor. However, once technology exists which allows computer users to create truly lifelike avatars, ageplayers could theoretically be charged with possessing or distributing child pornography for engaging in virtual ageplay.

COULD VIRTUAL AGEPLAY BE BANNED UNDER OBSCENITY LAW?

Though the new child pornography rules pose a distant threat to ageplayers, the most serious and immediate threat lurks in the PROTECT Act's addition to the obscenity statute—the section titled "Obscene visual representations of the sexual abuse of children." The statute explicitly applies to drawings and cartoons, and, thus, brings all virtual child pornography under its umbrella. This law ensures that even unrealistic images may be suppressed if they contain childlike figures. Therefore, two adult users of Second Life—one of whom created an avatar of an adult and the other of whom created an avatar of a child—who engaged in virtual sexual intercourse could be prosecuted under the Act for either producing, distributing, receiving, or possessing criminally obscene materials. Whether this action would most appropriately qualify as production, distribution, receipt, or possession is debatable, and the outcome would perhaps depend on a legal determination of where the images technically reside. Regardless, both participants in this exchange could be held to fall under one or more of these categories.

The two new offenses created by PROTECT through modification of the obscenity statute deal with (1) production, distribution, or possession with intent to distribute; and (2) mere possession. This two-part provision raises two distinct constitutional issues with regard to its application to virtual children. First, can the statute constitutionally proscribe the materials it describes without requiring satisfaction of all three prongs of the Miller test? Second, can mere possession of sexually explicit images of virtual children be criminalized?

Section 1466A of the PROTECT Act allows for the criminalization of images depicting children engaged in hardcore acts as long as they lack "serious literary, artistic, political, or scientific value." (he provision leaves out the community standards test included in Miller. In Free Speech Coalition, the Supreme Court commented that "CPPA [could not] be read to prohibit obscenity because it lacks the required link between its prohibitions and the affront to community standards prohibited by the definition of obscenity." Section 1466A lacks this link, which suggests that it, like CPPA, should be declared unconstitutional.

The "possession" prohibition in [section] 1466A is also vulnerable to constitutional attack. In Stanley v. Georgia, the Court passionately rejected the idea that the government could ban mere possession of adult pornography under obscenity law, stating "[o]ur whole constitutional heritage rebels at the thought of giving government the power to control men's minds." Meanwhile, the Court in Osborne v. Ohio explained that given the special interests of the government with respect to child pornography, and the inherent evil of the material itself, the government could ban mere possession under child pornography law. This does not mean, however, that the government may ban possession of virtual child pornography. Here, the government is not entitled to the leniency it had in regulating real child pornography, because the special circumstances that justified that leniency do not exist in the case of virtual child pornography. The point of banning possession of real child pornography is to further discourage people from supporting the market for it because the market requires the abuse of children—the ultimate harm that child pornography legislation is intended to prevent. Virtual child pornography does not similarly necessitate the abuse of children. Thus, the Supreme Court could find just cause to reject the PROTECT Act's criminalization of the private possession of pornographic materials that feature only virtual children.

Even assuming that the parts of the PROTECT Act that threaten virtual ageplay will be overturned before gaining enough momentum to affect activities in virtual worlds, one avenue remains open for those who wish to prosecute ageplayers. If the Supreme Court were to declare portions of the PROTECT Act unconstitutional for unjustifiably truncating the Miller standard, virtual ageplay could nevertheless probably be banned as obscene under the full Miller standard should the government choose to devote energy to prosecuting virtual child pornography under that theory. Though private possession of obscene materials cannot be criminalized, sexual interaction in a virtual world could be seen as not entirely private, since there is always at least one other person—the sex partner—viewing the onscreen activity. Indeed, the Supreme Court has good precedent for denying consenting adults access to such sights under Paris Adult Theatre I v. Slaton.

There are two reasonable arguments against the suppression of ageplay under Miller. The first argument would be to challenge the constitutionality of obscenity law in general. That argument acknowledges that the suppression of sexual images of children is justified when those images are incident to the abuse of an actual child, but proposes that sexual images that produce no real victims, such as virtual child pornography, should not be suppressed. Unfortunately, that argument would likely be futile given the long history of obscenity suppression in the United States and the solid standing of the Miller test in our legal system. The second argument distinguishes virtual child pornography from virtual ageplay, and compares virtual ageplay to the type of sexual activity protected under Lawrence v. Texas. It concludes that the Due Process Clauses of the Fifth and Fourteenth Amendments guarantee that online ageplay cannot be suppressed. That argument has two compelling characteristics: it is less earth-shattering than a general abandonment of obscenity law and it is supported by precedent. Both arguments deserve consideration.

THE OBSCENITY ARGUMENT

Obscenity laws are not based on fact, or policy, or harm done, but rather on a specific moral worldview. They serve to sustain the dominant moral tone and social order existing at a particular time and place in history. The Supreme Court seems to subscribe to the belief that pornographic speech of almost any kind does not contribute to the marketplace of ideas, so no democratic value is lost by suppressing it if the majority finds it offensive. But how does the court distinguish the value of sexual works from musical or artistic works, which also produce visceral and emotional responses, sometimes to the exclusion of coherent thought? First Amendment scholar Andrew Koppelman claims that obscenity laws are not really based on the idea that some speech is less valuable than others because it is non-cognitive or apolitical, as other scholars like Cass Sunstein have suggested, but rather on the irrational fear that "sexuality has a powerful tendency to distort our powers of perception and judgment," thereby corrupting the morals of otherwise healthy individuals and turning them into depraved criminals. Clearly, people are justified in their outrage over the prevalence of child sexual abuse and in their fear for their own children. However, although this horror is widely shared among most non-pedophiliac adults in Westernized nations, pacification of the morally-outraged alone cannot serve as the kind of compelling interest which would allow Congress and the judiciary to disregard the First Amendment. Holocaust deniers and the Ku Klux Klan (KKK) are allowed to march and write and say things that offend most of the civilized world, as long as they cause no physical harm in the process and their advocacy does not reach the level of a credible threat or incitement to imminent lawlessness. While those who endorse the ideas behind the words and symbols of white supremacists constitute a minority of the population, the majority permits them to burn crosses and disseminate hateful speech.

But in a culture where many consider child abuse "worse than murder," it seems that the government's tolerance of distasteful views in the name of free speech goes as far as the KKK but stops short of the very idea of a sexually explicit child. The First Amendment is used to protect racists with violent ideologies, but not pedophiles, because our nation's anxiety over sexual abuse is stronger than our anxiety over hate crimes. First Amendment scholar Amy Adler proclaims that fear of child abuse has in fact developed into a blinding hysteria so pervasive that it has produced lapses in judicial judgment, akin to those which weakened the government's commitment to free speech ideals during the McCarthy era.

Of course, the government has the right to prevent behavior when it creates real victims. As soon as a pedophile solicits or abuses a real child, or advocates the abuse of a child in a manner likely to incite imminent abuse, there is a reason to prosecute him. Further, images of real children can be criminalized for being involved in the crime of child abuse. But the government should not suppress speech based on its content when it has no proven harmful effects, as is the case with virtual child pornography. Short of establishing a strong link between virtual child pornography and some specific harm, a governmental ban on virtual child pornography as obscenity, especially the mere possession of it, would be unjustified.

It is hard to argue with the majority's observation in Young v. American Mini Theaters that "few of us would march our sons and daughters off to war to preserve the citizen's right to see 'Specified Sexual Activities' exhibited in the theaters of our choice." But perhaps this is the problem: if few step up to defend undesirable viewpoints, tyranny wins by default. While few have any interest in defending the right of pedophiles to fantasize about children amongst themselves, the same justifications given to suppress pedophiles' free speech rights could also be used to curtail the rights of gays, interracial couples, and any group not in the majority.

The thrust of the obscenity argument is that obscenity law, as distinct from child pornography law, runs counter to the First Amendment free speech ideal. If communities fear that potentially offensive materials might be forced upon unwilling listeners or viewers, laws may be tailored towards preventing such unwilling exposure, while not depriving willing adults of their right to decide what is and is not appropriate for themselves. If there is a certain type of speech that causes a particular, cognizable harm, then laws may be tailored to prevent that harm without unnecessarily affecting harmless speech. Laws premised on emotional and moral reactions to speech, however, gut democracy, and should not be tolerated simply because we have become habituated to them.

THE LIBERTY ARGUMENT

The less controversial argument against prohibiting online ageplay as obscenity is that online ageplay is simply not something that can be regulated by obscenity law. This argument recategorizes ageplay as something that does not fall within obscenity law's purview. The argument claims that online ageplay is essentially action, not depiction—sexual activity, not interactive pornography—and as such is protected by the Due Process Clauses of the Fifth and Fourteenth Amendments as a matter of liberty.

It is easy for two consenting adults to keep their sexual activity online in any form—whether by email, live chat, or contact between avatars-private, as long as no one goes out of their way to intrude on that privacy. The goal of the participants in creating a written dialogue or a scene between avatars is not the production of a pictorial sex aid, but rather the formation of an intimate connection, whether romantic or purely sexual. Participants are not in the business of producing pornography, but instead aim to create a pseudophysical connection, for very personal purposes. Long-distance couples who are unable to meet in person with great frequency can maintain their sexual connection through virtual trysts. For those who are physically disabled and incapable of having sex, or those whose psychological makeup prevent them from acting on their desires, virtual sex may be their only means of experiencing a sexual connection. Instead of conceptualizing online ageplay as a series of images which can be regulated by obscenity law, it should be seen as an intimate activity, albeit one conducted in an unconventional forum.

So if online ageplay is simply a type of sexual interaction that does not fall into the criminal categories of child abuse or child pornography, can it be regulated? A similar question was posed in Lawrence v. Texas. The issue in Lawrence was whether the Constitution guaranteed two adult men, charged with violating a Texas statute prohibiting same-sex intimacy, the freedom to engage in consensual sexual activity with one another. The Supreme Court held that the right of citizens to due process of the laws under the Fourteenth Amendment prevented the government from interfering with their sex lives, as long as the sexual activity "does not involve minors[,] ... persons who might be injured or coerced[,] or ... public conduct or prostitution." The reason for this, according to the Court, is that the Constitution grants citizens the liberty to decide how to conduct their most personal affairs, free from government intrusion. Though there may be a powerful majority who believe homosexuality, or ageplay, to be immoral, the Court in Lawrence correctly pointed out that the legal and the moral issues are distinct, with the legal question being whether "the majority may use the power of the State to enforce these views on the whole society through operation of the criminal law." The Court found the answer to the legal question to be no: there was no sound legal basis for prohibiting homosexual intimacy, apart from the erroneous Bowers v. Hardwick decision, which it took the opportunity to overrule. Citing Justice Stevens's dissent in Bowers, the court declared that a majority belief that a practice is immoral is insufficient grounds for criminalizing it, and that sexual intimacy is a form of liberty protected by the Due Process Clause of the Fourteenth Amendment.

Online ageplay is not fundamentally different from the sexual activity at issue in Lawrence. That is not to say, of course, that one type of sexual preference is similar to the other. Rather, both types of sexual activity are practiced by a minority of the population and involve the participation of consenting adults, and neither is thrust upon unwilling viewers nor harm third parties. The idea that some people are aroused by fantasies involving underage partners and that those people may act out these fantasies in private may be repulsive to many. But so long as those acting out the fantasy are both legal, consenting adults, the government should not interfere.

One might argue that prohibiting online ageplay would not deprive people of the liberty to express their sexuality in the same way prohibiting homosexual intimacy would, because virtual sex is not the inevitable instantiation of some unchangeable sexual preference, as is homosexual sex to homosexuals. But this argument undermines the centrality of virtual sex to some people's fantasy lives. For some, sexual satisfaction is only achieved by way of a specific sexual fantasy, and they cannot, or are not willing to, explore that fantasy with another person in the real world. Perhaps they do not have a partner who is willing to indulge them or are too afraid to ask. Or perhaps there is no legal, real-world outlet for their fantasy. For them, virtual sex is the only way for them to express their sexuality. Perhaps allowing them this safe, insular forum for fantasy even has a social benefit. Regardless, denying them this outlet would certainly be an unconstitutional deprivation of liberty.

CONCLUSION

Fantasies are not reality. The man who fantasizes about children or acts out those fantasies with his partner is often not the same man who molests actual children. Moreover, there is no proof that the man who is stimulated by cybersex with a virtual child is any more likely to seek out real sex with a real child. In fact, there may be some therapeutic value in indulging such fantasies. For instance, psychologist Michael J. Bader claims that sexual fantasies are specifically crafted by people's subconscious minds to help them feel comfortable expressing their sexuality. He argues that those fantasies should be explored rather than suppressed, and indulging them may be productive rather than psychologically detrimental. Bader further points out that fantasies involving youthful participants are not necessarily about children per se, but may be representative of something more subtle. Such fantasies, especially the tamer varieties, are not uncommon—consider, for example, the popularity of the sexy school girl look, the incidence of flirtatious baby-talk between adult couples, or the prevalence of advertisements featuring teenage girls in suggestive poses. Our culture is overflowing with these and similar images of sexualized youth. Is it really so strange that these same images feature in people's fantasies?

Congress has made numerous attempts to ban virtual child pornography and offered a multitude of justifications in defense of those efforts. Recently, Congress tried a different approach, adding virtual child pornography to the range of materials banned under federal obscenity law. Critics and court rulings have suggested that the provision of the PROTECT Act which criminalizes virtual child pornography as obscenity are likely unconstitutional. Some of these same critics have suggested that even if many provisions of the PROTECT Act are declared unconstitutional, virtual child pornography may still be suppressed as obscenity under the standard established in Miller. This Comment has argued that there is no sound constitutional basis for doing so, and at least one good argument, based on the concept of liberty, is refusing to honor any such intrusion into the private fantasy lives of consenting adults. Though the thought that a safe haven exists for pedophiles to act out their taboo fantasies may turn the collective stomachs of the government or civilian majority, unless the judiciary is willing to tolerate the prosecution of people for unpopular ideas, in violation of fundamental constitutional principles, citizens must be allowed to enjoy their harmless roleplay in peace.

Footnotes deleted.

5

Child Pornography Websites

Techniques Used to Evade Law Enforcement

Wade Luders

Illegal child pornography on the Internet is a huge industry. Recent studies estimate the number of child pornography Web sites at over 100,000, (1) capable of bringing in more than $3 billion annually. (2) While child pornography is predominantly illegal worldwide, many savvy pornographers make their content available to the Internet community, lacking fear of capture by law enforcement for several reasons.

First, child pornography Web sites often are so complex that efforts to identify the administrators become tedious and time consuming. Frequently, by the time investigators have taken the appropriate legal steps to track administrators, the suspect sites have moved from one place to another on the Internet. Such movement hinders law enforcement efforts because locating Web sites a second time in the vast, virtual world of the Internet proves difficult. And, if they can locate it again, the legal process usually must start over.

W. Luders, Child pornography Web sites: techniques used to evade law enforcement. *The FBI Law Enforcement Bulletin.* July 2007, p. 17-22.

Second, Web site administrators use methods to make their sites appear as though they are hosted overseas when, in fact, they are not. This technique often results in investigators ignoring these sites and searching for others they more easily can locate in their own country.

Finally, the manner in which people pay for child pornography Web site memberships often involves stolen credit cards, identity theft, and online financial transactions. Tracking these payment methods involves complex paper trails, spin-off investigations, and tedious legal processes that bog down and divert investigators' attention from the primary focus of the child pornography investigation. Armed with information about the technology and various techniques that child pornography Web site administrators use, investigators can better prepare to combat this international problem that targets the most precious and defenseless victims—children.

PROXY SERVERS

Each Internet user and Web site is identified by an Internet protocol (IP) address, such as 64.128.203.30, which is one of the IP addresses for the FBI's Web site. Readable text, or a domain name, often is displayed in lieu of this string of numbers for convenience and ease of Internet users. Since the beginning of cybercrime, law enforcement agencies have relied on this unique identifier to locate, and eventually prosecute, cybercriminals.

Clever pornographers, as well as anyone else wishing to conceal their online identity, use proxy servers to mask their true IP address on the Internet. A proxy server allows one computer on the Internet to act for another one or, in some cases, many others. Essentially, the proxy server shares its identifying IP address and allows other users to access the Internet through it. Therefore, any online act committed by someone using a proxy server appears as though the proxy server executed it. For investigators, this merely adds another step, usually in the form of an additional legal process, to obtain the true IP address of the end user. Whether investigators even can acquire it depends on if the proxy server keeps accurate logging information and if the proxy server's host will make the address available.

Online users who do not want anyone to trace them use an anonymous proxy server. Similarly, the proxy masks the IP address of potential offenders; however, no logs or other identifying information are kept. Therefore, they will not assist law enforcement agencies in determining the true identity of the original user.

Anonymous proxy servers are easy to use, and many are free, requiring no registration or identifying information from the end user. Also, many are located in other countries. While a typical proxy server may be available one day and offline the next, Web site administrators easily can locate another one to use.

HOSTING PROVIDERS

Like all Web sites, child pornography sites must be hosted somewhere for Internet users to access. Thousands of hosting providers exist, all offering space on the Internet and a myriad of other online and offline services. Most charge a fee based upon the amount of disk space used to host the Web site and the amount of traffic to that site.

Several online tools can determine a particular Web site's hosting provider, which, once located, can furnish valuable information regarding who registered it, who pays the monthly bill, and, often, the IP address they use to do so. Usually, law enforcement agencies must take legal action to obtain this information. A child pornographer who wants to remain anonymous may use a proxy server anytime they communicate online with the hosting provider. To avoid a money trail for law enforcement investigators to trace, free hosting providers often are used because they are relatively easy to find. Offering no-frills hosting, many of these providers make their revenue by placing advertisements on their customers' Web sites. Without accurate customer or IP address information, they provide little use to law enforcement with or without legal process.

WEB SITE STRATEGY

Like other for-profit Web sites, child pornography sites must advertise to prospective customers to stay in business. These advertisements benefit law enforcement because they are accessible to people searching the Internet for child pornography. Online pornography businesses usually separate the advertise-and-join Web site from the members area. The first one often contains a preview of what prospective members can expect to receive if they agree to pay a subscription fee, and it includes a hyperlink to use to obtain membership. In the members area, Web site administrators place content available to paying members. This location is not disclosed until after a person purchases a membership. While this strategy of separating the two Web sites helps prevent hackers from accessing members-only material without paying, it also deceives law enforcement regarding the actual location of the illegal content.

Child pornographers can create multiple advertise-and-join Web sites using free hosting providers outside the United States. The actual location of the illegal content will become apparent only after purchasing a membership. Because law enforcement agencies often are reluctant to make a covert purchase of a membership or access to a child pornography Web site apparently in another country, much illegal child pornography located in the United States evades investigation. By employing a strategy of separating the advertise-and-join Web site from the members area, child pornographers can effectively conceal a great deal of their illegal content from everyone but paying customers.

URL ENCODING

A Web site's uniform resource locator (URL) is the text typically typed into the top bar of a Web browser that directs a user to a Web site. The URL usually takes the form of access protocol (http), domain name (www.fbi.gov), and a path to a file or Web site on that server (/publications.htm).

URLs may appear straightforward and easy to interpret, but many individuals know that they can use hexadecimal codes, IP addresses, and other text in place of standard-looking domain names to confuse people attempting to track the source of the Web page content. Some tricks include placing misleading text followed by the @ symbol between the access protocol and the domain name. Any text placed prior to this symbol is not used to resolve the true URL. Next, URLs may be written in their corresponding hexadecimal codes (e.g., the letter "A" represents "%61," "B" is "%62" and so forth). The three URLs in the box look surprisingly different, but all point to the same location on the Internet. Using a combination of these and other URL encoding techniques, child pornographers use the Internet's underlying technology to obscure and conceal the actual location of their content.

REDIRECT SERVICES

Redirect services allow individuals to use another URL to access their Web site. The services redirect users to a Web site hosted in a particular country. These sites, however, have the outward appearance of being located in another country, rather than what the domain extension denotes. At this initial stage of exploring URLs, law enforcement agencies often elect to use their investigative resources to find sites obviously hosted within their own jurisdiction to avoid the additional legal hurdles of pursuing an international legal process.

CLEVER HTML

Hypertext markup language, or HTML, is the language of the Internet and most Web sites. People who know this language can exploit it enough to deceive even veteran Internet surfers when locating the source of Web content. Viewing the source HTML behind a suspected Web site may reveal images and other content located at a different URL and physical location, rather than the original Web site itself. HTML code even can be used covertly to redirect users to another URL or location on the Internet without their knowledge.

IP FILTERS

A Web site typically serves HTML code to a Web browser, resulting in a familiar Web page for each Internet surfer. However, some scripting languages allow different Web pages to be served to different users based upon qualifying factors, such as an IP address. For example, one search engine uses filtering technology to serve a German language version to anyone accessing their Web site from a German IP address. Similarly, pornographers could use this technology to serve different pages to users coming from differing ranges of IP addresses. For example, IP addresses within the United States or those known to be from law enforcement or government sources could receive non-pornographic content.

ANONYMOUS PAYMENT METHODS

Law enforcement agencies may prefer the strategy of tracing money when targeting for-profit child pornography enterprises. However, inventive child pornographers use several tools to profit from their ventures. The growth of Internet commerce has resulted in a new industry of online payment processors, which present an ideal solution for many online businesses seeking to collect revenue for a good or service. They collect significant customer data, including name, address, transaction information, and IP address logs. Processors in the United States assist law enforcement efforts worldwide to curb child pornography. But, obtaining records from processors in other countries can become a lengthy procedure. Some online payment processors do not require nor verify identifying information about their customers. They may only request users to choose a name and password to open an account. Many people who seek child pornography provide their credit card numbers and significant identifying information to such Web site operators. Quite often, administrators for these sites intentionally use their customers' credit cards to fund their own operations, such as purchasing another domain name or a location at another Internet hosting provider. This places the child pornography subscriber in the precarious position of not reporting the unauthorized use of their credit card to avoid betraying that they sought child pornography.

While law enforcement agencies more easily can track credit card purchases, credit card fraud presents a unique opportunity for Internet child pornographers. Hackers spend countless hours finding vulnerabilities in online banking software to seize identities of unsuspecting users. People lurking in the right places on the Internet can purchase vast lists of credit card numbers. Then, they use these compromised numbers and identities to pay for child pornography Web site memberships.

CONCLUSION

Illegal child pornography is one of the fastest growing businesses on the Internet, and online pornographers use numerous tactics to evade law enforcement's efforts to capture them. Attempts to identify administrators of these complex Web sites can prove frustrating for investigators. Advances in technology present even more challenges in shutting down these Web sites in the future. Law enforcement agencies must be aware of the techniques online child pornographers use to further their illegal activities—only with such knowledge will they be able to combat this critical international problem.

Footnotes deleted.

3

Transnational
Terrorist and Extremist
Groups in Cyberspace

6

Al Qaeda and the Internet

The Danger of "Cyberplanning"

Timothy L. Thomas

We can say with some certainty, al Qaeda loves the Internet. When the latter first appeared, it was hailed as an integrator of cultures and a medium for businesses, consumers, and governments to communicate with one another. It appeared to offer unparalleled opportunities for the creation of a "global village." Today the Internet still offers that promise, but it also has proven in some respects to be a digital menace. Its use by al Qaeda is only one example. It also has provided a virtual battlefield for peacetime hostilities between Taiwan and China, Israel and Palestine, Pakistan and India, and China and the United States (during both the war over Kosovo and in the aftermath of the collision between the Navy EP-3 aircraft and Chinese MiG). In times of actual conflict, the Internet was used as a virtual battleground between NATO's coalition forces and elements of the Serbian population. These real tensions from a virtual interface involved not only nation-states but also non-state individuals and groups eit her aligned with one side or the other, or acting independently. Evidence strongly suggests that terrorists used the Internet to plan their operations for 9/11. Computers seized in Afghanistan reportedly revealed that al Qaeda was collecting intelligence on targets and sending encrypted messages via the Internet.

T.L. Thomas, Al-Qaeda and the internet: The danger of cyber planning. *Parameters* 33 (1): 112-124, 2003.

As recently as 16 September 2002, al Qaeda cells operating in America reportedly were using Internet-based phone services to communicate with cells overseas. These incidents indicate that the Internet is being used as a "cyberplanning" tool for terrorists.

It provides terrorists with anonymity, command and control resources, and a host of other measures to coordinate and integrate attack options. Cyberplanning may be a more important terrorist Internet tool than the much touted and feared cyberterrorism option—attacks against information and systems resulting in violence against noncombatant targets. The Naval Postgraduate School (NPS) has defined cyberterrorism as the unlawful destruction or disruption of digital property to intimidate or coerce people. Cyberplanning, not defined by NPS or any other source, refers to the digital coordination of an integrated plan stretching across geographical boundaries that may or may not result in bloodshed. It can include cyberterrorism as part of the overall plan. Since 9/11, US sources have monitored several websites linked to al Qaeda that appear to contain elements of cyberplanning:

* alneda.com, which US officials said contained encrypted information to direct al Qaeda members to more secure sites, featured international news on al Qaeda, and published articles, fatwas (decisions on applying Muslim law), and books.

* assam.com, believed to be linked to al Qaeda (originally hosted by the Scranton company BurstNET Technologies, Inc.), served as a mouthpiece for jihad in Afghanistan, Chechnya, and Palestine.

* almuhrajiroun.com, an al Qaeda site which urged sympathizers to assassinate Pakistani President Musharraf.

* qassam.net, reportedly linked to Hamas.

* jihadunspun.net, which offered a 36-minute video of Osama bin Laden.

* 7hj.7hj.com, which aimed to teach visitors how to conduct computer attacks.

* aloswa.org, which featured quotes from bin Laden tapes, religious legal rulings that "justified" the terrorist attacks, and support for the al Qaeda cause.

* drasat.com, run by the Islamic Studies and Research Center (which some allege is a fake center), and reported to be the most credible of dozens of Islamist sites posting al Qaeda news.

* jehad.net, alsaha.com, and islammemo.com, alleged to have posted al Qaeda statements on their websites.

* mwhoob.net and aljehad.online, alleged to have flashed political-religious songs, with pictures of persecuted Muslims, to denounce US policy and Arab leaders, notably Saudi.

While it is prudent to tally the Internet cyberplanning applications that support terrorists, it must be underscored that few if any of these measures are really anything new. Any hacker or legitimate web user can employ many of these same measures for their own purposes, for business, or even for advertising endeavors. The difference, of course, is that most of the people on the net, even if they have the capabilities, do not harbor the intent to do harm as does a terrorist or al Qaeda member.

Highlighting several of the more important applications may help attract attention to terrorist methodologies and enable law enforcement agencies to recognize where and what to look for on the net. Sixteen measures are listed below for consideration. More could be added.

1) The Internet can be used to put together profiles. Internet user demographics allow terrorists to target users with sympathy toward a cause or issue, and to solicit donations if the right "profile" is found. Usually a front group will perform the fundraising for the terrorist, often unwittingly. E-mail fundraising has the potential to significantly assist a terrorist's publicity objectives and finances simultaneously.

Word searches of online newspapers and journals allow a terrorist to construct a profile of the means designed to counter his actions, or a profile of admitted vulnerabilities in our systems. For example, recent articles reported on attempts to slip contraband items through security checkpoints. One report noted that at Cincinnati's airport, contraband slipped through over 50 percent of the time. A simple Internet search by a terrorist would uncover this shortcoming, and offer the terrorist an embarkation point to consider for his or her next operation. A 16 September report noted that US law enforcement agencies were tracing calls made overseas to al Qaeda cells from phone cards, cell phones, phone booths, or Internet-based phone services. Exposing the targeting techniques of law enforcement agencies allows the terrorist to alter his or her operating procedures. The use of profiles by terrorists to uncover such material greatly assists their command and control of operations. The implication is that in a free society such as the United States, you can publish too much information, and while the information might not be sensitive to us, it might be very useful to a terrorist.

2) Internet access can be controlled or its use directed according to the server configuration, thus creating a true ideological weapon. In the past, if some report was offensive to a government, the content of the report could be censored or filtered. Governments cannot control the Internet to the same degree they could control newspapers and TV. In fact, the Internet can serve as a terrorist's TV or radio station, or his international newspaper or journal. The web allows an uncensored and unfiltered version of events to be broadcast worldwide. Chat rooms, websites, and bulletin boards are largely uncontrolled, with few filters in place. This climate is perfect for an underfunded group to explain its actions or to offset both internal and international condemnation, especially when using specific servers. The Internet can target fence-sitters as well as true believers with different messages, oriented to the target audience.

In the aftermath of the 9/11 attacks, al Qaeda operatives used the Internet to fight for the hearts and minds of the Islamic faithful worldwide. Several internationally recognized and respected Muslims who questioned the attacks were described as hypocrites by al Qaeda. Al Qaeda ran two websites, alneda.com and drasat.com, to discuss the legality of the attacks on 9/11. Al Qaeda stated that Islam shares no fundamental values with the West and that Muslims are committed to spread Islam by the sword. As a result of such commentary, several Muslim critics of al Qaeda's policies withdrew their prior condemnation. Ideological warfare worked.

3) The Internet can be used anonymously, or as a shell game to hide identities. Terrorists have access to Internet tools to create anonymity or disguise their identities. Online encryption services offer encryption keys for some services that are very difficult to break. The website spammimic.com offers tools that hide text in "spam," unsolicited bulk commercial e-mail. Speech compression technology allows users to convert a computer into a secure phone device.

Network accounts can be deleted or changed as required. For example, Internet users can create Internet accounts with national firms such as America Online (AOL), or can even create an AOL Instant Messenger (AIM) account on a short-term basis. In addition, anonymous logins are possible for many of the thousands of chat rooms on the net. If desired, the user can access cyber cafes, university and library computers, or additional external resources to further hide the source of the messages. An al Qaeda laptop found in Afghanistan had linked with the French Anonymous Society on several occasions. The site offers a two-volume Sabotage Handbook online.

Not only are anonymous methods available for the people who use the Internet, but at times Internet service providers (ISPs) unwittingly participate in serving people or groups for purposes other than legitimate ones. The al Qaeda web site www.alneda.com was originally located in Malaysia until 13 May. It reappeared in Texas at http://66.34.191.223/ until 13 June, and then reappeared on 21 June at www.drasat.com in Michigan. It was shut down on 25 June 2002. The ISPs hosting it apparently knew nothing about the content of the site or even the fact that it was housed on their servers. This shell game with their website enabled the al Qaeda web to remain functional in spite of repeated efforts to shut it down. Cyber deception campaigns will remain a problem for law enforcement personnel for years to come.

4) The Internet produces an atmosphere of virtual fear or virtual life. People are afraid of things that are invisible and things they don't understand. The virtual threat of computer attacks appears to be one of those things. Cyberfear is generated by the fact that what a computer attack could do (bring down airliners, ruin critical infrastructure, destroy the stock market, reveal Pentagon planning secrets, etc.) is too often associated with what will happen. News reports would lead one to believe that hundreds or thousands of people are still active in the al Qaeda network on a daily basis just because al Qaeda says so. It is clear that the Internet empowers small groups and makes them appear much more capable than they might actually be, even turning bluster into a type of virtual fear. The net allows terrorists to amplify the consequences of their activities with follow-on messages and threats directly to the population at large, even though the terrorist group may be totally impotent. In effect, the

Inter net allows a person or group to appear to be larger or more important or threatening than they really are.

The Internet can be used to spread disinformation, frightening personal messages, or horrific images of recent activities (one is reminded of the use of the net to replay the murder of reporter Daniel Pearl by his Pakistani captors). Virtually, it appears as though attacks are well planned and controlled, and capabilities are genuine. Messages are usually one-sided, however, and reflect a particular political slant. There is often little chance to check the story and find out if it is mere bravado or fact. The Internet can thus spread rumors and false reports that many people, until further examination, regard as facts.

Recently, the Arab TV station al-Jazeera has played tape recordings of bin Laden's speeches and displayed a note purportedly signed by him praising attacks on an oil tanker near Yemen, and on US soldiers participating in a war game in Kuwait. These messages were picked up and spread around the Internet, offering virtual proof that bin Laden was alive. Most likely bin Laden was seriously injured (which is why we haven't seen him in over a year), but his image can be manipulated through radio or Internet broadcasts so that he appears confident, even healthy.

5) The Internet can help a poorly funded group to raise money. Al Qaeda has used Islamic humanitarian "charities" to raise money for jihad against the perceived enemies of Islam. Analysts found al Qaeda and humanitarian relief agencies using the same bank account numbers on numerous occasions. As a result, several US-based Islamic charities were shut down. The Sunni extremist group Hizb al-Tabrir uses an integrated web of Internet sites from Europe to Africa to call for the return of an Islamic caliphate. The website states that it desires to do so by peaceful means. Supporters are encouraged to assist the effort by monetary support, scholarly verdicts, and encouraging others to support jihad. Bank information, including account numbers, is provided on a German site, www.explizit-islam.de. Portals specializing in the anonymous transfer of money, or portals providing services popular with terrorists (such as the issue of new identities and official passports) are also available.

The fighters in the Russian breakaway republic of Chechnya have used the Internet to publicize banks and bank account numbers to which sympathizers can contribute. One of these Chechen bank accounts is located in Sacramento, California, according to a Chechen website known as amina.com.

Of course, there are other ways to obtain money for a cause via the Internet. One of the most common ways is credit card fraud. Jean-Francois Ricard, one of France's top anti-terrorism investigators, noted that many Islamist terror plots in Europe and North America were financed through such criminal activity.

6) The Internet is an outstanding command and control mechanism. Command and control, from a US military point of view, involves the exercise of authority and direction by a properly designated commander over assigned and attached forces in the accomplishment of the mission. Personnel, equipment, communications, facilities, and procedures accomplish command and control by assisting in planning, directing, coordinating, and controlling forces and operations in the accomplishment of a mission.

Command and control on the Internet is not hindered by geographical distance, or by lack of sophisticated communications equipment. Antigovernment groups present at the G8 conference in Cologne used the Internet to attack computers of financial centers and to coordinate protests from locations as distant as Indonesia and Canada. Terrorists can use their front organizations to coordinate such attacks, to flood a key institution's e-mail service (sometimes as a diversionary tactic for another attack), or to send hidden messages that coordinate and plan future operations.

The average citizen, the antigovernment protester, and the terrorist now have access to command and control means, limited though they may be, to coordinate and plan attacks. Further, there are "cracking" tools available to detect security flaws in systems and try to exploit them. Attaining access to a site allows the hacker or planner to command and control assets (forces or electrons) that are not his. The Internet's potential for command and control can vastly improve an organization 's effectiveness if it does not have a dedicated command and control establishment, especially in the propaganda and internal coordination areas. Finally, command and control can be accomplished via the Internet's chat rooms. One website, alneda.com, has supported al Qaeda's effort to disperse its forces and enable them to operate independently, providing leadership via strategic guidance, theological arguments, and moral inspiration. The site also published a list of the names and home phone numbers of 84 al Qaeda fighters captured in Pakistan after escaping from Afghanistan. The aim presumably was to allow sympathizers to contact their families and let them know they were alive.

7) The Internet is a recruiting tool. The web allows the user complete control over content, and eliminates the need to rely on journalists for publicity.

Individuals with sympathy for a cause can be converted by the images and messages of terrorist organizations, and the addition of digital video has reinforced this ability. Images and video clips are tools of empowerment for terrorists. More important, net access to such products provides contact points for men and women to enroll in the cause, whatever it may be. Additionally, current versions of web browsers, including Netscape and Internet Explorer, support JavaScript functions allowing Internet servers to know which language is set as the default for a particular client's computer. Hence, a browser set to use English as the default language can be redirected to a site optimized for publicity aimed at Western audiences, while one set to use Arabic as the default can be redirected to a different site tailored toward Arab or Muslim sensibilities.

This allows recruiting to be audience- and language-specific, enabling the web to serve as a recruiter of talent for a terrorist cause. Recently, the Chechen website qoqaz.net, which used to be aimed strictly against Russian forces operating in Chechnya, changed its address to assam.com, and now includes links to Jihad in Afghanistan, Jihad in Palestine, and Jihad in Chechnya. Such sites give the impression that the entire Islamic world is uniting against the West, when in fact the site may be the work of just a few individuals.

8) The Internet is used to gather information on potential targets. The website operated by the Muslim Hackers Club reportedly featured links to US sites that purport to disclose sensitive information like code names and radio frequencies used by the US Secret Service. The same website offers tutorials in viruses, hacking stratagems, network "phreaking" and secret codes, as well as links to other militant Islamic and cyberprankster web addresses. Recent targets that terrorists have discussed include the Centers for Disease Control and Prevention in Atlanta; FedWire, the money-movement clearing system maintained by the Federal Reserve Board; and facilities controlling the flow of information over the Internet. Attacks on critical infrastructure control systems would be particularly harmful, especially on a system such as the Supervisory Control and Data Acquisition (SCADA) system. Thus any information on insecure

network architectures or non-enforceable security protocols is potentially very damaging.

Terrorists have access, like many Americans, to imaging data on potential targets, as well as maps, diagrams, and other crucial data on important facilities or networks. Imaging data can also allow terrorists to view counterterrorist activities at a target site. One captured al Qaeda computer contained engineering and structural architecture features of a dam, enabling al Qaeda engineers and planners to simulate catastrophic failures.

With regard to gathering information through the Internet, on 15 January 2003 Defense Secretary Donald Rumsfeld observed that anal Qaeda training manual recovered in Afghanistan said, "Using public sources openly and without resorting to illegal means, it is possible to gather at least 80 percent of all information required about the enemy."

9) The Internet puts distance between those planning the attack and their targets. Terrorists planning attacks on the United States can do so abroad with limited risk, especially if their command and control sites are located in countries other than their own. Tracing the route of their activity is particularly difficult. The net provides terrorists a place to plan without the risks normally associated with cell or satellite phones.

10) The Internet can be used to steal information or manipulate data. Ronald Dick, Director of the FBI's National Infrastructure Protection Center, considers the theft or manipulation of data by terrorist groups as his worst nightmare, especially if the attacks are integrated with a physical attack such as on a US power grid. Richard Clark, Chairman of the President's Critical Infrastructure Protection Board, said the problem of cyber security and data protection had its own 9/11 on 18 September 2001 when the Nimda virus spread through Internet-connected computers around the world, causing billions of dollars of damage. Nimda's creator has never been identified. This virus, hardly noticed in the wake of the airliner attacks and anthrax scares, set off a chain reaction among software companies (including Microsoft) to get very serious about plugging vulnerabilities. In the fall of 2001 a number of unexplained intrusions began occurring against Silicon Valley computers. An FBI investigation traced the intrusions to telecommunication switches in Saudi Arabia, Indonesia, and Pakistan. While none was directly linked to al Qaeda, there remain strong suspicions that the group was somehow involved.

11) The Internet can be used to send hidden messages. The practice of steganography, which involves hiding messages inside graphic files, is a widespread art among criminal and terrorist elements. Hidden pages or nonsensical phrases can be coded instructions for al Qaeda operatives and supporters. One recent report noted,

Al Qaeda uses prearranged phrases and symbols to direct its agents. An icon of an AK-47 can appear next to a photo of Osama bin Laden facing one direction one day, and another direction the next. The color of icons can change as well. Messages can be hidden on pages inside sites with no links to them, or placed openly in chat rooms.

In addition, it is possible to buy encryption software for less than $15. Cyberplanners gain an advantage in hiding their messages via encryption. Sometimes the messages are not even hidden in a sophisticated manner. Al-Jazeera television reported that Mohammed Atta's final message (another advantage of the Internet—the impossibility of checking sources) to direct the attacks on the Twin Towers was simple and open. The message purportedly said, "The semester begins in three more weeks. We've obtained 19 confirmations for studies in the faculty of law, the faculty of urban planning, the faculty of fine arts, and the faculty of engineering." The reference to the various faculties was apparently the code for the buildings targeted in the attacks.

12) The Internet allows groups with few resources to offset even some huge propaganda machines in advanced countries. The web is an attractive device to those looking for a way to attack major powers via the mass media. The "always on" status of the web allows these individuals not only to access sites day and night but also to scold major powers and treat them with disdain in a public forum. The web can be used to counter facts and logic with the logic of the terrorist. There is no need for the terrorist organization to worry about "the truth," because ignoring facts is a standard operating procedure.

Al Qaeda uses polemics on the net not only to offset Western reporting, but also to counter Muslims who don't toe the party line. It defends the conduct of its war against the West and encourages violence. The web is important to al Qaeda because it can be used to enrage people and neutralize moderate opinion. The website of the Center for Islamic Studies and Research (according to one source, a made-up name), for example, has 11 sections, including reports on fighting in Afghanistan, world media coverage of the conflict, books on jihad theology, videos of hijackers' testaments, information about prisoners held in Pakistan and Guantanamo Bay, and jihad poetry.

It does not pay for any major power to lie, as facts can be easily used against them. Even in the war in Chechnya, there were times when the Chechens would report a successful ambush of a Russian convoy, and the Russians would deny the event ever happened. To prove their point, the Chechens would show video footage of the ambush on the Internet, thus offsetting the credibility of the Russian official media and undercutting the power of their massive propaganda machine. Al Qaeda officials are waiting to do the same to Western media reporting if the opportunity presents itself.

13) The Internet can be used to disrupt business. This tactic requires precise timing and intimate knowledge of the business climate in the target country. It attempts to harm businesses by accusing them of guilt by association.

Hizbullah, for example, has outlined a strategy to cripple Israeli government, military, and business sites with the aim of disrupting normal economic and societal operations. Phase one might be to disable official Israeli government sites; phase two might focus on crashing financial sites such as those on the Israeli stock exchange; phase three might involve knocking out the main Israeli internet servers; and phase four might blitz Israeli e-commerce sites to ensure the loss of hundreds of transactions. A final phase could be to accuse companies that do business with a target government as guilty by association and call for a boycott of the firm's products. Arab terrorists attacked Lucent Technologies in a round of Israeli-Arab cyber skirmishes, for example. All of these plans require insider knowledge in order to carry out the operation in a timely and accurate manner.

14) The Internet can mobilize a group or diaspora, or other hackers to action. Websites are not only used to disseminate information and propaganda. They also are used to create solidarity and brotherhood among groups. In the case of Islamist terrorist organizations, the Internet substitutes for the loss of bases and territory. In this respect the most important sites are alneda.com, jehad.net, drasat.com, and aloswa.org, which feature quotes from bin Laden tapes, religious legal rulings that justify the terrorist attacks, and support for the al Qaeda cause. In addition, website operators have established a site that is "a kind of database or encyclopedia for the dissemination of

computer viruses." The site is 7hj.7hj.com, and it aims to teach Internet users how to conduct computer attacks, purportedly in the service of Islam.

15) The Internet takes advantage of legal norms. Non-state actors or terrorists using the Internet can ignore Western notions of law and focus instead on cultural or religious norms. At a minimum, they ignore legal protocols on the Internet. In addition, they use the net to break the law (when they hack websites or send out viruses) while at the same time the law protects them (from unlawful surveillance, etc.).

International investigations into such behavior are difficult to conclude due to the slow pace of other nations' investigative mechanisms, and the limited time that data is stored. However, in the aftermath of the events of 9/11 in the United States, the terrorists' actions actually initiated several changes in the US legal system that were not to the terrorists' advantage. For example, in the past, the privacy concerns of Internet users were a paramount consideration by the US government. After 9/11, new legislation was enacted.

The controversial USA Patriot Act of 2001 included new field guidance relating to computer crime and electronic evidence. The Patriot Act is designed to unite and strengthen the United States by providing the appropriate tools required to intercept and obstruct terrorism. It establishes a counterterrorism fund in the Treasury Department, amends federal criminal code that authorizes enhanced surveillance procedures, provides guidelines for investigating money-laundering concerns, removes obstacles to investigating terrorism (granting the FBI authority to investigate fraud and computer-related activity for specific cases), and strengthens criminal laws against terrorism.

The "Field Guidance on New Authorities that Relate to Computer Crime and Electronic Evidence Enacted in the USA Patriot Act of 2001" provides the authority to do several things. Authorizations include: intercepting voice communications in computer hacking investigations; allowing law enforcement to trace communications on the Internet and other computer networks within the pen register and trap and trace statute ("pen/trap" statute); intercepting communications of computer trespassers; writing nationwide search warrants for e-mail; and deterring and preventing cyberterrorism. The latter provision raises the maximum penalty for hackers that damage protected computers (and eliminates minimums); states that hackers need only show intent to cause damage, not a particular consequence or degree of damage; provides for the aggregation of damage caused by a hacker's entire course of conduct; creates a new offense for damaging computers used for national security and criminal justice; expands the definition of a "pro tected computer" to include computers in foreign countries; counts prior state convictions of computer crime as prior offenses; and defines computer "loss." In addition, the guidance develops and supports cyber-security forensic capabilities.

16) The Internet can be used to divert attention from a real attack scenario. Al Qaeda can plant threats on the Internet or via cell phones to mislead law enforcement officials. Terrorists study how the United States collects and analyzes information, and thus how we respond to information.

Terrorists know when their Internet "chatter" or use of telecommunications increases, US officials issue warnings. Terrorists can thus introduce false information into a net via routine means, measure the response it garners from the US intelligence community, and then try to figure out where the leaks are in their systems or what type of technology the United States is using to uncover their plans. For example, if terrorists use encrypted messages over cell phones to discuss a fake operation against, say, the Golden Gate Bridge, they can then sit back and watch to see if law enforcement agencies issue warnings regarding that particular landmark. If they do, then the terrorists know their communications are being listened to by US officials.

In conclusion, it should be reiterated that cyberplanning is as important a concept as cyberterrorism, and perhaps even more so. Terrorists won't have an easy time shutting down the Internet. Vulnerabilities are continuously reported and fixed while computers function without serious interference (at least in the United States). One hopes that law enforcement and government officials will focus more efforts on the cyberplanning capabilities of terrorists in order to thwart computer attacks and other terrorist activities. At a minimum, America can use such measures to make terrorist activities much harder to coordinate and control. Paul Eedle, writing in The Guardian, summed up the value of the Internet to al Qaeda:

Whether bin Ladin or al Qaeda's Egyptian theorist Ayman al-Zawahiri and their colleagues are on a mountain in the Hindu Kush or living with their beards shaved off in a suburb of Karachi no longer matters to the organization. They can inspire and guide a worldwide movement without physically meeting their followers—without knowing who they are.

Such is the power and the danger of cyberplanning.

Footnotes deleted.

7

Cyber Embargo

Countering the Internet Jihad

Gregory S. McNeal

If you are a young Muslim male, even a doctor, with a PC in Egypt, the Gulf states, Somalia, Morocco or Glasgow, as always with the Web you are marinating your mind in its content, and the content here is homicide on a mass scale. The answer—technical or political—is not obvious to me. But the one unacceptable answer is doing nothing.

Daniel Henninger

INTRODUCTION

As Daniel Henninger pointed out shortly after the attempted July 2007 Glasgow and London terrorist attacks, the solution to the problem of jihadist websites is not obvious. Nevertheless, doing nothing is no longer acceptable. Terrorists are engaged in an online jihad, characterized by the use of the internet to fundraise, distribute messages and directives, recruit, and proselytize. Although it is impossible to eliminate the presence of terrorists on the internet, this article details a proposal that would have a marked impact on the presence of terrorists on the internet. Using existing statutes, it is possible to regionalize terrorist websites, limiting them to a small number of countries from which they may receive internet services.

Gregory S. McNeal, Cyber embargo: Countering the internet jihad. *Case Western Reserve Journal of International Law* 39 (3): 789-827, 2007. Reprinted by permission.

Once the terrorist message is limited to a particular region, a modification of current laws can allow for a cyber embargo on jihadist websites and their supporters. These efforts, coupled with diplomatic cooperation, can further the attempt to curb the impact of jihadist websites, while simultaneously increasing the ability of governments to monitor these websites and, when necessary, shut them down.

This article is a thought piece, intended to create debate about my proposal. I have not exhaustively addressed all of the constitutional and policy issues associated with my proposal; instead, I hope this piece will serve as a platform for future scholarship. In this article, I outline my proposal for countering the internet jihad by using, as an example, the active and official website of Palestinian Islamic Jihad (PIJ), a designated terrorist organization. While I frequently reference PIJ, the principles I articulate have relevance to any other terrorist's website. In Part One I provide a brief overview of the status of Palestinian Islamic Jihad, and its brazen efforts to stay online despite government countermeasures. I outline a three-step process by which the PIJ web presence, and others like it, can be eliminated. Step one involves the use of the existing material support statute. Step two recommends the creation of a cyber embargo by modifying existing statutes to create a non-criminal "material supporter" designation that will prevent U.S. companies from conducting business with designated material supporters. Finally, step three involves diplomatic efforts to globalize the reach of the techniques detailed in steps one and two. Part One also explains the practical effect of each step of my proposed process on the official website of PIJ.

In Part Two of this article, I detail the threat posed by "cyber jihad." I explain how terrorists use the internet to recruit, train for attacks, and coordinate those attacks. I also describe the clear advantages terrorist organizations enjoy by using websites. This sets the stage for a discussion of the current statutory framework, which, to date, has only enjoyed moderate success.

In Part Three, I move beyond the threat and explore the legal and policy implications of using existing statutes to eliminate the web presence of terrorist organizations. I also detail the limitations of the current statute and prepare the reader for a discussion of how, with slight modifications, the existing statutory and policy framework can significantly diminish the advantages terrorist organizations enjoy through their web presence.

In Part Four, I present the critical next step in countering the cyber jihad. I explain the advantages of creating a cyber embargo on companies that provide "material support" to terrorist organizations, but that, for legal or policy reasons, may be beyond the reach of the material support statute. The creation of a cyber embargo rests upon a non-criminal "material supporter" designation that will prevent American companies from conducting business with designated "material supporters." In essence, this process involves the creation of virtual "persona non grata." I also detail the diplomatic efforts necessary to globalize the reach of this counter-terrorism strategy. Through cooperation with foreign governments, loopholes in the jihadist web presence can be closed and terrorist organizations can be forced to a limited number of potential host countries.

I conclude the article by discussing the implications of following my approach, and the new counterterrorism opportunities it presents.

I. THE PALESTINIAN ISLAMIC JIHAD EXAMPLE

PIJ is a designated terrorist organization, responsible for the deaths of Americans and others. They brazenly boasted in 2006 that the FBI could not shut them down, and their boasts, thus far, have proven true. In January 2006, PIJ's official website was present on the web through the support of three U.S. companies. After a public shaming campaign led by Internet Haganah, a web based watchdog group, PIJ changed network providers. As of May 2006, however, PIJ maintained six active websites, five of which were based on servers in the United States, with six American companies involved in keeping those sites online. A further check conducted at the time of this article's publication showed that the official websites of PIJ were still operational, although they have now located all of their internet services outside the United States, obtaining network services from businesses in Malaysia.

Some see the above example as support for the argument that efforts to counter the presence of terrorists on the internet are a fruitless endeavor. At first blush, the example of PIJ seems to support this assertion—despite actions taken to shut PIJ down in January and May of 2006 the cyber jihadists almost immediately resurfaced to mock authorities. Nevertheless, critics should not be so quick to dismiss efforts to shut down jihadist websites. The web, like other battlefields in the struggle against terrorist organizations, is dynamic, and efforts that keep the terrorists moving impose costs on their operations. These costs include preventing the distribution of the terrorist message, disrupting the organization's regular activities, and damaging the morale of the organization. Moreover, as the PIJ example illustrates, efforts to counter the terrorist presence on the web can force such organizations to overseas internet service providers, thus limiting their host options and increasing the likelihood that authorities will be able to track them.

Step one in the process of shutting down a website such as PIJ is to use shaming techniques and the threat of criminal sanctions to stop U.S. companies from providing services to a designated terrorist organization. Websites such as Internet Haganah posted the details of U.S. companies who were providing services to PIJ as part of a shaming campaign. The website encouraged readers to contact those U.S. companies and demand that they stop supporting terrorists. The U.S. companies have more at stake than just their reputation. Current statutes make it a crime to provide material support to terrorist organizations, and the list of prohibited forms of support includes the provision of computer services. Shortly after the shaming campaign, with its attendant potential for criminal liability, the PIJ website shifted its operation to overseas service providers that are beyond the reach of U.S. laws and less susceptible to shaming techniques. As a result, the PIJ website is still operating today.

The second step to further isolate and eventually shut down the PIJ website is the most critical one. As the facts detailed in step one illustrate, current laws and techniques are limited, and terrorist organizations are quick to adapt and avoid the reach of shaming techniques and U.S. laws. Nevertheless, once terrorist organizations make their home outside the United States, they must still rely on the support of service providers in their new jurisdiction. While the terrorist organization itself may not be deterred by U.S. efforts, their service providers are vulnerable to commercial pressure and the desire to maintain their business—the majority of which likely comes from non-terrorist clientele. These service providers are the critical and weakest link in the terrorist's web presence. Accordingly, a cyber embargo is the quickest and most effective way to cease their support of terrorist organizations. Such an embargo focuses on those service providers who are providing material support to PIJ in the form of web services.

The example of PIJ demonstrates the necessity of this cyber embargo. After being forced off of U.S. network service providers, PIJ now receives an IP address and connection to the internet from a Malaysian network service provider, Time Net Central. They also receive registrar services from Time Telekomm, a major telecommunications company in Malaysia. I propose a modification to existing statutes to create a new material supporter designation. U.S. companies and persons under this approach will be forbidden from doing business with a designated material supporter. The practical result of such a designation will be to create a cyber embargo, cutting off streams of income to overseas companies due to their affiliation with terrorist organizations.

With a cyber embargo in place, companies that support terrorists will be forced to choose between either losing all commercial services from the United States or continuing to provide services to the terrorist organization. The result in the case of PIJ is obvious. If Time Telekomm, a major international telecommunications company, were designated as a material supporter, then all U.S. commercial services would be cut off, including internet and financial services. In the face of this potential loss of income, Time Telekomm would likely cease providing services to PIJ immediately. Moreover, the network service provider Time Net Central, may also have ties to U.S. commercial activity, and would be reluctant to find itself designated a material supporter.

Nevertheless, it is still possible that Time Net Central is a much smaller organization and may not be deterred by a material supporter designation. As such, a further step is necessary to isolate these terrorist organizations and their overseas webhosts. The third step involves diplomatic efforts to standardize the creation of "designated material supporter" lists by urging nations to adopt the list and implement necessary domestic enforcement mechanisms. Such an adoption will expand the number of nations participating in a cyber embargo, and will foreclose overseas safe havens for terrorist websites. In the example above, Time Net Central, as a small, mostly domestic company, may not be concerned if commercial activity between it and the United States is disrupted. Time Net Central will likely be very concerned, however, if Malaysia has a similar designation process that cuts commercial ties between itself and a major Malaysian company such as Time Telekomm, for example. Thus, expanding the cyber embargo is key because as PIJ continues to shift its operations to countries it believes are safe havens the cyber embargo will continue to isolate them geographically.

II. RECRUITMENT, COORDINATION, TRAINING, AND CYBER JIHAD

OVERVIEW OF WEBSITES, WEBHOSTS, AND THE INTERNET JIHAD

Why should we be concerned with the presence of terrorists on the internet? Unlike cyberterrorism, which is the use of computers to attack networks and create chaos, the cyber jihad is information presented on behalf of terrorist organizations, and is seemingly less

94

threatening than cyberterrorism. There is no evidence to indicate that cyberterrorist techniques have been used for serious destructive activity. On the other hand, the cyber jihad can be used for many activities that directly support war. For example, Joseph Shahda, an expert in cyberterrorism, explains that "[t]errorist leaders including Bin Laden have stated that 'media Jihad' is as important as 'battlefield Jihad' and in this case the most common and powerful medium for the terrorists 'media Jihad' is the internet." The internet is used on a daily basis to support the ongoing jihad. Via the internet, terrorist groups set up operation centers, raise money, recruit, spread propaganda, and communicate their ideologies. All of this is accomplished with minimal effort and resources, and without geographical limitation. Thus, the internet jihad is quite successful and has serious consequences. Officials would not allow PIJ or other terrorist organizations to operate a downtown recruiting center or headquarters; similarly, terrorists should not be allowed to engage in the same activity on the internet.

RECRUITING AND COMMUNICATING THE IDEOLOGY

The internet provides an inexpensive recruiting tool for terrorists to win supporters and members from any part of the world.

Because the internet can be accessed easily by those at home or in public places, the number of potential recruits has gone up exponentially since the rise of the internet. Websites and chat rooms provide an instant connection between recruiters and interested sympathizers.

Technology has made instantaneous recruitment simple. With the internet capabilities of digital imaging and video, terrorists can broadcast powerful messages to a mass audience of sympathetic viewers. Bandwidth costs continue to decrease, thereby reducing streaming video costs. Furthermore, terrorists can use browsers to check language settings and direct the viewer to a site customized to his language and culture. Interested viewers can then contact the terrorists by way of the contact information listed on the web. Once contact is established, terrorists can assess and recruit members for their cause. Through steganography, the process of embedding messages in graphic files, terrorists can use their websites to provide instructions to their recruits.

Again, anonymity plays a large role in the internet's efficacy as a terrorist tool. The anonymity of the internet has been found to foster higher levels of violence in people. This rise in violent feelings is understandable, when one considers that anonymity allows people to act freely, unfettered by a fear of consequences. Terrorists can encourage these feelings of violence, drawing people to their cause.

Additionally, terrorists are using the internet to target younger members of society. According to a congressional report, "web sites are often flashy and colorful, apparently designed to appeal to a computer savvy, media-saturated, video game-addicted generation." One such example was a website that presented the video game "Quest for Bush." The object of the game is to conquer Americans in the name of the jihad. Levels of the game include "Jihad Growing Up" and "American's Hell." Other sites play youth-oriented music like rap and hip-hop.

With the advent of internet recruitment, terrorists have been able to lower their costs while customizing their search for potential members on a global level. Furthermore, terrorists can stir web visitors into action by raising their feelings of violence and indignation. Thus, the internet has increased the pool of recruits for terrorist organizations.

Related to recruiting, one of the jihadists' main goals is to pass on their ideology and provide a sense of community and belonging. Because the internet is capable of generating a virtual community, jihadists can reach supporters in any corner of the world. Ultimately, the community strengthens the bond of individuals to the group.

On the internet, communication is not unidirectional. Rather than issuing a statement that reaches group members, jihadist leaders can invite interactive participation. By doing so, leaders can answer questions, address issues, and engage in discussions to create unity within the group. Once unity has been established, leaders can invite small groups of people to exchange strategies and work together toward the same goal. These strategies are often aimed at moving against the United States. One example is a jihadist Yahoo! message board that presented a strategy to compel United States-led coalition forces to leave Iraq.

In another, more recent example, six Muslim men living in the United States were charged with plotting to attack Fort Dix in New Jersey. The men had planned to sneak onto the base as military personnel. The accused were united via the internet, where they all downloaded videos of Osama bin Laden preaching inspirational jihadist messages. Their capture resulted from a tip by a store clerk who was hired by the men to dub video of their training and practice attacks onto a digital disk for internet use.

The internet has proven to be a simple, effective way for jihadists to communicate their ideology and create strong communities of supporters that strategize together. With its ability to eliminate geographical constraints, the interact allows jihadists from abroad to unite and work together with those on the homefront. The Fort Dix plot demonstrated that jihadists, with intent to contribute to the international cause, could join and construct a plot within U.S. borders.

Official websites of al Qaeda and other designated terrorist groups are not just hosted in the Arab world. In fact, many are registered or hosted in Europe, Asia, or the United States. These sites offer articles that condemn America, give biographies of Islamists killed in battle, and relate biased accounts of the current war in Afghanistan. They communicate an ideology with the intent to recruit members to the terrorist organization's cause.

COMMAND AND CONTROL

Beyond recruiting, terrorist websites can also act as virtual command and control centers. The ease of accessibility and information exchange make websites ideal for serving some of the administrative functions of terrorist organizations. Terrorists are able to exert control over their missions through the internet with few geographic and communication limitations. A terrorist in Iran, for example, can coordinate attacks in the United States from afar. The convenience of the internet has made terrorist operations "cheaper, faster, and more secure." Terrorist organizations are dynamic, and the internet has become the medium of choice for centralizing their operations. Communication and training is much easier to accomplish with the speed of the internet, and without the limitations of geography.

Prior to the age of the internet, terrorists were limited to communicating with each other by way of available electronics, such as telephones or radios. As a result, they were always at risk of being monitored by electronic surveillance tools, such as wiretaps. The internet solved that problem by providing anonymity. For example, complex encryption keys, nearly impossible to break, mask terrorist messages. Terrorists can use spamming tools that hide messages in bulk commercial email. Network accounts can be easily set up under false names, and many internet access locations have anonymous logins. Often, hosting internet service providers are unaware of their clients' site content.

TRAINING SITES

Terrorists also use websites as training sites by posting training materials online. For example, the training pamphlet, How Can I Train Myself for Jihad, was originally posted on Azzam.com, a website run by a British company and affiliated with Sheikh Abdullah Azzam, a mentor to Osama Bin Laden. The document provided information on various aspects of battle, including martial arts, survival training, and firearm use.

The Azzam.com subscriber list included Said Bahaj, who is believed to be a key planner in the September 11, 2001 terrorist attacks, which peripherally demonstrates the use and effectiveness of internet training sites. Another example of detailed online training comes from al Battar, al Qaeda's online journal. At one point, the constantly relocating al Battar was posted on www.alm2sda.net, a jihadist internet forum. Topics included methods of intelligence gathering, discussions of bin Laden's political genius, and explanations of public kidnapping procedures. One article provided a "how to" guide for dealing with hostages, instructing site visitors to "[s]eparate the young people from the old, the women and the children. The young people have more strength, hence their ability to resist is high. The security forces must be killed instantly. This prevents others from showing resistance."

Dozens of sites feature information on how to build chemical and explosive weapons. The Mujahadeen Poisons Handbook, posted on the official Hamas website, included instructions for homemade poisons, poisonous gases, and other deadly materials for use in terrorist attacks. Other websites, like alneda.com, offered motivational tidbits, religious support, and strategies for attack. Additionally, the media has speculated that such sites are written in Arabic to direct al Qaeda to other sites. Some websites even trained readers to wage attacks through the computer system itself. For example, the site 7hj.7hj.com taught viewers how to damage computer systems with viruses.

Terrorists are able to run training websites more effectively by using video demonstrations. Videos train viewers to make explosive devices, gunpowder, mines, and suicide bomber vests. One website that featured links to such videos, Al Qalah, claimed responsibility for several terrorist attacks. The website also featured Arabic voiceovers and written instructions. In keeping with the anonymity of the internet, the videos did not show any faces.

The example of "Irahabi007," also known as Younis Tsouli, supports these conclusions. Tsouli was an information technology student in London, and was one of al-Qaida's most notorious cyber facilitators. He distributed online weapons manuals and videotapes of bombings and beheadings. He taught seminars on how to operate online anonymously, and how to hack into vulnerable websites and upload material onto them.

The internet serves as the ultimate center of operations for terrorist organizations. Not only does the internet provide terrorist organization websites with a safe location to train and communicate with their members, but it also provides global access. This kind of access facilitates fundraising, as well as recruiting, and allows propaganda to be spread all over the world in a very inexpensive and efficient manner.

FUNDRAISING

Terrorist organizations use the internet to raise funds for their murderous activities. They rely on donations given through charities and nongovernmental organizations that conduct business online. Terrorist groups often establish websites that front as charities, but serve as fundraising centers for their cause. For example, Al Qaeda employs charities under the guise of Islamic humanitarianism. The Benevolence International Foundation (BIF), based in the United States, touts itself as an organization that provides relief to war-torn areas. BIF gave $600,000 to Al-Qaeda trainees and funded activities for Osama bin Laden and other Islamists involved with the September 11, 2001 attack.

Contributors are often unaware that the ultimate destinations of their donations are terrorist organizations. Moreover, terrorists have become adroit at soliciting donations. The webmaster can pull demographic information from online questionnaires that contributors fill out when donating to the charity. They then use this information to send out emails tailored to the contributor in the hope of gaining more sympathy and, ultimately, contributions.

The example of Irahbi007 supports these conclusions. Two days before his arrest, Irahbi007 had the following encrypted web chat with a colleague:

Abuthaabit: This media work, I am telling you, is very important. Very, very, very, very.

Irhabi007: I know, I know.

Abuthaabit: Because a lot of the funds brothers are getting is because they are seeing stuff like this coming out. Imagine how many people have gone [to Iraq] after seeing the situation because of the videos.

Imagine how many of them could have been shaheed [martyrs] as well.

This admission confirms that the internet is one of the weapons terrorists use to raise funds and personnel to aid their cause.

EXECUTIONS AND PROPAGANDA

Terrorist organizations have also begun to employ websites as a form of information warfare. Their websites can disperse inaccurate information that has far-reaching consequences. Because internet postings are not regulated sources of news, they can reflect any viewpoint, truthful or not. Thus, readers tend to consider internet items to be fact, and stories can go unchecked for some time. Furthermore, streaming video and pictures of frightening scenes can support and magnify these news stories. As a result, the internet is a powerful and effective tool for spreading propaganda.

The usefulness of the internet for propaganda is similar to its usefulness for operation headquartering. Anonymity and global capability permit terrorists to spread their message quickly to all areas of the world with minimal risk of detection. Al Qaeda's use of the internet provides a good illustration. Rather than using official websites that are easier to pinpoint and shut down, al Qaeda uses semi-official sites to broadcast its propaganda. The people who maintain such sites are al Qaeda members or supporters, and they are almost impossible to identify. Registering websites can be accomplished easily with fabricated information, and the ability of terrorists to remain anonymous lends to the allure of using the internet.

Azzam.com, an al Qaeda site, features more than four-dozen flattering biographies of foreign Mujahideen who were killed in the jihad. Many of these biographies are supplemented with images, audio, and video, and they aim to inspire readers to join the cause. Other al Qaeda websites, such as jehad.net, give interested readers their perspective on the conflict in Afghanistan. Using such websites, Al Qaeda is able to broadcast a biased version of the news, while claiming to be a news source. One such example involves an insurgent "black propaganda" operation called "Lee's Life for Lies";

[t]his operation involved fabricating the false history of American soldier Lee Kendall, whose USB flash drive was found by insurgents. The insurgents utilized the information contained in the USB to write a fake letter that described the desperate situation of the foreign soldier in Iraq and the existence of abuses and unpunished war crimes.

Al Qaeda can, thus, downplay negative stories about unsuccessful attacks and highlight unfair treatment of Afghan (and other) civilians by Americans. These sites commonly use a tactic in which they report high death tolls for American troops to rally support. In reality, however, death tolls are hundreds of times smaller than the sites claim. These tactics make readers and supporters believe that al Qaeda stands strong against the United States.

Many sites also feature statements made by Osama bin Laden or al Qaeda. Some post public executions, like that of kidnapped American Nick Berg. In fact, an increasing number of websites have included graphic video testimonials of suicide bombers. These websites, which tap into visual imagery, are likely to have more power to connect with their audience. A recent report from The United States Military Academy at West Point's Combating Terrorism Center reinforces this conclusion, stating "[v]isual imagery provides a key aspect of the terrorists' message in that it allows these groups to paint a picture of their objectives, their enemies, and their strategy through graphics, photographs, and symbols."

In light of the clear advantages terrorist organizations enjoy by using websites to recruit, coordinate, and enhance their operations, new and creative ways to diminish the terrorist web presence are necessary. To date, extant efforts have enjoyed only moderate success. Nevertheless, with slight modifications, the existing statutory and policy framework can markedly diminish the advantages terrorist organizations enjoy on the internet.

III. UNDERSTANDING THE EXISTING STATUTORY AND POLICY FRAMEWORK AND ISOLATING THE THREAT

OVERVIEW OF INTERNET ARCHITECHTURE AND JIHADIST TECHNIQUES

The internet's ubiquity and resilience allows for seamless global communications thereby making it difficult to control its use by terrorists. The interconnected nature of the web means that for a website to operate effectively, it must rely on intermediaries to carry any individual message. These intermediaries are U.S. and foreign companies that support the internet jihad by providing domain names to, and hosting the websites of terrorist organizations. Some may be doing so unwittingly, while others may be turning a blind eye. The internet jihad, however, can be countered by enlisting corporate cooperation, and where cooperation fails, sanctioning companies that support terrorist organizations.

The first step is to identify terrorist websites; some claim to be "the official" website, while others merely post supportive information. While the task of identifying terrorist websites is difficult, small, private watchdog groups that police the internet for potential threats are emerging. As previously mentioned, one particularly well-known watchdog website is Internet Haganah, run by Aaron Weisburd. Keeping his costs low, Weisburd operates out of his home office and has a network of supporters who contribute time and money to the voluntary counterterrorism endeavor. By going undercover as an interested party, Weisburd is able to discover jihadist sites that pose a high risk. Once Weisburd locates terrorist activity, he tracks down the host of the website and either shames the internet service provider (ISP) into shutting the site down, or provides the information to the appropriate authorities who can, in turn, notify the ISP.

While this solution is beneficial given its low cost, Weisburd's method has its weaknesses. The main problem is that when he shuts a website down, that same website will reappear somewhere else. The terrorists who run these sites merely move to a new ISP. Because ISPs are numerous, the time-consuming tracking process must begin all over again. Unfortunately, jihadists are often able to jump from site to site much more quickly than the sites can be shut down.

Moreover, Jihadists have gone one step further. Not only do they switch ISPs, but they also take on new domains. Finding new domains is a fairly easy task. Al Qaeda, for example, uses mailing lists, chat rooms, and sympathizer websites that immediately broadcast the new domain name to al Qaeda members. Because these sources are password protected and fairly secure, jihadists ensure that only their group receives the information.

As in the example of PIJ, once a terrorist organization is shut down by its ISP the jihadists pack up and move to a new ISP. There are many ISPs in business, and thus relocating the website is akin to finding a needle in a haystack. Nevertheless, terrorist organizations are interested in recruiting, spreading their message, fundraising, and coordinating their efforts. Thus, a website that cannot be found does not benefit them, and therein lies the first of their weaknesses.

Moreover, all website or domain names (*.com, *.gov, *.org, etc.) are controlled by a domain name registrar, and the domain name servers maintain directory maps to each domain.

Simply put, to create a website with a domain name, one must register and pay for it. Once the name is registered, the company that owns the name can keep track of which ISP is hosting their domain name. When PIJ decided to operate their website, they selected the domain name saraya.ps. This domain name, like all domain names, is owned by a company called a domain name registrar (DNR). Different companies own the rights to a unique set of domain names, so PIJ had to approach the appropriate company to purchase the use of the name saraya.ps. Once they received their domain name, PIJ needed to find an ISP to host their actual site. Because the DNR can trace the location of its domain names, it is always able to track saraya.ps to its ISP.

Knowing this, the jihadists have begun not only switching ISPs, but also changing domain names to avoid detection. This is because the DNR's directory details each new ISP of a given name, the sites are often shut down in quick succession by tracing the domain name to the next ISP. The mere act of changing names is enough to thwart the tracking process and begin the tedious hunting anew; however, it also results in a temporary loss of the terrorist organization's ability to communicate with their followers.

SHUTTING DOWN DNRS

One step toward immobilizing the internet jihad is to ignore the ISP and go straight to the DNR to shut down domain names themselves. Many jihadist sites purchase their names from U.S.-based companies, and hence would be easy to regulate. Once a site is identified as affiliated with a terrorist group, the DNR can be found without difficulty. Several sites, like whois.com and godaddy.com, maintain a listing of DNRs for domain names. For example, after entering alhanein.com, number three on Weisburd's current top twelve list of terrorist websites, the search turns up Fast Domain, Inc., a DNR based out of Utah.

Once a domain name is shut down, the site no longer appears in web searches. Web crawlers, such as Google and Yahoo! Search, limit their crawl space with rules. These rules forbid search returns of IP addresses, limiting returns to domain names only. Hence, jihadist networks without domain names would be crippled by an inability to recruit interested parties who use such web crawlers to search the internet.

Nevertheless, internet companies have proven that, due to the nature of the web business, they can neither be forced nor expected to police the hundreds of thousands of websites with which they are affiliated. For ex ample, in 2004 the American company, Network Solutions, hosted PIJ. When a current customer complained about the company's support of a terrorist organization, the company's response was "Network Solutions has no responsibility or duty to police the rights of trademark owners concerning domain names." Network Solutions further added, "If the domain owner in question is conducting criminal activity we would ask you to defer to either the police or the proper authorities."

Despite the difficulties associated with shutting down websites, and the impossibility of eliminating the entire terrorist web presence, there are good reasons to make efforts. While some companies may be unwilling to cut off their clients, others may simply be unaware that they are hosting terrorist websites. In 2005, Weisburd alerted the U.S. government that forty-eight Iranian government websites, including the official website of Iran's Supreme Leader, were hosted by the American company CI Host. Because of a trade embargo enacted in 1980, U.S. companies are not permitted to be in business with Iran, which has been denoted by President Bush as being a member of the "Axis of Evil." CI Host was unaware that they were hosting such clients, and immediately shut down all forty-eight sites once they were informed of the issue.

THE PROBLEM AND THE LACK OF A COHERENT STRATEGY

Shutting down websites hosted within the United States is possible, but companies are sometimes reluctant to do so. Consider again the example of PIJ and one of their websites, qudsway.net. This site is hosted in Iran and has a domain name registered with a U.S. company, Network Solutions.

The most direct and effective option for shutting the site down would be to enlist the cooperation of Iran as the law enforcement arm in the country where the site is hosted. Since Iranians are the main backers of the PIJ, however, any attempt to work with them would be unsuccessful. The only other option would require Network Solutions to sever PIJ's registration with the domain name qudsway.net. Weisburd tried to shut the website down by contacting Network Solutions, but he met with serious resistance. A representative of Network Solutions sent him the following message:

In reviewing your site located at http://haganah.org.il/haganah/ I noted that my company is called out as being a company that is keeping qudsway.net online. Honestly, do you really think that there is not a good reason that the site is still up. Use your brain, I know that you must be more intelligent than your postswould have people believe. I find blogs like yours loathsome because you are criticizing the actions of a company when you have no idea what is actually happening.

As one can infer from the Network Solutions message, there may be "good reasons" that the website was still up. Perhaps the government chose to monitor the site and requested Network Solutions keep the site in operation, or it may just represent the lack of a clear policy. Either way, qudsway.net continues to flourish.

While it would certainly consume substantial government resources to attempt to shut down individual websites, service providers can shut down sites and domain names with relative ease. Many of these service providers do not even physically house the servers. Rather, they provide an IP address and network access. As Professor Orin Kerr points out, however, there are serious flaws in assuming that ISPs can monitor and control their property like a physical property owner, who can monitor and control their property. Kerr states that "[t]he common theme is that computer owners can know and control what is happening within their networks; civil liability can lead to less crime because computer owners have the power (and, with civil liability, the incentive) to minimize criminal activity." He states that the problem with this reasoning is that

[C]omprehensive ISP monitoring appears to be extremely difficult, even putting aside the very important privacy questions it raises. ISPs can have hundreds of thousands or even millions of customers; it is very difficult and time consuming for an ISP to watch just one or two customers in a comprehensive way; and it is easy for any customer to circumvent or defeat ISP monitoring.

Kerr has accurately stated the common theme—a theme related to my proposal. Nevertheless, my proposal is distinguishable from his suggesting civil liability, as mine adds both a notification requirement and watch dog monitoring. Thus, while sifting through websites for terrorist activities is beyond the reasonable capability of service providers, they would have no difficulty shutting down websites or domain names upon notification by government officials or third party monitors. Notwithstanding this, without some threat of penalty, be it criminal sanction, civil penalty, or shaming, there is little incentive for the service providers to act after notification.

MATERIAL SUPPORT STATUTE AS A TOOL
TO STOP THE INTERNET JIHAD

Following September 11, 2001, Congress and the justice system responded to the threat of terrorism through a dramatic increase in prosecutions under the material support statutes. The material support statutes have been two of the most frequently charged terrorism related offenses since 9/11, culminating in ninety-two individuals facing allegations that they violated either Section 2339A or Section 2339B. One of the key aspects of the material support statutes is their independence from any specific event, creating a separate offense for those attempting to support terrorism. Furthermore, they allow the charges to be made early in the terrorist plot. Section 2339A provides the government with tools to prosecute individuals and organizations that are actively supporting terrorist activities, either financially or otherwise. Expanding this concept of material support, Congress enacted Section 2339B, which focused on "providing material support or resources to designated foreign terrorist organizations." The two statutes share the definition of "material support" found in Section 2339A and incorporated by reference into Section 2339B.

Section 2339A was originally passed in the early 1990s after the first bombing of the World Trade Center while Congress was actively seeking a way to cut off funds given for the support of terrorist actions. The purpose of Section 2339A is to stop the furnishing of resources to any individual or group with the knowledge or intention that it be used to lend support to any of more than two dozen different terrorist activities. Within Section 2339A, material support is defined as any property, tangible or intangible, or service, including expert advice or assistance and communications equipment.

The scope of Section 2339A is often considered to be very narrow and unattainable by practical standards. Thus, only a short period after Section 2339A was passed, Congress added Section 2339B, making it a crime to knowingly provide material support or resources to a specifically "designated foreign terrorist organization." Because Section 2339B does not require that support be tied to a specific terrorist act as in Section 2339A, the material support statute's applicable use is significantly broadened by providing a way to prosecute indirect terrorist conduct. Furthermore, Section 2339B only requires that the "defendant knowingly provide material support or resources to a foreign terrorist organization." If a donor gives a designated foreign terrorist organization material support of the kind listed in the statute, even if it is meant to be used for peaceful nonviolent means, the donor is still in violation of Section 2339B. The policy position is that all support, regardless of its intended use when given to a designated terrorist organization, will ultimately free funds that can be used to further violent terrorist activities.

Section 2339B is the most used of the two material support statutes, as well as the most debated. Defendants often challenge section 2339B on the constitutional basis of freedom of association and the due process clause. Challengers claim that the right of association includes the fight to support that idea or group through the donation of money and goods. In Humanitarian Law Project v. Gonzales (HLP) the defendants claimed that without a specific intent requirement written into Section 2339B, the statute violates the Fifth Amendment. The plaintiffs relied upon precedent set by Scales v. United States. Scales was a conviction based on the Smith Act, which specifically criminalized being a member in an organization whose goal was to overthrow the government. The court in HLP disagreed with Scales, stating Section 2339B is fundamentally different by not criminalizing the membership, but instead the actions which would "materially support" the group's intentions. The effect of this distinction is that the court found that the specific intent requirement does not defeat the purpose and constitutionality of Section 2339B.

Although the validity of the statute itself has been upheld, courts have found portions of the statute to be impermissibly vague. In US v. Sattar, a terrorist organization called the Islamic Group (IG) operated within the United States as a radical Islamic group opposing any "infidels" who did not agree with either the IG's interpretation of Islamic law or the sentence and detention of the Islamic leader of the IG, Sheikh Abdel Rahman. The indictment against the defendants included a charge of facilitating correspondence between Rahman and third parties, namely other IG leaders. The court found that the "provision of communications equipment" was unconstitutional because "a criminal defendant simply could not be expected to know that the conduct alleged was prohibited by the statute." In addition, the court in Sattar stated the "provision" of "personnel" was also interpreted as impermissibly vague due to the lack of notice or standards for its application. Nevertheless, the court denied the defendant's claim that the statute was also overbroad and thus unconstitutional in light of its sweeping purpose and applicability. Section 2339B is content-neutral, and Congress has the ability to prohibit the "supply of tangible support."

DESIGNATION AS A FOREIGN TERRORIST ORGANIZATION

A variety of lists compiled by U.S. government agencies designate groups or individuals as terrorists. The Secretary of State has the power to declare a group a "foreign terrorist organization" (FTO) pursuant to 8 U.S.C. [section] 1189. The Secretary is authorized to make such a designation if three conditions are met: the organization is foreign, the organization engages in terrorist activity, and the terrorist activity threatens the security of U.S. citizens or the national security of the United States. If the Secretary finds that the organization meets these requirements, the Secretary can add the organization to the FTO list by informing Congress seven days before the designation, and then publishing a notice in the Federal Registrar. As of October 2005, there have been forty-two listed foreign terrorist organizations identified.

Section 2339B(g) defines the term "terrorist organization" as "an organization designated as a terrorist organization under section 219 of the Immigration and Nationality Act" which is codified at 18 U.S.C. 1189. Once an organization has been designated an FTO, the effects of that designation are in two important areas: finance and immigration. Under the Antiterrorism and Effective Death Penalty Act of 1996, it is a crime to donate money, assets, or any other "material support" to a designated FTO. Members of an FTO are also forbidden from entering the country and, if already present, are often subject to removal. Furthermore, if any bank or financial institution finds that it controls an FTO's money or has interests in the FTO's assets, they must retain possession of, or control over, the funds and report them to the Office of Foreign Assets Control of the U.S. Department of the Treasury. Most importantly, Section 2339B applies specifically to any donation of "material support" to a designated FTO on the State Department's list.

The U.S. Department of the Treasury compiles its own list of terrorist organizations, but the list also includes individuals designated as terrorists. Pursuant to Executive Order 13224, all property, and interests in property, within the United States owned by certain persons are blocked. According to the U.S. Department of Treasury website, these persons/organizations include: (foreign individuals or entities listed in the Annex to E.O. 13224; foreign individuals or entities that "have committed or ... pose a significant

108

risk of committing acts of terrorism that threaten the security of U.S. nationals or the national security, foreign policy, or economy" of the United States; individuals or entities that either are "owned or controlled by" or "act for or on behalf of" those parties already designated under sub-sections l(a), l(b), l(c), or l(d)(i) of E.O. 13224; individuals or entities that "assist in, sponsor, or provide financial, material, or technological support for, or financial or other services to or in support of such acts of terrorism or those" parties already designated under E.O. 13224; and individuals or entities that are "otherwise associated" with those parties already designated under sub-sections l(a), l(b), l(c), or l(d)(i), of E.O. 13224. This list includes the criteria the Department of State uses to determine whether or not to block financial assets of terrorists and their affiliated members. There are currently over three hundred persons identified as "Specially Designated Global Terrorists" (SDGT) including the original "specially designated terrorists" list.

The main distinction between the Department of State's FTO list and the Department of Treasury's SDGT list is the lack of an immigration element. Another distinguishing feature of the SDGT list is that the designation has no time limit, while the designation of an FTO contains a provision for re-evaluation after five years (if one has not been petitioned for before that time). Furthermore, the lists are founded in separate legislation, and each department takes the lead on adding new organizations or individuals to their respective lists. Currently, the SDGT list contains more than two hundred organizations and individuals who have had their assets frozen under E.O. 13224.

The FTO list has been challenged as facially unconstitutional for denying groups their fight to due process. In U.S. v. Rahmani, the court decided that the legislation's restriction on a court's ability to review the constitutionality of 8 U.S.C. 1189 was impermissible. The court went on to declare that a group's exclusion from and inability to challenge their designation as an FTO denied them due process. On appeal, the circuit court overruled the first finding because "[m]any administrative determinations are reviewable only by petition to the correct circuit court." The circuit court also held that a third party does not have the power to challenge the designation on a constitutional due process basis. Therefore, while the systems have been challenged and critiqued, the court has generally held that the designation of organizations as terrorist organizations is facially constitutional.

TREASURY REGULATIONS AND IEEPA AS TOOLS

The Treasury's authority to confront and counter terrorists in cyberspace stems largely from the powers provided to the President by IEEPA. The IEEPA allows the President to declare a national emergency in response to a threat to national security, foreign policy, or economy of the United States. With such a declaration the President can exercise a broad set of powers including blocking property, investigating, and regulating and prohibiting transactions. On September 23, 2001, President Bush invoked this power, declaring a national emergency with respect to the threat posed by al-Qaida, and issued E.O. 13224, "Blocking Property and Prohibiting Transactions With Persons Who Commit, Threaten to Commit, or Support Terrorism."

The Order included an initial list of twenty-seven targets, including Osama bin Laden and al-Qaida. In addition, it provided that the Secretaries of State and Treasury could add specified categories of persons (individuals and entities) to the list. The categories of individuals and entities "designatable" by the Secretary of the Treasury are:

(a) persons determined to be owned or controlled by, or to act for, or on behalf of, those persons either listed in the Annex to the EO [Executive Order] or determined to be subject to the EO;

(b) persons determined to assist in, sponsor, or provide financial, material, or technological support for, or financial or other services to or in support of, those persons listed in the Annex to this order or determined to be subject to this order;

(c) persons determined to assist in, sponsor, or provide financial, material, or technological support for, or financial or other services to or in support of, acts of terrorism as defined by the EO, or

(d) persons determined to be otherwise associated with those persons listed in the Annex to the EO order or those persons determined to be subject to the EO.

Placement on the list requires U.S. persons, which for purposes of this article would also include ISPs and DNRs, to block property and interests in property—including "services of any nature whatsoever," belonging to the designated sanctions targets. In addition, U.S. persons are also prohibited under E.O. 13224 (and its implementing regulations) from engaging in "any transaction or dealing ... in [blocked] property or interests in property," including the provision of services to or for the benefit of persons designated pursuant to the E.O.

This means that Treasury Regulations may be an extremely effective tool in countering the internet jihad. Those companies organized under the laws of the United States, or any ISPs physically located in the United States, are thus prohibited by law from providing internet service to or for the benefit of al-Qaeda, Hezbollah, Hamas, PIJ, and any other entities or individuals designated pursuant to the Order.

Furthermore, treasury regulations found in 31 C.F.R. [section] 594, as well as those available on Office of Foreign Assets Control's (OFAC) internet homepage, also apply to potential sanctions for internet providers supporting jihadist websites. According to OFAC guidance, those who wish to provide services to targets of Treasury sanctions may not do so without ex ante case by case authorization by Treasury. The potential civil penalties for violations of IEEPA regulations are $250,000.

Acting pursuant to these authorities, the Treasury may issue Cease and Desist orders (C&Ds) to U.S.-based internet companies providing services in violation of existing sanctions programs. The C&Ds would be issued pursuant to IEEPA, E.O. 13224 (or possibly E.O. 13438), and 31 C.F.R. [section] 594. If systematically employed as part of a long-term program targeting terrorist websites, jihadists will be forced to seek domain names and ISPs from overseas hosts.

Under the same laws and regulations, OFAC can also demand information from internet service providers' client lists, such as those clients receiving domain names or web-hosting. Signing up for an account with an ISP generally involves providing your name, address, telephone number, and billing information, which invariably includes a credit card number. The example of Irhabi007 supports this; investigators there found stolen credit card information and confirmed that the cards were used to pay American internet providers, on whose servers Irhabi007 had posted jihadi propaganda. According to the Washington Post, that lead demonstrated to authorities that "they had netted the infamous hacker."

SHAMING AND WATCH-DOG GROUPS: STEPS SHORT OF USING THE STATUTE

Despite the fact that designated foreign terrorist organizations are publicly listed on the Department of State and Department of Treasury websites, internet companies are either undeterred by the threat of prosecution, or are unaware of their client's terrorist status. As such, and as the PIJ example illustrates, these companies continue to do business with them. The material support statute may be a means for government officials to shut down the phenomenon of cyber jihad, although doing so would be an extreme step.

While the government has a legitimate interest in keeping terrorists from recruiting, they do not want to be seen as attempting to censor the internet. A wiser interim policy is to persuade internet service providers and domain name registrars to voluntarily take down or suspend services when those services are assisting terrorist organizations. Network Solutions, which I wrote critically about earlier in the article, often avoids acknowledging the fact that it has retained through their User Policy Agreement, the ability to regulate and take down a site that it deems "unlawful," "threatening," or which "constitutes an illegal threat, hate propaganda, profane, indecent or otherwise objectionable material of any kind or nature." Of course, Network Solutions is not the only web service provider that hosts extremist websites, another site based in Dallas, thePlanet.com has also been accused of hosting three different PIJ websites, as well as a Hamas monthly news magazine, each run by designated FTOs.

Because it is difficult for companies and the government to monitor whom internet services are being provided to, independent watch-dog sites stand in the best position to fill the gap. A number of watch-dog sites already monitor the interact for terrorist activity and information. This brings me back to the example of Internet Haganah. While Internet Haganah is primarily run by Weisburd out of his home, it enjoys the help of groups from around the world. After finding a terrorist website, Weisburd determines which internet companies are providing the site support and either "shames service providers into shutting down the sites that host them or gathers what he terms 'intel' for interested parties." These interested parties include both government and private entities. Internet Haganah encourages individuals to take action by learning about both the terrorist website and the group, understanding the terms of service of the host company, and finally making a calm, informed complaint to the company. Often these complaints go unanswered, at which point Internet Haganah recommends that an individual go to the local media for publicity. No company wants to see its name smeared across the morning news as a supporter of terrorism, especially in their key market.

Tactics such as these have successfully encouraged sites to take down other questionable material, such as websites that cater to pedophiles. For example, in April 2007, Network Solutions shut down a website after receiving complaints from customers. The site had been publicly broadcasted in the Bellingham Herald newspaper, prompting the complaints. Company spokeswoman, Susan Wade, responded by saying that although there is no way they could possibly "police the content of everything that's going up because hosting providers can sell thousands of sites a day," they appreciate when third parties get involved or "when we get served legal papers that say, 'Hey, take a look at this.'"

WHAT IMPACT WILL USING THE STATUTE HAVE ON THE INTERNET JIHAD?

When shaming, complaints, and bad publicity fail, government officials may need to bring legal action against companies that are providing support to terrorist organizations. The U.S. Senate Committee on Homeland Security and Governmental Affairs has conducted hearings on violent Islamic extremism, covering various aspects of the problems including how the internet fosters recruitment and propaganda dissemination. At the hearings, the George Washington University Homeland Security Policy Institute endorsed the use of "[l]egal means for disrupting extremist use of the Internet[, which] may be useful against websites that directly advocate violence or provide material support to known terrorist organizations, crossing the line from protected speech to illegal acts of violence." The House of Representatives has also begun to take notice of the presence of terrorism on the internet. House Resolution 224 has been referred to committee, calling on all corporate owners of websites that share user-posted videos to take down terrorist and jihadist propaganda. Yet, even without this express resolution, the government already has a powerful legal tool available in the form of Section 2339.

Prosecutors can use Section 2339 to stop U.S. internet providers from providing their services as "material support" to FTOs. Ignoring the threat of prosecution exposes companies to prison, fines, and significant public outcry. Section 2339 holds that if a person is found to have materially supported a designated foreign terrorist organization, they "shall be fined under this title or imprisoned not more than 15 years, or both, and, if the death of any person results, shall be imprisoned for any term of years or for life." While to date no case has been brought against an ISP, a plain reading of the statute suggests that those who provide services to terrorist websites have satisfied the definition of providing "material support."

While most prosecutions under the Section 2339 have centered upon individuals who have physically provided material support, either through the provision of objects such as weaponry or funding, the statute has only recently been used to prosecute individuals who use computers and the internet as a means of providing material support. In 2004, The District Court of Connecticut indicted Babar Ahmad on terrorism charges including a violation of Section 2339A, providing material support. The charges allege that Ahmad created websites in order to "recruit mujahideen, raise funds for violent jihad, recruit personnel ... solicit military items," and to give instructions on how to travel to Pakistan to fight for the Taliban, and for the "surreptitious transfer of funds" to terrorist groups. Some of the websites opened and maintained by Ahmad were serviced through a U.S. company, OLM, which was headquartered in Connecticut at the time.

The Ahmad case proves that a material support prosecution for providing internet services is at least conceivable; yet, no such actions have been brought against internet service providers. This is likely due to the fact that most companies want to cooperate, and when they are reluctant to do so, their reluctance is short-lived when faced with the threat of prosecution.

Despite the utility of threatening prosecution, there are legal challenges to successfully using the material support statute. Some may argue that targeting internet service providers amounts to censorship by proxy. According to Professor Kreimer of the University of Pennsylvania:

If unrestrained by First Amendment doctrine, the "material support" statutes, or other similar criminal prohibitions that might be adopted, will threaten to recruit a federally conscripted corps of censors. Webmasters, site owners, or technicians could find themselves the subjects of criminal prosecution for facilitating the transmission of any message originating with federally proscribed organizations. A risk-averse Internet intermediary would not need to descend into paranoia to conclude that the most prudent course would be to proactively censor messages or links that might prove problematic, and to respond to official "requests" with alacrity.

Professor Kreimer goes on to argue that First Amendment protection should be read "at a minimum ... [to] provide similar protection to those who innocently associate with illicit actors or provide links in the chain of communications over the Internet." I do not disagree with Professor Kreimer's assertion; in fact, this is why I argued above that the first step should be, as some watchdog groups advocate, to first contact the internet company, then conduct a public shaming and media campaign. Only when those methods fail should the government consider prosecuting those companies who support terrorist websites. It is only then that the government can argue that the company was aware of its support of terrorist organizations. It is critical to bear in mind that the government in such a prosecution is not targeting the company's speech; it is instead targeting the company's provision of services to a designated terrorist organization.

Similarly, Treasury regulations have undergone First Amendment scrutiny and survived. For example, an examination of case law involving the constitutionality of OFAC actions involving First Amendment claims by U.S. persons indicates that courts overwhelmingly rule in favor of the agency, especially when the cases involve counterterrorism-related enforcement actions. As stated in a D.C. Circuit Court of Appeals decision, "there is no First Amendment right nor any other constitutional right to support terrorists." Despite this fact, the Treasury has not aggressively attempted to cut off cyber-services to terrorism supporters—not even to key al-Qaida facilitators.

One example of Treasury action was the December 2006 designation of Kuwaiti Hamid al-Ali, a cleric who supported al-Qaeda in Iraq and funded terrorist cells in Kuwait. At the time of Hamid al-Ali's designation, the Treasury, under Secretary Stuart Levey, declared that these "individuals support every stage of the terrorist life-cycle, from financing terrorist groups and activity, to facilitating deadly attacks, and inciting others to join campaigns of violence and hate. The civilized world must stand united in isolating these terrorists" Rather than isolating these terrorists, however, Hamid al-Ali has continued to operate his website outside of Washington state. His operations have included the religious sanctioning of suicide bombings and the incitement of individuals to "join the armed resistance of the jihadi movement[.]"

Two barriers to Treasury action may be found, not in the First Amendment, but instead in decades old pieces of legislation. In 1988, Representative Howard Berman (D-CA) proposed The Berman Amendment, which limited the President's powers under IEEPA by creating an exemption for "informational materials." Also, in 1994 Congress passed the Free Trade in Ideas Amendment which expanded the Berman Amendment to non-tangible forms of information. The Conference Report on the bill stated that the language of the Berman Amendment was explicitly intended to have broad scope.

Given the age of these pieces of legislation, a case can be made that their silence regarding terrorism and internet services supporting terrorism may provide for an exception to their broad scope. Even in the absence of an exception, one may argue that terrorist websites provide more than information, that is by allowing fundraising, training, recruiting, and operational details these websites provide "instrumental uses" that are distinguishable from "communicative uses."

Moreover, in U.S. v. O'Brien, the Supreme Court declared that government actions which advance "sufficiently important governmental interests" may allow for incidental limitations on the First Amendment for speech and nonspeech. The O'Brien Court held that a government regulation is sufficiently justified if it is within the Constitutional power of the Government; if it furthers an important or substantial governmental interest; if the governmental interest is unrelated to the suppression of free expression; and if the incidental restriction on the alleged First Amendment freedoms is no greater than is essential to the furtherance of that interest.

Federal Courts applying this test to OFAC activity have allowed the Treasury to restrict the import of books from sanctioned nations. Courts have also upheld Presidential action on the grounds that barring provision of financial support to terrorists was unrelated to suppression of free expression, and that any incidental restrictions on First Amendment freedoms were "no greater than necessary."

Finally, Supreme Court precedent buttresses the view that not all speech is protected. For example, speech which is likely to incite violence, or which creates a clear and present danger of a substantive evil, is unprotected. The content neutral nature of statutes, regulations and other government activity that can counter the cyber jihad makes a successful First Amendment challenge less likely. Accordingly, more government action against terrorist websites and their supporters is necessary to counter the cyber jihad and to fully define the limits of the First Amendment in this critical area of governmental concern.

IV. A CYBER EMBARGO OF DESIGNATED MATERIAL SUPPORTERS

Even if the use of shaming and the threat of the material support statute or Treasury regulations can be successful in driving jihadist websites from U.S.-based service providers, the jihadist web presence will still remain. As the PIJ example demonstrates, a terrorist organization may maintain its web presence by utilizing the

116

services of foreign companies. These companies are, in essence, providing material support, although they have not yet been charged or convicted of the specific offense. Merely forcing jihadist websites overseas is not a sufficient counterterrorism strategy given the ubiquity of the internet, and the fact that sites hosted outside the United States appear as seamlessly as those hosted within the United States. Therefore, new policy and legal proscriptions are necessary to further counter the cyber jihad.

An aggressive application of current statutes may suffice to counter the cyber jihad by targeting "material supporters." The Department of the Treasury's designation process, if liberally and aggressively applied, may provide an adequate remedy. As detailed above, sub paragraph three of E.O. allows the Department of the Treasury to block both property and interests in property, which "act for or on behalf of' those parties already designated as terrorist organizations. Furthermore, sub paragraph four allows similar techniques to be applied to "individuals or entities that 'assist in, sponsor, or provide financial, material, or technological support for, or financial or other services to or in support of 'such acts of terrorism or those parties already designated.'" A broad interpretation of these rules would result in the blocking of both property and interests in property for "material supporters." In the PIJ example, the practical effect of this designation would be to block the assets of Time Telekomm and the Malaysian network service provider supporting the PIJ website.

Nevertheless, this process is limited because these entities may not have assets worth blocking. Thus, a true cyber embargo would entail creating a new process whereby those foreign communications companies that provide material support to terrorist organizations may be designated as "material supporters." Such a designation would prevent U.S. companies from conducting business with designated entities. This process would create virtual "persona non grata." The interconnected nature of the world wide web necessitates that even those overseas companies that provide web services to terrorist organizations (the material supporters) must still rely on other web service providers, many of which are in the United States, to communicate. This reliance is the weak link in the cyber jihadist's web presence. Designating overseas web providers as "material supporters" forces those companies to choose between either losing all commercial services from the United States or continuing to provide services to the terrorist organization.

How would such a designation work? I propose amending the U.S. Code to create a category of "designated material supporter." U.S. companies would be forbidden from engaging in commercial services with entities bearing such a designation. The designation would include elements of the material support statute, but would limit itself to internet companies. Moreover, the designation could include a provision that allows companies to sever ties to terrorist organizations to avoid being designated a "material supporter."

Diplomatic efforts could further expand the cyber embargo. Initially this diplomatic effort need not be expansive. Rather, it could focus on the nine countries that control 95.58% of all registrars. Preventing these registrars from engaging in commercial activity with "material supporters" would have a dramatic impact on the "designated material supporter," likely forcing them out of business if they do not cease their ties to jihadists. Diplomatic efforts have worked in the past, albeit on a small scale. For example, the U.S. Department of Defense reportedly used its leverage to shut down Palestinian resistance sites hosted by the Ukraine in 2004. In another instance "the British government, responding to the U.S. request under the Mutual Legal Assistance Treaty between the two countries, ordered the closure of twenty media websites in seventeen countries that advocated terrorism." Working through diplomatic channels to shut down foreign companies that serve as material supporters is the critical next step in countering the cyber jihad.

As each country cuts off internet support within their jurisdiction, terrorist websites will be forced to find support in new jurisdictions. Continued monitoring and diplomatic efforts would thus remain critical. Additionally, because 95.8% of all domain registrars are located in nine countries with which the United States has strong diplomatic ties, the internationalization of these efforts is achievable. Furthermore, internationalizing an agreement that will ensure that other countries shut down "designated material supporters" is the next step in countering the internet jihad.

Continuing diplomatic efforts to prohibit dealing with "designated material supporters" will create a system whereby terrorist organizations will have extremely limited choice of locations where they can register and operate their websites. In most cases, the internet jihadists will be forced to register in small, already ostracized countries such as Iran or Libya, which maintain control over their respective .IR and .LY domain names. By limiting internet jihadists to these countries, diplomatic measures, such as trade restrictions or even the dramatic step of blocking internet traffic to those countries, can be brought to bear. Those countries that host jihadist websites will then have to decide if they are willing to protect the internet jihadists at the cost of losing their legitimate commercial internet traffic.

CONCLUSIONS AND IMPLICATIONS

Given the ubiquity of the internet, and the challenges of tracking down constantly moving websites, domain name registrars, and internet service providers, one may be left to conclude that efforts to counter the internet jihad are pointless. Nevertheless, the only truly effective way to counter the internet jihad is to continually make efforts to shut them down. Doing so can dramatically impact the terrorist web presence. For example, Aaron Weisburd claims to have been responsible for shutting down 80% of jihadist websites.

The limited efforts of watchdog groups prove that the fight against cyber jihadists is not a fruitless one. Through increased support of watchdog groups, expanded shaming techniques, and the use of existing statutes, terrorist websites can be forced to overseas service providers. This first step is not enough, however, as the world wide web is dynamic, and the move to overseas service providers will allow cyber jihadists to seamlessly maintain their web presence. Thus, more aggressive use of existing designation techniques, and the creation of a new "material supporter" designation are necessary to create a cyber embargo of jihadist websites and those companies that provide them services. Diplomatic efforts are necessary to fully realize the potential of the cyber embargo, as cyber jihadists can continually move and find new "material supporters" in other jurisdictions. Through continued diplomatic efforts, terrorist websites can be forced to exist in a geographically limited number of jurisdictions.

Furthermore, even if only some jihadist sites are closed down, the jihadists will still be restricted to a few overseas hosts. These few hosts would no longer be needles in a haystack; with fewer places to go, the major jihadist sites with direct links to terrorism could be quickly identified and monitored by investigators. The end result of this process will not eliminate the cyber jihadist presence, but geographically limiting terrorists allows for government and civilian orchestrated monitoring, as well as for offensive actions to shut down these sites. Some websites may, for intelligence reasons, be identified as sites that the government will not want to shut down. Instead, the government may choose to monitor or compromise these sites as they may contain valuable intelligence information, such as user names, locations, and messages that users believe to be encrypted but are in fact being monitored. This technique is not universally accepted though, as some contend "getting real actionable intelligence from a terrorist website or forum is extremely difficult and requires a lot of time and a lot of luck[,] and in many cases the small amounts of available actionable intelligence would only be noticed after the act is done." Thus, geographically limiting these sites will corral the cyber jihadists onto a limited number of web servers, effectuating monitoring and other counterterrorism techniques.

While some may argue that the anonymity of the internet makes locating and shutting down jihadist websites too challenging, one must bear in mind that jihadists use websites for the specific purpose of dispersing information and connecting with each other. To a large extent, jihadists are forced to relinquish anonymity in order to reach their own audience. In addition, anonymity is a two-way street. Trackers and investigators can infiltrate the jihadist ranks by acting as interested jihadists, avoiding detection through anonymity.

The key to countering cyber jihad is to relentlessly target jihadist websites by keeping them continually on the move, cutting off their resources by targeting "material supporters," and finally limiting their potential areas of operation so that increased monitoring and other counter-terrorism techniques can be applied to them. Following these steps will go a long way toward addressing the technical and political issues inherent in the internet jihad, that have plagued lawmakers and policy experts.

Footnotes deleted.

8

Terror on YouTube

The Internet's Most Popular Sites are Becoming Tools for Terrorist Recruitment

Ingrid Caldwell

S ince its creation, the Internet has been viewed as a symbol of democracy and free speech, a tool for communicating, networking, and learning. But there is a dark side to the unregulated sprawl of the World Wide Web, and it doesn't take a computer forensics expert to find it. The very same features that make it convenient for the average user to socialize with friends or research for a school paper are now being used by terrorist organizations to recruit, raise funds, and attract a whole new generation of supporters.

The terrorist presence on the Web concerned Homeland Security and Governmental Affairs Committee chairman Joe Lieberman (ID-Conn.) so much that he wrote a letter to Google chairman Eric Schmidt, urging him to remove from YouTube all videos with ties to terrorist organizations.

Ingrid Caldwell, Terror on YouTube: the Internet's most popular sites are becoming tools for terrorist recruitment. *The Forensic Examiner* 17(3): 80-84. Reprinted by permission of The Forensic Examiner and Dr. Robert L. O'Block.

"Protecting our citizens from terrorist attacks is a top priority for our government," Lieberman continued. "The private sector can help us do that. By taking action to curtail the use of YouTube to disseminate the goals and methods of those who wish to kill innocent civilians, Google will make a singularly important contribution to this important national effort."

MANY TERRORIST VIDEOS

YouTube responded to Lieberman's request by taking down some videos that the company said violated its policies on content. But The Forensic Examiner found that on June 18, weeks after the Lieberman initiative, many videos remained on YouTube that appeared to promote or affiliate with terrorist groups such as Hamas, Hezbollah, Al-Qaeda, and the Iraqi insurgency.

One disturbing YouTube video featured Star Wars action figures recreating the beheading of American journalist Daniel Pearl. Though the actual Pearl execution is not on YouTube, it can easily be found elsewhere on the Internet.

YouTube videos posted by supporters of the Iraqi insurgency show American soldiers being shot and flag-covered coffins en route to the United States.

Other YouTube videos found by The Examiner included tributes to suicide bombers, propaganda promoting Hamas and Hezbollah leaders, and statements alleging that the U.S. is covering up its actual casualties in Iraq. One cartoon image showed a bloody U.S. soldier caught in a mousetrap that featured the Iraqi flag.

Osama bin Laden's message praising the attacks of 9/11/2001 also can be found on YouTube.

FREE SPEECH DEBATE

Lieberman's plea re-ignited the nationwide debate about when—if ever—security should override freedom. Civil libertarians ask: Terrorists on the Web pose a very real threat, but would harshly regulating Internet content in an attempt to stop them do more harm than good?

In his report "How Modern Terrorism Uses the Internet," Gabriel Weimann (2004a, p. 2) states that security agencies have focused too much on potential acts of cyberterrorism (such as virus attacks and hacking) and have failed to widely address the more common ways terrorists use the Internet every day. Although cyberterrorism is a real threat that needs to be handled seriously, terrorists more commonly use the Internet to recruit new supporters, mobilize current supporters, raise funds, find information on potential targets, and wage campaigns of intimidation and disinformation.

Weimann (2004a, p. 2) states that in 1998, "around half of the 30 organizations designated as 'Foreign Terrorist Organizations' under the U.S. Antiterrorism and Effective Death Penalty Act of 1996 maintained Web sites; by 2000, virtually all terrorist groups had established their presence on the Internet."

Modern terrorist organizations have changed with the times, operating more like a PR-savvy corporation than a stereotypical bunch of nomads hiding in a back room. One of Hezbollah's sites targets international journalists directly and encourages them to contact the organization's press office (Weimann, 2004a, p. 4). According to Weimann, Web sites maintained by terrorist groups use similar methods of propaganda, aiming their messages at current and potential members, the global public, and citizens of enemy states in order to gain sympathy and financial support.

"Typically, a (terrorist organization) site will provide a history of the organization and its activities, a detailed review of its social and political background, accounts of its notable exploits, biographies of its leaders, founders, and heroes, information on its political and ideological aims, fierce criticism of its enemies, and up-to-date news," said Weimann in his report. "Despite the ever-present vocabulary of "the armed struggle" and "resistance," what most sides do not feature is a detailed description of their violent activities" (p. 4).

Using sophisticated rhetorical methods, online terrorists attempt to convince their audiences that their violent acts are necessary to achieve "greater peace," that they have no other choice. Their tactics are undeniably successful: Since Sept. 11, numerous threats of big attacks on U.S. soil have appeared on al Qaeda's Web site, and while none of these threats came into fruition, they attracted significant media attention and managed to perpetuate the nationwide feelings of fear and insecurity that arose post-9/11.

In a 2003 speech, former Secretary of Defense Donald Rumsfeld read the following passage from an al Qaeda training manual recovered in Afghanistan: "Using public sources openly and without resorting to illegal means, it is possible to gather at least 80 percent of all information required about the enemy" (as cited in Weimann, 2004b). "Public sources," of course, refer primarily to the Internet, where the average user can find anything from maps of the New York subway system to commercial flight schedules to the current whereabouts of a particular U.S. politician—all without sacrificing anonymity.

Because there is no question that terrorists use the Internet every day to further their plans, the solution seems fairly straightforward: shut down their sites, take their videos off YouTube, closely monitor their chat rooms, and censor their blogs and news articles. But, as Dan Gillmore, a panelist at the 2005 International Summit on Democracy, Terrorism, and Security in Madrid, pointed out, it's often more complicated than that. In some countries, the line between terrorist rebellion and legitimate political dissent is hard to distinguish, and heavy regulation of the Internet could actually backfire and endanger innocent people.

"We believe that an attempt to end anonymity would be highly unlikely to stop a determined terrorist or criminal of any kind, but it would certainly have a deeply chilling effect on political activity in places where speaking one's mind is dangerous and where certain kinds of unpopular speech could jeopardize someone's livelihood or perhaps life," Gillmore said (as cited in Ito, 2005).

Another case for a free and open Internet rests on the idea that it is best to keep enemies in plain sight. As long as terrorist organizations uphold their presence on the Web, it is possible to keep track of their whereabouts, plans, and new campaigns. Rebecca MacKinnon, also a panelist at the 2005 summit, argued that the general public can play a useful role in the fight against terrorism— keeping a watchful eye on those corners of the Web that security agencies are not able to monitor constantly.

"Terrorism is a problem of armies, it is a problem faced by police forces, but it is also a problem faced by ordinary citizens everywhere," she said. "The best way to combat terrorism is to involve the general public in that fight and the best way to do that is though the open Internet" (as cited in Ito, J, 2005).

On May 8, 2008, the Senate Committee on Homeland Security and Governmental Affairs released a report, "Violent Islamist Extremism, The Internet, and the Homegrown Terrorist Threat," detailing the threat of terrorists on the Internet. Authored by Lieberman and Ranking Minority Member Susan Collins (R-Maine), the report calls on federal agencies to unify their scattered attempts into a single, comprehensive plan for responding to the terrorist web presence.

"Despite recognition in the National Implementation Plan (NIP) that a comprehensive response is needed, the U.S. government has not developed nor implemented a coordinated outreach and communications strategy to address the homegrown terrorist threat, especially as that threat is amplified by the use of the Internet," Lieberman and Collins (2008, p. 16) wrote.

The committee's report proposes no specific solution but stresses the immediacy of the problem, concluding that the "use of the Internet by al-Qaeda and other violent Islamist extremist groups has expanded the terrorist threat to our homeland. No longer is the threat just from abroad, as was the case with the attacks of September 11, 2001; the threat is now increasingly from within, from homegrown terrorists who are inspired by violent Islamist ideology to plan and execute attacks where they live. One of the primary drivers of this new threat is the use of the Internet to enlist individuals or groups of individuals to join the cause without ever affiliating with a terrorist organization" (Lieberman & Collins, 2008, p. 15).

Because complete censorship is difficult and dangerous, perhaps what we need to do is not regulate but reign in the Internet as a tool—not impose heavy restrictions, which could hurt everyone, but utilize the freedom and global connection provided by the Internet to further the goals of democracy and peace.

"The fundamental democratic values that are embedded in the architecture of the Internet are the same fundamental democratic values that will enable us to defeat terrorism," said Andrew McLaughlin, head of Global Public Policy and Government Affairs for Google, Inc., at the 2005 summit. "They are openness, they are participation, they are distribution of authority, accountability; these are the essential features of the Internet, and if we view this medium properly, we can see that it is in fact the best ally that we have in fighting the scourge of terrorism."

REFERENCES

Ito, J., moderator. (2005, March 10). Democracy. Terrorism and the Internet. International Summit on Democracy, Terrorism and Security. Retrieved June 9, 2008, from http://english.safe-democracy.org/keynotes/ democracy-terrorism-and-the-internet.html#transcrip

Lieberman, J., and Collins, S. (2008, March 8). Violent Islamist extremism, the Internet, and the homegrown terrorist threat. Senate Committee on Homeland Security and Governmental Affairs. Retrieved June 9, 2008, from http://hsgac.senate.gov/ public/_files/IslamistReport.pdf

Senate Committee on Homeland Security and Governmental Affairs. (2008, May 19). Lieberman calls on Google to take down terrorist content. Senate Committee on Homeland Security and Governmental Affairs. Retrieved June 8, 2008, from http:// hsgac.senate.gov/public/index.cfm?Fuseaction=PressReleases. Detail&PressRelease_id=8093d5b2-c882-4d12-883d-5c670d 43d269&Month=5&Year=2008&Affiliation=C

Weimann, G. (2004a, March). How modern terrorism uses the Internet. U.S. Institute of Peace. Retrieved June 10, 2008, from http://www.usip.org/pubs/specialreports/sr116.html

Weimann, G. (2004b, April 30). Terrorism and the Internet. Computer Crime Research Center. Retrieved June 8, 2008, from http://www.crime-research.org/news/30.04.2004/254/

Named Works: YouTube (Website) - Military aspects

9

United States Homeland Security in the Information Age

Dealing with the Threat of Cyberterrorism

James F. Pasley

ABSTRACT

This paper examines the threat of cyber-terrorism and the steps taken by the administration of George W. Bush to deal with this significant threat. It contends that the terrorist actions of September 11, 2001 would have been worse had they occurred in tandem with a sustained cyber attack against the United States. Therefore, the United States must be vigilant in its efforts to defend against cyber-terrorist actions. The paper suggests that while the Bush administration is moving in the right direction, more can be done to ensure U.S. cyber security. In particular, the newly developed National Strategy to Secure Cyberspace needs to be strengthened. No defense is likely to provide absolute security against future cyber-terrorist actions, but the United States can do more to ensure its protection when such attacks occur.

James F. Pasley, United States homeland security in the information age: dealing with the threat of cyberterrorism. *White House Studies* 3 (4): 403-411. Reprinted with permission from Nova Science Publishers, Inc.

128

INTRODUCTION

he remarkable level of technological achievement the states
of the North now enjoy has propelled these countries to
higher and higher levels of economic standing. Technology
has created a brave new world in which information is the key to
security. Control of information must be a major goal of the United
States in the years ahead because it is the new currency of power.
Access to information drives the U.S. economy, informs citizens, and
provides intelligence to U.S. policymakers; it must be guarded
diligently.

The events of 9/11 vividly displayed to the citizens of the
United States that war is no longer limited to far away lands. The
long shadow of terrorism now casts its dark shade over U.S. shores
and it must be addressed. Understanding what form future terrorist
actions will take is key to U.S. policymakers as they work to develop
measures to defend against future terrorist actions. This article
explores the threat of cyber-terrorism to U.S. homeland security and
then examines the Bush administration's response to dealing with this
threat.

CYBER WORLD

In an evolving system, as is the case with the current state-centric
international system, the passage of time generally reflects the
growth of order within the system. Successful behaviors are learned
or mimicked as the system members adapt to what has proven to be
beneficial behavior in the past. Thus successful institutions are
generally adopted, as has been the case for democracy following the
victory of the democratic institutional structures of the West during
the Cold War.

A secondary proliferation has become one not of
institutions, but rather, one of technology. Kenneth Waltz notes,
"Self-help is the principle of action in an anarchic order, and the most
important way in which states must help themselves is by providing
for their own security." Therefore, the proliferation of technology is
inevitable, as states strive to ensure their own survivability.

However, this technology threatens the very order it has
produced. The September 11, 2001 terrorist attacks on the United
States were a horrific display of the nation's own technology being-
used against it. With devastating results, commercial airliners were
hijacked and utilized as precision guided bombs.

The fog of war for U.S. policymakers as these attacks
happened was significant. It was unclear how many planes had been

hijacked and where they might be heading, despite the fact that the FAA was monitoring the location of all the commercial airliners aloft. But imagine if, in tandem with the hijackings, terrorists had attacked the digital infrastructure of the United States by temporarily taking down the FAA's computers, or by inserting erroneous information into their databases. The terrorist acts of 9/11 easily could have been augmented by such cyber attacks.

Over the course of only a few decades, the developed world has become more and more dependent upon computers to function. This dependence has spread to the general public of the United States in the past two decades, with the introduction of the personal computer and the explosive growth of the Interact. As the digital world has grown in terms of the level of its integration into national infrastructures and the number of participants, so too has the threat of cyber-terrorists.

The United States is vulnerable to cyber attacks because it is so dependent upon technology. Figure one shows that the United States is the most wired country in the world in terms of the level of Internet connections per 1,000 inhabitants.

The vulnerability of the United States to cyber attacks suggests that the next significant terrorist event in this country may be coupled with some form of cyber-terrorism. Therefore, it is important to understand what cyber-terrorism refers to, what such acts might involve and what the United States is doing to lessen the impact such attacks might produce.

CYBER-TERRORISM

To paraphrase Dorothy Denning, a professor of computer science at Georgetown University, cyber-terrorism is considered to be unlawful attacks or threats against computers and networks in order to further some political or social objective. The disruption of nonessential services typically does not fall into this larger heading. Denning argues that while past cyber attacks have caused billions of dollars in damage, they cannot be characterized as terrorism. Rather, past events are better described as fraud, theft, sabotage or vandalism. True cyber-terrorism is something far more devastating in terms of its scope and impact on a society.

Effective cyber-terrorism is unlikely to occur separate from other terrorist attacks. The most likely scenario for cyber attacks to happen is in tandem with physical attacks. There are at least four forms the cyber attack could take: 1) web defacements; 2) domain name service attacks; 3) distributed denial of service attacks; and 4) worms.

Web defacements come in two forms: 1) overt; and 2) semantic attacks. Overt actions involve the altering of targeted web sites to display some pro-terrorist propaganda. Such actions are clear and, while embarrassing for operators of the victimized site, they pose no immediate threat. Semantic attacks, however, are an example of cyber-terror because they are significantly more threatening. This is because semantic attacks involve the subtle alteration of a site's content. A compromised site, therefore, would provide incorrect information, at a potentially critical moment, which could lead to faulty decision-making with potentially disastrous consequences.

Domain Name Service (DNS) attacks are similar to web defacements in that their goal is to provide false information in the guise of a legitimate source. Domain name servers connect the name of a system (or website) to its numerical address. Every website has a system on which the server runs. A DNS attack simply funnels those seeking a particular website to a different numerical address. This removes the need for the terrorist(s) to break into the actual web server while providing the same result as a semantic web defacement attack.

Distributed Denial of Service (DDS) attacks use groups of 'zombie' machines controlled by a master computer to victimize other computers with data. Commercial web sites have been attacked and shut down because of the technique, as the attackers overwhelm sites with multilateral attacks. By controlling enough machines, attackers can effectively shut down targeted sites.

Worms are digital destroyers designed to burrow into a host computer and disrupt its functioning. The current design of most worms is to create buffer overflows, which crash the computer or allow for unauthorized access. Worms employed in the past typically have exploited well-known vulnerabilities unpatched on enough systems to make them a nuisance.

There is a concern by some cyber-terrorism analysts that new types of worms are being developed that could spread in minutes or less. Because of the speed of these new worms little time would be left for administrators to react and, therefore, the damage the worms incur would be much more widespread.

All these types of attacks threaten the national infrastructure and proper functioning of the U.S. government. Recent tests by the Pentagon and others have shown that the United States is potentially vulnerable to cyber-terrorism. For instance, the Pentagon's 1008 "Eligible Receiver" exercise, which simulated a cyber attack on the nation's power distribution grid, revealed that hackers "could have a dramatic impact on the nation's infrastructure, including the electrical power grid."

A Dartmouth University study on the threat of cyber-terrorism in the wake of the 9/11 attacks suggested targets in the United States vulnerable to cyber attacks include: 1) banking and financial institutions; 2) voice communication systems; 3) electrical infrastructures; 4) water resources; and 5) oil and gas infrastructures.

These types of attacks were examined by the Center for the Study of Terrorism and Irregular Warfare at the Naval Postgraduate School in Monterey, California, in August 1999. Their report assesses the ability of terrorist organizations to use effectively the forms of cyber attacks previously discussed.

The report assigned three levels of capability to potential attackers. The first was defined as "simple-unstructured." These included terror groups who could engage in only basic hacking techniques to threaten individual systems.

The second category was known as "advanced-structured." These groups could engage in more sophisticated attacks against multiple systems. They also would engage in target analysis and command and control.

The third level was called "complex-coordinated." These types enjoyed a high capability for coordinated attacks threatening massive disruption against high-level defenses (including encrypted systems). They placed a large emphasis on target analysis and command and control.

The report estimated that a new group would require 2-4 years to achieve the level of "advanced-structured" and 6-10 years to reach the "complex-coordinated" level. The study concluded that, in the near-term, the prospects for effective cyber attacks were low, but the threat is growing and is most significant from radical religious groups. Considering that this report was completed in 1999, al-Qaeda and others might be well on the way to "complex-coordinated" level attack capabilities.

NATIONAL STRATEGY FOR HOMELAND SECURITY

In the wake of the 9/11 terrorist attacks, the Bush administration began the development of a Homeland Security office that would be responsible for coordinating the implementation of a national strategy to secure the United States from further terrorist actions. Appreciating that technology will play a major role in any successful homeland security effort, The National Strategy for Homeland Security states:

Five principles will guide our country's approach to developing information systems for homeland security. First, we will balance our homeland security requirements with citizens' privacy. Second, the homeland security community will view the federal, state, and local governments as one entity. Third, information will be captured once at the source and used many times to support multiple requirements. Fourth, we will create databases of record, which will be trusted sources of information. Finally, the homeland security information architecture will be a dynamic tool, recognizing that the use of information technology to combat terrorism will continually evolve to stay ahead of the ability of terrorists to exploit our systems.

Basically, the Bush administration's goals with respect to cyber security are: 1) improvement of security buffers in the private sector; 2) increased cooperation, communication, and information sharing among the federal, state, and local levels; and improvement of existing database records.

The focal point of the Bush administration's efforts to combat cyber-terrorism in the private sector is the National Strategy to Secure Cyberspace (NSSC). The NSSC seeks to integrate the larger public into the government's quest to protect the nation's information technology infrastructure. Its goal is to keep cyberspace disruptions to a minimum and to protect against cyber vulnerabilities terrorists might exploit. Nearly sixty recommendations for government, academia, and home computer users are put forward by the NNSC. For instance, beginning in 2004, it recommends (though does not mandate) IT security personnel and audit firms to be tested and certified regularly by a national public-private board.

The Bush administration is moving in the right direction in developing effective measures to protect the nation's economy from a debilitating terrorist attack but, unfortunately, lobbying groups have succeeded in limiting what might have been done. Because the NSSC is only a strategy and not an implementation plan, it remains unclear what it will accomplish. The Bush administration's philosophy is to make its cyber security recommendations voluntary for private industry, rather than mandating them. This is in line with the administration's conservative ideals promoting limited government influence, but concerns that these recommendations threaten business by impacting market forces seem misplaced. The goal of the NSSC and the Bush administration's efforts in the area of homeland security should be to increase the nation's security. Thus mandating the use of cyber security efforts such as firewalls and anti-virus utilities seems necessary.

CYBER COUNTERTERRORISM

The United States, though, is not merely intending to defend against cyber attacks. It also will use information technology to pursue terrorists and to further enhance the security of the country. The Bush administration's Department of Homeland Security will create a Collaborative Classified Enterprise effort to share sensitive information among government entities at the federal level. State and local governments also will be permitted access to a secure intranet service to increase the flow of relevant information regarding potential terrorists.

Technology must be used to assist in detecting terrorists before they act. In this regard, data sharing between agencies is vital to uncovering potential terrorists operating within the United States. By combining criminal records and intelligence information, individual threats can be identified more readily.

For instance, if one examines the actions of Mohammed Atta (the apparent ringleader of the 9/11 attacks) less than a year before the September 11, 2001 attacks, a startling series of events is revealed. On May 28, 2001, a warrant was issued for his arrest after he failed to appear in court for a traffic violation. Yet, on July 5, 2001, an officer who had pulled Atta over for speeding found no evidence of outstanding warrants following a computer search. Atta then left for Spain to meet with other conspirators, but was permitted entry back into the United States on July 19 despite his outstanding warrant. Reports indicate that Atta was on a CIA watch-list and therefore his entry back into the United States should have been prevented. However, no one at INS or the FBI was notified.

These examples of information sharing shortcomings are troubling and need to be corrected. In an effort to begin to correct problems exemplified by the Atta case the Bush administration has mandated the INS to create a new entry-exit system in order to track the arrival and departure of non-U.S, citizens. While this may do a better job of preventing terrorist access to the United States (at least legally), there also must be a more active governmental role for removing non-U.S, citizens whose visas have expired, or who are not doing what their visas permitted them entry to do (such as attending school).

The second issue of concern with respect to the Atta case, is the lack of information sharing between U.S. agencies and departments. Information sharing is a must in any new national effort to combat terrorism. The Bush administration is addressing this issue directly, calling for an increase in funding to more effectively share information vertically (among federal, state, and local agencies) and horizontally (among Federal and agencies and departments). Additionally, the administration will establish a national threat advisory system to inform Federal, state, and private sector officials of terrorist threats and appropriate protective actions.

Some additional components of the homeland security strategy serve to augment existing counter-terrorist efforts and create new ones. The National Infrastructure Protection Center (NIPC) is the main cyber-threat center within the FBI. It will receive additional funding. A cyberspace warning intelligence network is to be created in order to link main players in government and private industry should a cyberspace crisis arise. A priority wireless hierarchy will be created to ensure that first responders will be able to communicate in the event of a crisis. A National Infrastructure Simulation and Analysis Center is to be created at the Department of Energy to study the dependencies between government and the private sector in order to identify potential vulnerabilities. Finally, cybercorps scholarships encouraging college students to become high tech computer security professionals within government will strive to enhance the level of information security in the United States for the future.

CONCLUSION

The Bush administration's response to the threat of cyber-terrorism has been positive, but there is room for improvement. Measures are being taken to enhance the security of governmental computer networks and systems and there is an active effort to promote more cooperation in the fight against terror among federal, state, and local departments and agencies.

The cyber security shortfall appears to be in the private sector. The administration's much trumpeted National Strategy to Secure Cyberspace provides an outline for how private users can improve cyber security without any mandates by the government regarding security enhancements. The NSSC stresses voluntary cooperation and education and does little else. This is a concern because the government needs to provide leadership on this issue so that the private sector can be organized to limit the damage any future cyber attacks will incur.

Nevertheless, the United States is focused on the issue of defending against cyber-terrorism more than at any time since the information revolution began. Progress is being made to augment the country's defenses against cyber attacks, but the long road ahead has many more steps.

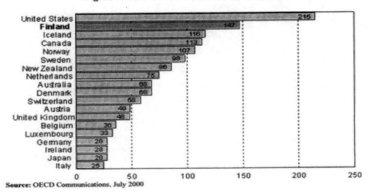

Figure 1. Internet Connections Per 1000 Inhabitants

Source: OECD Communications, July 2000

Footnotes deleted.

4

Online Predatory Intimidation and Harassment

10

Cyber-bullying

Creating a Culture of Respect in a Cyber World

Susan Keith and Michelle E. Martin

I n the 1990s, many incidents revolved around student-on-student violence, usually involving guns. Schools implemented many programs to keep guns and gangs out of schools. In the 21st Century, school violence is taking on a new and more insidious form. New technologies have made it easier for bullies to gain access to their victims. This form of bullying has become known as cyber-bullying. This article provides a window on this little known world and offers practical suggestions for dealing with this new challenge.

When we think about school violence, events like Columbine come to mind. Looking back at the incident, Andy Carvin for The Digital Beat reminds his readers that one of the killers, Eric Harris, had his own web site that contained "conspicuous threats against fellow students" (Carvin, 2000). It was brought to the attention of the police and led to both Harris and Klebold being questioned about the incident and was an early example of what is now called "cyber bullying."

Susan Keith and Michelle E. Martin, Cyber-bullying: creating a culture of respect in a cyber world. Reprinted with permission from *Reclaiming Children and Youth*, Volume 13, Number 4, Winter 2005, p. 224-229. For subscription information see www.reclaimingjournal.com.

Bill Belsey, a nationally recognized educator from Alberta, Canada, gives this definition:

> Cyber-bullying involves the use of information and communication technologies such as e-mail, cell phone and pager text messages, instant messaging (IM), defamatory personal Web sites, and defamatory online personal polling Web sites, to support deliberate, repeated, and hostile behavior by an individual or group, that is intended to harm others. (Belsey, 2004)

Cyber-bullying, while being similar in its intent to hurt others through power and control, is different due to the use of these new technologies. Nowadays, kids are always connected or wired, and communicate in ways that are often unknown by adults and away from their supervision. This can make it hard for parents and school administrators to both understand the nature of the problem and do something about it.

Several surveys have been taken to get a handle on the number of children across the country who have experienced cyber-bullying. It is estimated that 91% of kids 12 to 15 years old and almost all teens (99%) ages 16 to 18 use the Internet (UCLA Internet Report, 2003). Much of their time online is spent talking with other kids. i-SAFE America, an internet safety education foundation, conducted a nationwide survey of 1,566 students from grades four to eight to find out their experiences with bullying online (National i-Safe Survey, 2004).

The survey found:

* 57% of students said that someone had said hurtful or angry things to them online with 13% saying it happens "quite often"

* 53% of students admit saying mean or hurtful things to someone online and 7% admit to doing it "quite often"

* 35% of students have been threatened online with 5% saying it happens "quite often"

* 42% have been bullied online with 7% saying it happens "quite often"

* 20% have received mean or threatening e-mails

* 58% have not told their parents or another adult about their experiences online

Another survey conducted by the Crimes against Children Research Center at the University of New Hampshire (Wollack & Mitchell, 2000) found that along with sexual solicitations and approaches online (19% of children surveyed received unwanted sexual solicitation), six percent of the young people surveyed experienced harassing incidents, including threats, rumors, or other offensive behavior, and two percent reported episodes of distressing harassment that they described as making them feel very or extremely upset or afraid.

Most parents tend to think that this kind of bullying is uncommon and that their child would never do something this mean. Unfortunately not so, according to Alane Fagin, the executive director of Child Abuse Prevention Services (CAPS). On-line bullying has become very common and is particularly easy for girls to do. This is an example of relational aggression where girls use relationships as weapons. Imagine, she says, a group of girls sitting around a computer. The person being instant messaged thinks she is only talking to one person. Before she knows it, the "target" has said something negative about one of the group. The group then starts gossiping about her. "This leads to social isolation," says Fagin (cited in Wolfe, 2004).

In general, girls inflict virtual abuse more than boys through instant messaging, online conversations, and e-mails. A survey of girls ages 12 to 18 found that 74% of adolescent girls spend the majority of their time online in chat rooms or sending instant messages and e-mail (Migliore, 2003). Boys are more likely to make online threats and build websites targeting others. It can be much more difficult to identify bullies in cyberspace. Online screen names and e-mail addresses can hide a person's true identity. It is easier to bully someone you don't have to face. With no boundaries or tangible consequences, children are using technology to vent normal frustrations in ways that can become very destructive.

Traditionally, home was a place where a kid could go to escape his bully. With advances in technology, home is no longer a haven. Glenn Stutzky, a School Safety Violence Specialist at Michigan State University, said that today's bullies use technology to spread rumors and threats, making life miserable for their victims throughout the day and night. Today's kids have to deal with bullying in its newest forms: text messages, e-mail, websites, on-line voting booths, and blogs. They cannot escape their bully because he can now follow them home. This is the new reality.

142

In the past several years, parents have provided cell phones for their children in order to keep track of them and to keep them safe. The same cell phones that make parents feel more connected to their children have become tools of harassment. And the newest forms of cell phones include the ability to send text messages, pictures, and even live video. In the hands of bored teenagers, these additions can become weapons for bullies to spread rumors as well as pictures of unsuspecting kids in locker rooms. Stutzky provides examples of a middle school girl and a straight high school boy. The girl returned from vacation in Canada to find out that someone had spread rumors through text messages that she had contracted SARS. The boy was harassed by text messages implying he was gay. Stutzky states that "(children) are at a very vulnerable time in their development, and while these comments may seem silly to people who have matured, they are very devastating to the young people on the receiving end" (Wendland, 2003).

Websites can provide places where children can gain knowledge and communicate with others who share the same interests. This same benefit can also be used to do harm. Some children are now using Websites to mock, harass, and torment others. Bullies post slurs on Websites where kids congregate, or on personal on-line journals, called Web logs or Blogs. They can post pictures of students they don't like or create online voting booths. An example of the latter was set up by a group of Manhattan (New York) students who decided to create a Website to determine who was the biggest "ho" (Benfer, 2003). Called the Interschool Ho and posted on a free Website called freevote.com, this voting booth accumulated a list of 150 students along with their rank. It took a call by the Brooklyn district attorney to force freevote.com to shut down the site.

Alane Fagin (cited in Wolfe, 2004) also writes about Jay, who, along with some friends, created a "hit list" of kids from their middle school that they "just didn't like" and put it on the Internet. Jay describes a bunch of bored, 13-year-old kids who just started "fooling around." They wanted to change their image from being "clean-cut kids" to being "tough guys." On the site, he and his friends wrote about wanting to "weed out the people we didn't like. Anybody that we didn't hang out with was on the list. We titled it 'People We're Gonna Whack.'" When other students started visiting the site, one of the people on the list brought it to the attention of the principal. Initially, Jay and his friends only received a verbal reprimand by the school. Because their names were on the site, though, a parent brought it to the attention of the police. After four months, the police filed no charges. The consequence for the boys was the loss of trust from their parents, teachers, and peers.

An extreme case of Website bullying took place in Dallas (Benfer, 2003). A sophomore at a local high school was harassed about her weight. She was called a "fat cow MOO BITCH" on the school's message boards. Besides making fun of her weight, the anonymous writer also made fun of the fact that she suffered from multiple sclerosis, saying, "I guess I'll have to wait until you kill yourself which I hope is not long from now, or I'll have to wait until your disease [MS] kills you." This bullying escalated to action, with the student getting her car egged and a bottle of acid thrown at her front door, resulting in injury for her mother.

Part of the problem in combating cyber-bullying, say experts, is that parents and kids relate to technology very differently. Most adults approach computers as practical tools, while for kids the Internet is a lifeline to their peer group. "Cyber-bullying is practically subterranean because it lives in the world of young people," says Belsey (2004). "Kids know there is a gap in the understanding of technology between themselves and their parents, and their fear is not only that the parents' response may make the bullying worse, but that the adults will take the technology away."

So what are some signs that your child or student is being cyber-bullied? The Australian Government (2004) lists the following signs as things to look for:

* Spending a lot of time on the computer;

* Having trouble sleeping or having nightmares;

* Feeling depressed or crying without reason;

* Mood swings;

* Feeling unwell;

* Becoming anti-social; and

* Falling behind in homework.

It is a fascinating time in history. Children have opportunities for learning that previously seemed like science fiction. Schools, parents and children gain much from these advances in technology, but at the same time, they create unique challenges. The primary thing that adults need to do is to be more knowledgeable regarding the use of current technology and the ways and means that children are using them. Many parents and teachers, who were not raised in a cyber world, do not feel comfortable with the tools children are using. By guiding children to use the technology in ways that promote respect, understanding, and responsibility, we can lessen the impact of this new form of bullying. (See Figure 1.)

Figure 1. What You Can DO

Tips for children:

* Never share or give out personal information, PIN numbers, phone numbers, etc.

* Tell a trusted adult.

* Do not read messages by cyber bullies.

* Do not delete messages; they can be used to take action.

* Bullying through instant messaging and chat rooms can often be blocked.

* Do not open a message from someone you don't know.

* Do not reply to the person bullying or harassing you.

Tips for parents:

* Pay attention! Know how and when your children are using the Internet.

* Become more tech savvy.

* Install blocking or filtering software.

* Encourage your child to talk to you if they are being bullied.

* Limit your child's time using the Internet.

* Develop a family online agreement including:

Where kids can go online and what they can do there

How much time they can spend on the
Internet

What to do if anything makes them uncomfortable

How to protect their personal information, stay safe in interactive
environments and behave ethically and responsibly online.

Tips for schools:

* Develop school policies for acceptable
Internet and cell phone use. Enforce them.

* Zero tolerance for bullying in any form.

* Ensure that children and young people are aware that all bullying
concerns will be dealt with sensitively and effectively.

* Ensure that parents/guardians expressing bullying concerns have
them taken seriously.

Glossary of Some Common Terms Taken from
www.webopedia.com:

E-mail: Short for electronic mail, the transmission of messages over
communications networks. The messages can be notes entered from
the keyboard or electronic files stored on disk. Most mainframes,
minicomputers, and computer networks have an email system. Some
electronic-mail systems are confined to a single computer system or
network, but others have gateways to other computer systems,
enabling users to send electronic mail anywhere in the world.
Companies that are fully computerized make extensive use of e-mail
because it is fast, flexible, and reliable.

Instant Messaging: A type of communications service that enables you to create a private chat room with another individual. Typically, the instant messaging system alerts you whenever somebody on your private list is online. You can then initiate a chat session with that particular individual.

Chat rooms: Real-time communication between two users via computer. Once a chat has been initiated, either user can enter text by typing on the keyboard and the entered text will appear on the other user's monitor. Most networks and online services offer a chat feature.

Text-messages: Sending short text messages to a device such as a cellular phone, PDA (personal digital assistant), or pager. Text messaging is used for messages that are no longer than a few hundred characters. The term is usually applied to messaging that takes place between two or more mobile devices.

Websites: A system of Internet servers that support specially formatted documents. The documents are formatted in a markup language called HTML (HyperText Markup Language) that supports links to other documents, as well as graphics, audio, and video files. This means you can jump from one document to another simply by clicking on hot spots. Not all Internet servers are part of the World Wide Web.

Voting booths: Some Websites such as www.freevote.com offer users the opportunity to create online polling / voting booths.

Blogs: Short for Web log, a blog is a Web page that serves as a publicly accessible personal journal for an individual. Typically updated daily, blogs often reflect the personality of the author.

Prevention Institute, Inc. Prior to joining the Crisis Prevention Institute, she was a Sign Language interpreter for the Milwaukee Public Schools. She has also worked in residential care settings with emotionally disturbed and developmentally delayed adults and children and served as a Peace Corps volunteer. She may be reached at skeith@crisisprevention.com

Michelle E. Martin, MA, is a professional staff instructor with the Crisis Prevention Institute, Inc. Prior to joining the Crisis Prevention Institute, she worked for 10 years as an educator, teaching mathematics and ESL, and providing counseling and orientation to foreign students at Northeastern University in Boston. She may be reached at mmartin@crisisprevention.com

References deleted.

11

Extending the School Grounds?

Bullying Experiences in Cyberspace

Jaana Juvonen and Elisheva F. Gross

BACKGROUND: Bullying is a national public health problem affecting millions of students. With the rapid increase in electronic or online communication, bullying is no longer limited to schools. The goal of the current investigation was to examine the overlap among targets of, and the similarities between, online and in-school bullying among Internet-using adolescents. Additionally, a number of common assumptions regarding online or cyberbullying were tested.

METHODS: An anonymous Web-based survey was conducted with one thousand four hundred fifty-four 12- to 17-year-old youth.

RESULTS: Within the past year, 72% of respondents reported at least 1 online incident of bullying, 85% of whom also experienced bullying in school. The most frequent forms of online and in-school bullying involved name-calling or insults, and the online incidents most typically took place through instant messaging.

Jaana Juvonen and Elisheva F. Gross, Extending the school grounds? Bullying experiences in cyberspace. *Journal of School Health*, September 2008, p. 496-505. Reprinted by permission of Wiley-Blackwell.

When controlling for Internet use, repeated school-based bullying experiences increased the likelihood of repeated cyberbullying more than the use of any particular electronic communication tool. About two thirds of cyberbullying victims reported knowing their perpetrators, and half of them knew the bully from school. Both in-school and online bullying experiences were independently associated with increased social anxiety. Ninety percent of the sample reported they do not tell an adult about cyberbullying, and only a minority of participants had used digital tools to prevent online incidents.

CONCLUSIONS: The findings have implications for (i) school policies about cyberbullying, parent education about the risks associated with online communication, and youth advice regarding strategies to prevent and deal with cyberbullying incidents.

Bullying that entails emotional or physical intimidation is associated with a number of mental health problems and hence is considered a major public health concern facing youth. Approximately 70% of youth report having experienced bullying at some point during their school careers, and at any 1 time, about 20-25% of youth are identified as being directly involved in bullying at school. With the rapid growth of communication technology especially among adolescents, cyberspace has been implicated as a new risky environment for bullying. However, relatively little is known about where and how youth encounter bullying online, risk factors associated with repeated intimidating online experiences, and the possible overlap and connection between bullying encountered in school and online.

Given the revolutionary increase in Internet use of 12- to 17-year-old youth within the past 5-6 years and the lack of adult supervision online, there are many reasons to be concerned that cyberspace provides a fertile ground for bullying. Public concerns have focused mainly on the risks associated with the technology enabling quick and anonymous spreading of messages to potentially large audiences. Accordingly, cyberbullying is broadly defined as the use of the Internet or other digital communication devices to insult or threaten someone. Cyberbullying is portrayed as a pervasive intimidation method that can happen to any youth using electronic communication tools, such as instant messaging (IM) or e-mail. The current prevalence estimates of youth experiencing at least 1 incident of cyberbullying range from 9% to 49% within a school year. This wide range of estimates depends in part on the sample characteristics and the types of technologies examined. Although the estimates of online bullying experiences are not as high as those of bullying incidents encountered at school (up to 70%), the steep increase in reported incidents across the past 5 years documented in the latest Youth Internet Safety Survey (YISS-2) is a reason for concern.

How do youth get bullied online? Does bullying in cyberspace take qualitatively different forms than bullying in school? On one hand, widespread forms of electronic communication, such as e-mail or IM, are well suited for direct verbal insults (eg, name-calling) that are most frequent at school. On the other hand, digital communication technology readily lends itself to particular forms of privacy violations, such as sharing or forwarding the contents of a private communication to others or stealing someone's password. For example, Ybarra et al found that approximately one third of the victims of cyberbullying were threatened or embarrassed because information was sent or posted about them to others. Thus, at least some cyberbullying tactics capitalize on the particular features of online communication technology.

Although some forms of cyberbullying experiences are likely to vary depending on the type of technology used, it is not clear whether particular communication tools are riskier than others. The most recent evidence suggests that any use of IM, blogging, and chat rooms elevates the odds of being cyberbullied. However, these data do not tell us whether youth experience cyberbullying mainly through these particular communications tools or whether their usage pattern merely reflects risky online behavior. Information about which communication tools are likely to be used for online harassment is critical to educate youth, parents, and schools about risks.

Cyberbullying may appear especially frightening to parents because it involves communication technologies with which they are unfamiliar. Yet, cyberspace may not function as a separate risky environment but rather as an extension of the school grounds. For example, Li found that one third of the seventh graders were bullied both at school and online, whereas one quarter reported having experienced bullying only online (and more than half of the respondents reported having been bullied only at school). The possible connection between bullying experiences in school and online is consistent with data showing that when most schoolmates have Internet access at home, electronic communication is conducted largely within school-based peer networks.

Another main reason underlying concerns over cyberbullying pertains to its potentially harmful psychological effects. The connection between bullying experiences in school and emotional distress is well established. Even a single incident of bullying encountered at school is associated with elevated daily levels of anxiety. Similarly, single episode of cyberbullying has been shown to be related to emotional distress. If cyberbullying is an extension of school-based bullying, then the question is whether online incidents are independently associated with distress. Online intimidation might be particularly distressing, inasmuch as youth are likely to confront cyberbullying incidents alone at home. Moreover, youth may be especially reluctant to tell adults about incidents confronted online if they are concerned about parents restricting their use of these increasingly popular forms of social contact. Hence, cyberbullying might be especially painful because it can go unnoticed for long periods of time.

The characterization of cyberbullying as offering victims "no escape" likely reflects the dearth of data available on how youth respond to or prevent further online harassment. Unlike school, cyberspace affords (potential) victims of cyberbullying an array of tools to prevent further incidents. For example, youth can avoid receiving messages from alleged bullies by blocking their screen names or restricting their buddy lists to their closest friends. Li reports that a majority of youth appear to be familiar with these tactics that ought to reduce or stop persistent harassment. Yet, to date, we do not know whether youth indeed rely on these tactics. This is an especially intriguing question in light of evidence that victims of school-based bullying rarely resort to any active tactics to prevent further incidents and that inaction may be associated with increased risk.

The current study extends prior research on cyberbullying in several important ways. New details about the frequency and nature of online incidents as well as electronic tools implicated in cyberbullying are examined. Most notably, this investigation is designed to test whether cyberspace operates as a risky environment separate from the confines of the school. Because recruitment methods and sample characteristics likely affect rates of cyberbullying and the estimates of the proportion of youth being targeted both online and in school, the recruitment procedures and sample characteristics were carefully considered. To complement small school-based convenience samples and large nationally representative phone surveys requiring parent consent, our sample was recruited via a Web site. This recruitment tactic enabled us to obtain relatively heavy Internet users—for whom the risks of cyberbullying might be higher than for infrequent users. Also, it was vital to conduct the current investigation as an anonymous survey not requiring parental consent because concerns over parental restrictions about Internet use (eg, admitting visits to a Web site to become a participant in the study) may prevent youth most at risk from taking part in the study.

Although many of our analyses pertained to descriptions of single incident of bullying, we also examined the risks associated with the plight of victims of repeated online intimidation. These analyses are consistent with Olweus' school-based definition of bullying as a persistent plight. We predicted that when controlling for the time spent online (ie, opportunity to get targeted), repeated school-based bullying experiences would increase the probability of becoming a target of repeated online bullying. Additionally, we tested whether the use—or relatively heavy use—of any specific electronic tool or communication method (eg, IM, chat rooms) might place youth at additional risk for repeated online victimization. In addition, we examined the validity of specific assumptions discussed earlier about the distress associated with cyberbullying, the anonymity of online harassment, and the low frequency of reporting incidents to adults. Finally, we explored to what extent Internet-using youth rely on methods afforded by electronic communication technology (eg, switching screen names or blocking someone from a buddy list) to prevent further online intimidation.

METHOD

Participants were recruited through a popular teen Web site (http://www.bolt.com) from August through October 2005. Through a link on the site, youth were invited to respond to a survey designed "to find out about teens' experiences communicating with one another on the Internet, in school, and using cell phones." Participants were informed that we were "especially interested in things that happen online that are mean or rude." To minimize self-selection bias (eg, sampling primarily bullied youth), we did not refer to "bullying" or "cyberbullying." Upon completion of the survey, interested participants were entered into a raffle for either an iPod (with lower odds) or a $30 gift certificate to Amazon.com (with higher odds). No parental consent was required because the recruitment took place via the Internet and because the survey was anonymous. We assumed that parental consent would have discouraged participation of individuals concerned about their parents' monitoring their Internet use—the very group that might be most at risk for cyberbullying. Participants were informed that they could refuse to answer any question or withdraw from the study at any time, an act facilitated by the study's online format, in which they

154

could simply log off the study Web page at any point and immediately withdraw from the research without having to explain themselves or be identified in any way.

SAMPLE

The analysis sample consisted of one thousand four hundred fifty-four 12- to 17-year-olds (mean = 15.5, SD = 1.47), 75% of whom were female. Sixty-six percent of survey respondents were Caucasian, 12% African American (or African), 9% Mexican American or Latino, and 5% Asian, including Pacific Islanders. All 50 states were represented in the current sample. With the highest proportion from California and New York (102 and 100 respondents, respectively), 30 states contributed 10 or more respondents. Apart from the 4% of participants who were homeschooled, the majority of schools attended by participants were public (84%) and served communities in which, according to participants, most or all students had home access to the Internet (94%). Only 6% (n = 92) of participants who did not complete the survey finished prior to reaching any questions concerning bullying experiences. This group did not differ from the analysis sample on any demographic variables and was excluded from the final sample of 1454 participants.

MEASURES

Online Experience and Communication Tool Use. To be able to control for any possible differences based on history of online experiences, we asked respondents to indicate on a 5-point scale how long they have used the Internet ("6 months" to "more than 3 years"). To obtain an estimate of daily Internet use consistent with previous surveys, we also asked participants how long they spent online the day prior to completing the survey on a 6-point scale (response options ranged from "did not go online" to "more than four hours"). Using a 5-point scale ranging from "never" to "every day," participants indicated how often they use the following electronic communication tools: e-mail, IM, chat rooms, blogs (ie, online journals or opinion pages that are available for others to read), personal profile Web sites (eg, Myspace.com), message boards (ie, asynchronous text-based dialogue about specific topics), cell phones (through which text messages and pictures may be sent), and Webcams (devices that can record and broadcast both still pictures and video).

Bullying Experiences. Rather than use the term bullying (with its potentially narrow connotations), we referred to mean things defined as "anything that someone does that upsets or offends someone else," including name-calling, threats, sending embarrassing/ private pictures, and sharing private information without permission. The types of experiences assessed were based on adolescent focus groups and research on bullying with middle and high school students. Certain forms of in-school bullying, such as physical attacks, were not included in the survey because they are less common among adolescents than among younger children and do not correspond directly to online experiences. Specifically, youth reported how frequently they had experienced name-calling or insults, threats, spreading of embarrassing or private pictures, sharing of private communications (also known online as "copy-and-pasting," as in when the contents of a private IM conversation are copied and forwarded to multiple others), and password theft (eg, gaining access to one's e-mail or IM account without permission). By relying on a 5-point scale ranging from "never" to "more than 12 times," participants were asked separately about corresponding school-based (ie, "off-line") and online incidents, a total of 9 questions. In order to reduce response bias and confusion, questions concerning online experiences were separated as much as possible from those concerning in-school experiences. Additionally, respondents reported whether they encountered online mean things via e-mail, IM, cell phone text messaging, in a chat room, blog, personal profile site, and/or message boards; multiple responses were allowed.

Assumptions About Cyberbullying. To test the assumption that cyberbullying is especially detrimental to the psychological well-being of youth, we examined the association between experiences of online intimidation and social anxiety when taking into account school-based bullying experiences. Social anxiety was assessed with 6 items (eg, "I worry what others think about me") from a scale ([alpha] =.84) developed for use with adolescents. To test the anonymity assumption, respondents rated their degree of certainty about the identity of the person who had bullied them online using a 5-point scale ranging from "not at all" to "totally sure." In addition, they rated whether they knew the person or people involved from school, offline but not school (eg, from after-school activities, camps, neighborhood) and online only, or whether they did not know the perpetrator. Participants also indicated whether they "did something to get even" or "got back at them so they'd leave me alone" in response to being bullied and, if so, whether they had retaliated online, off-line (ie, in school or elsewhere in person), or both. Youth were also asked whether they usually told adults when they were bullied online and, if not, why not. Answer choices included concern over parental restrictions concerning Internet use as well as a belief in need to learn to deal with such incidents themselves.

Reliance on Prevention Tactics. Finally, we probed about prevention tactics provided by the technology (ie, blocking someone, sending a warning, switching a screen name, restricting a buddy list to those whom they wish to hear from) that help youth avoid mean messages online.

All the above questions allowed respondents to indicate multiple responses. For example, participants might indicate that they had been bullied both by peers at school and by people whom they know only from online or that they had relied on more than 1 prevention tactic.

DATA ANALYSIS

Because 15- to 17-year-old girls were overrepresented in our sample, participants' Internet use and experience are analyzed by age and sex using chi-square tests. Rates of reported school-based and online bullying incidents and their overlap are also assessed by relying on chi-square statistics. To be able to examine risk factors for repeated cyberbullying, odds ratios are computed through logistic regression analyses. The associations between social anxiety and school-based as well as online bullying are, in turn, tested by relying on hierarchical regression analyses. All other data regarding the types of cyberbullying incidents, electronic communication tools involved, assumptions about cyberbullying, and the respondents' reliance on prevention strategies are summarized in percentages. Gender and age differences are noted only when they are statistically significant.

RESULTS

The Results section is divided into 4 main sections: electronic communication use and prevalence of bullying, risks associated with repeated cyberbullying, assumptions about cyberbullying, and prevention tactics used.

ELECTRONIC COMMUNICATION
AND PREVALENCE OF BULLYING

The vast majority of the respondents had used the Internet for more than 3 years and had gone online the day prior to completing the survey (Table 1). Compared to 12- to 14-year-olds, 15- to 17-year-old youth were significantly more likely to have more than 3 years' experience using the Internet, [chi square] $(91, 1454) = 27.4$, p < .001. E-mail and IM were the communication tools most frequently used by respondents. (Of the sample, 49% reported daily e-mail use and 58% reported daily IM.) More than half of the sample at least occasionally used profile sites, blogs, cell phone text messaging, chat rooms, and message boards (Table 1). Webcam use was least common within this sample of youth. Chi-square test by age and gender revealed that 15- to 17-year-olds and girls were significantly more frequent users of e-mail, profile sites, blogs, and cell phones than were 12- to 14-year-olds and boys ([chi square] = 7.5 and 28.7, respectively).

To assess the reliability of reported incidents, prevalence estimates for online and in-school bullying were computed by relying on 2 methods. First, based on the single item assessing the number of incidents encountered within the past year, 72% of the youth reported having experienced at least 1 incident of bullying in cyberspace, and 77% of youth reported a minimum of 1 situation of bullying in school. A second estimation method entailed summing across the 5 different forms of bullying experiences. The resultant estimate for online bullying was identical to that obtained by the single frequency count (ie, 72%). The composite across the 4 types of in-school incidents yielded a 3% higher estimate (80%) than the single item assessing the frequency of school-based bullying within the past year. When comparing the overlap among reports of online vs in-school bullying, a chi-square test indicated that 85% of youth who reported experiencing at least 1 incident of online bullying also reported experiencing at least 1 incident in school within the past year, [chi square] $(1, 1217) = 105.0$, p < .001. Hence, the probability of getting bullied online was substantially higher for those who were bullied in school.

Most youth reported that incidents occurred infrequently: 41% of respondents reported 1-3 incidents, and 13% reported 4-6 incidents in the past year. Almost one fifth of participants (19%), however, experienced 7 or more incidents of online bullying in the past year. A paired t test comparing the number of bullying incidents each participant reported in school and online in the past year revealed that respondents encountered school-based bullying with significantly greater frequency, mean school-based = 1.45, SD = 1.26 and mean online = 1.33, SD = 1.26 (on a 0-4 Likert-type scale indicating frequency in the past year), t(1217) = 3.27, p < .002. The frequency of online and in-school bullying experiences was significantly correlated, r = .45, p < .001.

The most prevalent forms of bullying online and in school involved name-calling or insults (Table 2). Password theft was the next most common cyberbullying tactic. Other than password violations, additional forms of online bullying were similar in type to those taking place at school. According to participants, even the unauthorized sharing of embarrassing or private pictures or other private information, which might be expected to be higher online, occurred at similar rates in school.

Across the entire sample of Internet users, the most likely communication tools implicated in cyberbullying involved IM (19%) and message boards (16%). Because the sample was rather selective in relying on certain tools less frequently (eg, message boards, Webcam) than others (eg, e-mail, IM), we analyzed the likelihood of encountering incidents via specific tools. When adjusting for the use of a particular communication tool, cyberbullying experiences remained most common among those who use message boards (26%) and IM (20%) and were least frequently encountered among those who have profile sites (4%) (Table 2).

RISK ASSOCIATED WITH REPEATED CYBERBULLYING

We used logistic regression analyses to predict the risk of repeated experiences of cyberbullying. Based on previous research, we defined repeated experiences as 7 or more incidents in the past year. Using this criterion, the group of repeatedly cyberbullied consisted of 19% of the entire sample. In addition to testing the predictive effects of age, gender, and repeated school-based bullying experiences, we examined whether heavy Internet use (more than 3 hours the day prior to survey) and reliance of each of 7 communication tools predicted repeated cyberbullying.

Heavy Internet use indeed significantly increased the likelihood of repeated online intimidation (Table 3). When controlling for Internet use, repeated school-based bullying experiences (7 or more times during the past year) increased the likelihood of cyberbullying almost 7-fold. Moreover, the analyses indicated that those who used IM and Webcams were each about 1.5-2.8 times as likely to be repeatedly cyberbullied compared to nonusers of these communication tools.

To be able to further understand the risks of repeated cyberbullying involved with each electronic communication tool, we also computed separate logistic regressions among the users of each tool by comparing light and heavy users. Because the distributions of the amount of time spent across the tools varied considerably, we identified light and heavy use in relative terms based on the respective distribution of time spent on each tool. These analyses replicated the effects of repeated school-based bullying and heavy Internet use. Consistent with the previous analyses comparing users and nonusers, Webcam users who reported using the tool at least once or twice a week were 1.75 times more likely to report repeated cyberbullying in the past year. In addition, these analyses revealed that among message board users, use of boards "most days of the week or more" significantly increased the likelihood of repeated cyberbullying (ORs = 1.67). Thus, the risk of repeated cyberbullying was significantly predicted not only by the use (vs nonuse) of IM and Webcams but also by relatively heavy (vs light) use of Webcams as well as message boards.

Table 1.

Internet Experience and Electronic Communication
Tool Use by Frequency (and Percentage)

12- to 14-Year-Olds

	Sample (%)	Total Boys (%)	Girls (%)
Internet use			
More than 3 years of use	1203 (83)	126 (77)	277 (75)
Internet use the day before	1294 (89)	146 (90)	333 (91)
Electronic communication * tool use			
E-mail	1402 (97)	145 (90) ([dagger])	353 (96)
IM	1357 (94)	147 (93)	344 (94)
Profile sites	925 (65)	67 (43)	232 (63)
Blogs	915 (64)	75 (48)	234 (64)
Cell phone (text messaging)	868 (60)	67 (42)	211 (58)
Chat rooms	840 (59)	89 (57)	221 (61)
Message boards	793 (55)	67 (43)	182 (50)
Webcam	348 (24)	34 (22)	85 (23)

* Respondents were asked to indicate how often they currently use each tool, from never to every day. All those who indicated greater frequency than never were defined as users.

([dagger]) The percentage scores are adjusted to the number of no-responses varying (n = 6-27) across the electronic communication tools.

15- to 17-Year-Olds

	Boys (%)	Girls (%)
Internet use		
More than 3 years of use	175 (87)	625 (87)
Internet use the day before	190 (95)	625 (87)
Electronic communication * tool use		
E-mail	189 (95)	715 (99)
IM	188 (95)	678 (94)
Profile sites	120 (61)	506 (71)
Blogs	309 (56)	111 (56)
Cell phone (text messaging)	112 (56)	478 (67)
Chat rooms	121 (61)	409 (57)
Message boards	111 (56)	433 (61)
Webcam	55 (28)	174 (24)

* Respondents were asked to indicate how often they currently use each tool, from never to every day. All those who indicated greater frequency than never were defined as users.

([dagger]) The percentage scores are adjusted to the number of no-responses varying (n = 6-27) across the electronic communication tools.

ASSUMPTIONS ABOUT CYBERBULLYING

Distress. The above analyses suggest that online and off-line experiences of bullying largely overlap. The question is whether cyberbullying incidents are related to social anxiety over and above school-based bullying experiences. To examine this question, we conducted hierarchical regression analysis. When controlling for gender and age, the number of bullying incidents experienced in school and in cyberspace each independently increased reported levels of social anxiety (Table 4). In other words, online experiences of bullying are associated with elevated level of distress much like encounters of bullying encountered in school.

Anonymity. Contrary to common assumptions about the anonymity of cyberbullies, 73% of the respondents were "pretty sure" or "totally sure" of the identity of the perpetrator. About half of the participants (51%) reported experiencing online bullying by schoolmates, 43% by someone they knew from online only, and 20% by someone known off-line but not from school (recall that participants were free to indicate multiple responses to this question). Thus, the Internet does not seem to protect perpetrators' identity—or, at least, the victims of cyberbullying think they know who is harassing them. Moreover, perpetrators are likely to be peers from school or other off-line contexts.

Retaliation. Were victims of school-based bullying especially likely to retaliate online? Among the 48% of school-based victims who reported retaliating against their presumed aggressor(s), the most likely site for retaliation was school (60%), not cyberspace (12%); 28% of school-based victims reported retaliating both in school and online. Thus, these data do not support the assumption about youth taking advantage of the anonymity of cyberspace but provide further evidence for the integral connection between the online and school lives of youth.

Reporting to Adults. As presumed, most youth (90%) reported not telling adults about cyberbullying incidents. The most common reason for not telling an adult, cited at equal rates across age and gender, was that participants believe they "need to learn to deal with it" themselves (50%). In addition, almost one third of the sample (31%) reported that the reason they do not tell is because they are concerned that their parents might find out and restrict their Internet access. This concern was significantly more common among 12-to 14-year-old girls (46% of 12-to 14-year-old girls vs 27% of 12- to

14-year-old boys), [chi square] $(1, 282) = 8.57$, $p < .004$. Also, one third of 12- to 14-year-olds reported that they do not tell an adult out of fear that they could get into trouble with their parents. Thus, the fear of restrictions may deter youth, especially younger girls, from sharing their negative experiences with adults.

PREVENTION TACTICS USED

Of the prevention strategies enabled by the technology used, blocking a particular screen name was the most common tactic used. Sixty-seven percent of the sample had blocked someone in the past. One third (33%) had restricted particular screen names from their buddy list. About one fourth of the sample had switched a screen name (26%) and had sent a warning (25%) to someone to prevent cyberbullying. Because most of these tactics are particularly relevant to IM as one of the most prevalent forms of electronic communication, we also compared the rates of tactics used specifically among those who had encountered cyberbullying on IM. These analyses showed that 75% of those who encountered an IM incident had blocked a screen name, 45% had restricted their buddy list, 44% had switched their own screen name, and 34% had sent someone a warning. Thus, although youth who have encountered a cyberbullying incident on IM rely on these tactics more frequently than those who have not experienced such encounters, the tactics appear underutilized. For example, one quarter of youth who had experienced online intimidation on IM had never blocked a screen name.

Table 2.
Percentage of Youth Reporting 5 Forms of Bullying Online and in School (Upper Part); Online Incidents via 7 Electronic Communication Tools (Lower Part)

Form of Bullying	Online (%)	In School (%)
Insults	66	75
Threats	27	33
Sharing embarrassing Pictures	18	18
Privacy violation ("cut-and-pasting")	25	21
Password theft	33	N/A

Communication Tool	Frequency (%)	
Message boards	199 (26)	*
IM	270 (20)	
E-mail	175 (13)	
Cell phone (text messaging)	55 (6)	
Chat rooms	50 (6)	
Blogs	47 (5)	
Profile sites	35 (4)	

* Frequencies and percentages are adjusted to reflect only users of each tool, N/A, not applicable.

Table 3.

Logistic Regression Analysis Predicting Repeated Cyberbullying
(7 or More Times During the Past Year) *

Predictors	Odds Ratio (95% Confidence Interval)	p
Age group (12-14 vs 15-17)	1.04 (0.74-1.48)	n.s.
Gender	0.97 (0.66-1.44)	n.s.
Heavy Internet users ([dagger])	1.45 (1.04-2.02)	.03
Repeatedly bullied at school ([double dagger])	6.87 (4.90-9.62)	.001
E-mail user	6.13 (0.77-49.00)	n.s.
IM user	2.84 (1.08-7.49)	.03
Webcam user	1.50 (1.04-2.14)	.001
Blog user	1.05 (0.71-1.56)	n.s.
Profile site user	1.37 (0.92-2.04)	n.s.
Message board user	1.32 (0.91-1.92)	n.s.
Cell phone user	1.15 (0.82-1.62)	n.s.

* All predictors are categorical.

([dagger]) Heavy Internet use was defined as 3 or more hours of use the previous day.

([double dagger]) Repeated bullying at school was defined as reporting 7 or more incidents during the past year.

n.s., nonsignificant.

DISCUSSION

There are many reasons to be concerned that cyberspace may provide a fertile ground for bullying beyond the confines of school grounds. The present findings provide novel information about where and how cyberbullying takes place; how online experiences are similar to, and connected with, incidents encountered in school; and who is most at risk for repeated cyberbullying. Most notably, our findings suggest that (1) among heavy users of the Internet, cyberbullying is a common experience; (2) the forms of online and in-school bullying are similar and the experiences overlap across the 2 contexts; (3) although some electronic communication methods and devices are associated with elevated risk of cyberbullying, they are merely tools, not causes of mean behavior; (4) independent of school-based bullying, cyberbullying is associated with increased distress, and (5) youth rarely tell adults about their experiences of online bullying and do not fully capitalize on the tools provided by communication technologies to prevent future incidents.

There is cause for concern about the pervasiveness of online intimidation in light of our prevalence estimates. Almost one fifth of 12- to 17-year-old Internet users reported repeated cyberbullying experiences during the past year. This figure is somewhat higher than estimates of more than occasional cyberbullying obtained in Canada and Britain. However, our finding of 72% of Internet users reporting at least 1 online bullying encounter within the past year is much higher than in other recent surveys in the United States. Several methodological differences between one of the most well-known surveys (YISS-2) and our study are likely to contribute to the discrepant findings. For example, the YISS-2 was conducted as a national telephone survey that included younger (10- to 12-year-old) youth and required parental consent, whereas our sample consisted of self-selected, slightly older sample recruited by a popular Web site and requiring no parental consent. Also, the YISS-2 participants were classified as Internet users if they had used the Internet at least once during the past 6 months, whereas almost 90% of our sample used the Internet on a daily basis. Thus, when estimating the prevalence of cyberbullying, the sample recruitment and characteristics (eg, age), Internet use, and methods used to investigate online incidents may considerably affect the findings.

The 85% overlap between online and in-school bullying experiences and the 7-fold higher risk of online incidents among repeatedly targeted youth at school suggest that cyberspace is not a separate risky environment. Rather, cyberspace seems to be used as a forum that extends the school grounds. Although heavy use of the Internet and communication tools such as IM and Webcams are implicated as risk factors for cyberbullying, they pose less risk than do school-based experiences. Thus, it is critical to recognize that electronic communication devices are not the cause of problem behavior among youth, but they are literally tools: they can be used to interact with peers in both anti- and prosocial ways. For most youth, electronic communication entails prosocial behavior aimed at developing and sustaining friendship networks and romantic relationships. Mean behaviors may therefore be just as inevitable online as they are in other in social contexts.

Certain electronic communication tools increase the risk of cyberbullying experiences more than others. Among the most common communication tools, IM increased the risk of cyberbullying by about 3-fold. When considering the relative frequency of use of particular technologies (ie, heavy vs light or none), the Webcam, which allows sharing of pictures and video, was the riskiest tool among the 8 studied. Heavy use of message boards was also found to significantly increase the risk of repeated cyberbullying. It is possible that these particular communication technologies facilitate more derogatory communication or "flaming." (27) Alternatively, the risks involved in using certain technologies might be related to the peer communities more than any inherent

166

aspect of a particular communication tool per se. When youth cannot connect online with their schoolmates, intimidation might be more likely to be carried out by unknown others on message boards.

Table 4.
Hierarchical Regression Analysis
Predicting Social Anxiety

Predictors	B	SE B	B	Total [R.sup.2]
Step 1				.002
Age	.53	.31	.05	
Gender	.25	.35	.02	
Step 2				.018 ***
Frequency of in-school bullying incidents	.34	.13	.08 **	
Frequency of online bullying incidents	.31	.13	.08 *	

* p < .05; ** p < 01; *** p < .001.

In theory, electronic communication tools enable bullies to remain anonymous. The present findings, however, do not support the assumption that the potential shield of anonymity is dramatically changing the nature of bullying. The forms of bullying online and in school remain more similar than different. We also find no support for the assumption that school-based victims use cyberspace to retaliate against their perpetrators. Quite the opposite: cyberbullied youth were more likely to retaliate in school than online. While about three quarters of youth reported knowing their perpetrators, approximately half of the cyberbullied suspected the perpetrators to be peers from school. These findings further underscore the continuity between adolescents' social worlds in school and online.

Our findings suggest that independent of school-based bullying, the frequency of cyberbullying experiences is related to increased distress. It is important to keep in mind, however, that the mere association between distress and cyberbullying cannot tell us if these bullying experiences are causing emotional distress or whether distressed youth spend more time online or use the riskier communication tools compared to their peers who are not distressed. To understand the emotional impact of cyberbullying, longitudinal studies with multiple data waves are needed.

Consistent with research on in-school bullying, we found that participants in our study do not tell adults about their online experiences. Ninety percent of the current sample reported that they do not tell an adult when they have been cyberbullied. This estimate is disconcerting inasmuch as this form of bullying may be very difficult for adults to detect: they are not "there" to witness events themselves, and peers who observe such online incidents are unlikely to intervene or let anyone know because their knowledge about what happened at a particular Web site may implicate them in a questionable activity (eg, something from which their parents had restricted them). Fear of parental restrictions of Internet access concerned at least one third of the youth in the current sample. This finding may also partly explain why prevalence estimates obtained in studies that require parental consent (eg, Ybarra et al) show lower rates of cyberbullying.

Unlike in school-based bullying, in the case of online intimidation, there is a range of preventative tools available to youth. Although more than half of the current sample of 12- to 17-year-old youth had used these tactics, one would expect these rates to be much higher, especially among youth who have encountered online intimidation. In future studies, it would be important to examine if there are specific reasons why youth do not rely on available electronic tactics to try to prevent bullying. For example, if embarrassing information is spread within a school about an individual, this person may want to at least know what is being said and shared about her/him.

Similar to any (Web-based) survey, the current study solely relied on self-reports. Although informative, self-reports are limited when no other data sources can be utilized. Hence, in subsequent research, complementary data from peers, teachers, or parents (eg, about school-based bullying, level of distress) would be invaluable. Data from different sources could also be used for systematic methodological studies to establish reliability and validity of survey instruments. In the current study, we assessed the reliability of the prevalence estimates by comparing reports of the number of total incidents experienced within the past year to the reports of specific types of incidents encountered. Whereas the estimates obtained through these 2 methods were identical for online bullying, the 3% discrepancy found in school-based incidents likely reflects incidents involving more than 1 form of bullying (ie, insults, privacy violations).

Our female-dominated, mostly European American, public school sample restricts the generalizability of the findings. For example, we cannot make inferences about online experiences of youth younger than 12 years. It is possible that parents monitor the computer-related behaviors of children more closely than those of adolescents and therefore online and in-school bullying experiences would overlap less among students in elementary grades than in middle and high school. Although the ethnic composition of our sample reflects the persistent gap between European Americans and other ethnic groups in home Internet access nationwide, additional data are needed on online experiences across a wider demographic spectrum of youth—and especially youth who are not electronically as connected with their schoolmates as the current sample.

POLICY IMPLICATIONS

The belief that youth should deal with cyberbullying alone is one of the reasons likely to contribute to the reluctance of telling parents about cyberbullying incidents. No less than half of our sample endorsed the belief that they need not tell an adult about a cyberbullying experience because "I need to learn to deal with it myself." This belief, combined with fears of parental restrictions on Internet use (especially among 12- to 14-year-old girls), may indeed ultimately increase the stress associated with cyberbullying. Until the generation gap in the use and understanding of communication technology narrows, it may be especially difficult for young people to turn to adults for help with cyberbullying.

Parents and youth would also benefit from increased knowledge about the positive functions of online communication among peers, which may help to allay fears that only harm can result from youth interacting online. Recent experimental research shows that compared to a solitary computer activity, IM with an unknown peer can alleviate the distress caused by social exclusion. Moreover, based on the most recent tragic campus shooting in Virginia Tech, it appears that an online community of peers can also help healing the aftermath of a tragic event. Parental restrictions on Internet use should therefore be made with the awareness that although they may help protect youth from cyberbullying, they may also limit the ways that youth can rely on communication technology to better cope with distressing events.

Another issue concerns whether parents and other adults may both overestimate the risk of bullying online and downplay the risk of bullying in school. Moreover, parents as well as school personnel may fail to see the connection between bullying in school and in cyberspace. The links and similarities between school-based and online bullying documented in this study need to be recognized. There is no reason why cyberbullying should be "beyond" the school's responsibility to address. Rather, it seems that schools need to enforce intolerance of any intimidation among students, regardless of whether it takes place on or beyond the school grounds.

Footnotes deleted.

12

A Study on Cyberstalking

Understanding Investigative Hurdles

Robert D'Ovidio and James Doyle

By enabling human interaction without the constraints of physical barriers and with the perception of anonymity, the Internet has become the ideal instrument for individuals who wish to intimidate, threaten, and harass others. A stalker can use the Internet to send alarming messages anywhere, within a matter of moments, under the guise of a fictitious screen name or pseudonym. Understanding how offenders use the Internet to stalk victims in cyberspace can provide law enforcement officers with solutions when they encounter impediments investigating these types of cases.

DEFINITION OF CYBERSTALKING

As the Internet becomes the communication device of choice for millions of people worldwide, news headlines, such as "Killer Keeps Web Pages on Victim, Stalks Her Through Internet" and "Penn Opens Hate E-mail Inquiry," have begun to appear more frequently. These headlines depict stories of criminal intimidation, harassment, fear, and suggestive violence where individuals use the Internet as a tool to stalk another person.

Robert D'Ovidio and James Doyle, A study on cyberstalking: understanding investigative hurdles. *The FBI Law Enforcement Bulletin* 72 (3): 10-18, March 2003.

The term cyberstalking has emerged to describe the use of such technology to harass or stalk. (3) Cyberstalking is defined as the repeated use of the Internet, e-mail, or related digital electronic communication devices to annoy, alarm, or threaten a specific individual or group of individuals.

All 50 states and the federal government have enacted statutes aimed at protecting the victims of stalking. Many of these statutes have existed for a long time, while others have originated recently. Some of the older statutes were broad enough to cover any type of stalking behavior, including cyberstalking; others had to be amended to do so.

In some jurisdictions, new laws specifically addressing the problem of cyberstalking have been enacted. In adapting general stalking and harassment statutes to cover instances of cyberstalking, legislators have expanded the means by which offenders commit this crime to include electronic communication devices.

Several states currently include specific protections against threatening electronically transmitted communications in their stalking or harassment statutes. Additionally, Title 18, Section 875, U.S. Code, criminalizes threatening messages transmitted electronically in interstate or foreign commerce. The use of federal legislation to prosecute cases of cyberstalking, however, is limited, by law, to instances where the harassing messages are transmitted across state lines or outside the United States. Despite the existence of Title 18, Section 875, the federal government historically has limited its involvement in prosecuting cases related to electronically transmitted threatening messages to cases involving special circumstances, such as threats made against the president of the United States. As with stalking that does not involve the Internet, local authorities investigate and prosecute most cyberstalking cases in either the jurisdiction where the victim resides or in the jurisdiction where the messages originated.

With the rapid pace of technological advancement that exists in today's society, legislation should take an evolutionary approach toward defining electronic communication devices and systems of transmission. Legislation that limits electronic devices and transmission systems to specific technologies, such as telephones and land-based wires, risk becoming antiquated with the emergence of new technologies, such as computers and wireless transmission systems.

THE STUDY

Background

Anticipating the significant role computers would play in the commission of crimes in the future, the New York City Police Department (NYPD) developed the Computer Investigation & Technology Unit (CITU) in 1995. CITU investigates cases where offenders use a computer or the Internet as an instrument to commit a crime or where a computer represents the target of a crime or constitutes a source of evidence relating to a crime. The unit also performs outreach services to business and community groups to educate people on computer ethics, safe Internet practices, and data security issues related to the most current practices of computer hackers. Additionally, CITU provides training and technical assistance to local, state, and federal law enforcement and prosecutorial agencies.

Methodology

The authors used official police records from NYPD's CITU to capture data on the extent and nature of cyberstalking for this study. Specifically, the data for this study were drawn from information contained within standardized forms filed by the complainant at the time of the initial complaint and standardized investigative forms that detail the progress of the investigation from beginning to end. Data were gathered using all closed cases of aggravated harassment investigated by NYPD from January 1996 through August 2000 in which criminals used a computer or the Internet as the instrument of the offense. In addition to the date of the offense, descriptive information was gathered on the victim, the offender, the outcome of the case, the method used to harass, and whether the victim and suspect resided in the same jurisdiction.

Extent of the Problem

When compared to other cybercrimes, cyberstalking has been the most prevalent crime reported to and investigated by CITU since the unit's inception. During the 56-month period from January 1996 through August 2000, 42.8 percent of the cases investigated by CITU involved aggravated harassment by means of a computer or the Internet. Additional CITU investigations during this period involved grand larceny, computer and network trespassing, forgery, petty larceny, criminal impersonation, child pornography, crimes against children, and schemes to defraud. Understanding the distribution of cybercrimes is essential to allocating a computer crime unit's resources in a cost-efficient manner. Training that provides investigators with the technical knowledge and procedural experience needed to successfully investigate cyberstalking should be a priority for a computer crime unit. Agencies should note that the technical training needed to successfully investigate cases of cyberstalking is not entirely crime specific and w ill prove useful when investigating other types of computer-related crime.

An examination of case outcomes revealed that 192 of the 201 cyberstalking cases investigated by CITI.J were closed during the 56-month period of this study. Approximately 40 percent of the cases were closed with an arrest, and almost 11 percent of the cases failed to produce evidence that a crime was committed. CITU closed the remaining cases after finding evidence to support the victim's complaint due to a jurisdictional issue, an uncooperative complainant, a case transfer, or exhausting all investigative leads without positively identifying a specific offender.

The Offender

Offender characteristics were examined using the 134 closed cases where a suspect was arrested or where evidence to support an arrest existed but a suspect was not arrested because of an uncooperative complainant or a jurisdictional issue. The results revealed that males (approximately 80 percent of the cases) were more likely than females to commit aggravated harassment using a computer or the Internet. Approximately 74 percent of the offenders were white, 13 percent Asian, 8 percent Hispanic, and 5 percent black. The average age of the offender was 24, with the oldest offender being 53 years old and the youngest being 10 years old. Approximately 26 percent of offenders were juveniles, according to New York State law, or under the age of 16.

The Victim

Victim characteristics were examined using the 171 closed cases where investigators determined that a threatening or alarming message6 was transmitted using a computer or the Internet (excluding cases with unfounded outcomes). Females, the most likely recipients, were victimized in about 52 percent of the cases, whereas males were the victims of aggravated harassment in approximately 35 percent. Educational institutions represented the next most likely target with 8 percent. Offenders chose private corporations in almost 5 percent of the cases. Public-sector agencies were targeted in about 1 percent of the cases.

Approximately 85 percent of victims were white, 6 percent Asian, 5 percent black, and 4 percent Hispanic. The average age of the victims was 32, with the youngest victim being 10 years old and the oldest being 62 years of age.

Technological Methods

In 92 percent of the cases, offenders used only one method to stalk their victims. E-mail was used most often. Offenders used email to harass their victims in approximately 79 percent of the cases. The second method most often used by offenders was the instant messenger. Offenders used instant messengers to harass their victims in about 13 percent of the cases. Chat rooms were used in approximately 8 percent of the cases, while message boards and Web sites were used respectively in 4 percent and 2 percent of the cases. Last, offenders employed newsgroups and false user profiles in approximately 1 percent of the cases.

Knowing the type of Internet technology used most often by cyberstalkers can prove beneficial to law enforcement administrators who must decide how to allocate the training budget for computer crime investigators. Because e-mail constitutes the method most often used by cyberstalkers, unit administrators should prioritize technical training that provides investigators with the knowledge needed to perform e-mail-related forensics.

Issues Facing Law Enforcement and Potential Solutions

Technical features of the Internet and procedural issues with the law present problems for criminal justice agencies when investigating and prosecuting cyberstalking cases. These problems, however, are not crime specific and generally occur when agencies investigate and prosecute cases involving any type of computer crime.

Jurisdiction

The global reach of the Internet and the instantaneous nature of computer-mediated communication present law enforcement with jurisdictional issues that could negatively impact the investigation and the subsequent prosecution of computer crimes. With the Internet, stalkers no longer need physical proximity to have contact with their victims. They just as easily can harass a person in another state or country as they can a person who lives in close proximity.

The majority of CITU's aggravated harassment cases involved investigations where both the offender and victim resided within the jurisdiction of the NYPD. In approximately 72 percent of the cases, the offender and the victim resided within the five boroughs of New York City. In comparison, 26 percent of the cases involved either an offender or a victim who resided outside the jurisdiction of the NYPD but within the United States, while 2 percent of the cases involved an offender from a foreign country.

An offender residing outside the jurisdiction of the investigating agency can negatively impact the outcome of a case. In New York City, the District Attorney's Office is less inclined to prosecute aggravated harassment cases if the arrest of the suspect requires extradition from another jurisdiction. Such policies have prevented the apprehension of offenders by the NYPD in cases where investigations by CITU have produced evidence supporting their arrests. In 20 aggravated harassment cases investigated by CITU, the NYPD did not arrest the suspects, despite supporting evidence, because their arrests would require extradition from another jurisdiction. In these cases, the NYPD made referrals to the police departments that had jurisdiction over the offenders.

Differences in statutory definitions of stalking across states may complicate the investigation and prosecution processes when offenders reside outside the jurisdiction of the investigating agency. Jurisdictions that do not recognize Internet communication as a viable method to stalk or harass may deny or ignore the extradition request, search warrant, or subpoena of a jurisdiction where such methods do constitute a criminal offense.

To minimize the negative impact jurisdictional issues have on the successful investigation and prosecution of cyberstalking cases, computer crime investigation units should develop working relationships with their counterparts in other jurisdictions. Such relationships can prove essential to securing the arrest of out-of-state or foreign offenders in their home jurisdictions when the victim's jurisdiction will not arrest if extradition is required. In addition, cross-jurisdictional relationships between computer crime investigation units can help secure the execution of out-of-state subpoenas and search warrants and facilitate relationships with out-of-state Internet service providers, computer manufacturers, and software developers. Over the past decade, various professional organizations have formed for those involved with the investigation of computer-related crimes. Participation in these organizations can provide law enforcement with invaluable links to out-of-state resources.

Because of the ease with which cyberstalkers may attack across jurisdictional lines, legislatures should carefully define the venue of the offense. In cases where threatening communication originates from another state or country and the statute of the investigating jurisdiction defines the venue of the offense in terms of where the communication originated, the criminal justice community will not be able to properly serve the victim. When creating legislation to combat cyberstalking or when revising existing stalking legislation to include Internet communication, states should define the venue of the offense in a manner that includes both the place where the communication was received and the place where the communication originated.

Account and User Information

The unwillingness of some Internet service providers to readily grant law enforcement access to subscriber records further complicates the investigation of a cyberstalking case. Not all Internet service providers agree on what constitutes subscriber records, which are obtainable by subpoena, as opposed to transactional records, which require a search warrant. When compared to obtaining telephone records from a telephone company, obtaining a suspect's Internet account information from a service provider can prove far more complicated and involve an increase in the amount of paperwork and time an investigator spends on a case.

178

Out-of-date and missing account, subscriber, or user information also presents problems to law enforcement agencies when investigating cases of cyberstalking. Without toll records or transactional data, investigators can have a difficult time establishing an electronic link between the suspect and the victim. The financial and human costs associated with gathering and maintaining account information decreases the possibility that Internet service providers will voluntarily collect and maintain such data for a useful period of time. Missing toll records, transactional data, user information, or account content resulted in a negative case clearance in approximately 18 percent of the cyberstalking cases investigated by CITU. In these cases, the content of the communication contained a threatening message, but no arrest occurred because detectives could not gain access to the electronic evidence to legally support apprehending a specific individual. To ensure that account, subscriber, and user information are collected and saved long enough to help law enforcement, legislation that regulates Internet service providers should include data collection requirements.

Anonymizing Tools

The continued development and increased availability of anonymizing Internet tools (i.e., devices that ensure a person's anonymity when using the Internet) can complicate the investigation of cyberstalking cases. Anonymous remailers allow individuals to send electronic mail without transmitting any information that would enable others to determine the identity of the author. Remailers strip identifying information from the e-mail header and erase any transactional data from servers that would enable law enforcement to trace the message back to the author. Consequently, cyberstalkers who use an anonymous remailer as the sole means to send threatening or harassing e-mail messages will remain virtually undetectable to the victim and law enforcement. The danger raised by the use of anonymous remailers, as depicted by CITU's caseload, does not stem from the frequency in which these tools are used, but from the effect these tools have on the investigative process. Anonymous remailers were used in only 4, or 2.1 percent, of the 192 cyberstalking cases investigated by CITU. Investigators, however, could not trace the harassing e-mail messages sent through the anonymous remailers back to their authors in all four cases where these tools were used.

Anonymous Web-browsing services also offer cyberstalkers the opportunity to harass or threaten victims while remaining virtually untraceable to law enforcement. Some companies provide users with the ability to surf the Internet, participate in public chat channels, send instant messages, and post messages to newsgroups without transmitting any identifying information. The exclusive use of such services to send harassing messages would prevent investigators from establishing an electronic link between the victim and the offender. An examination of CITU's cyberstalking caseload found no instances where offenders used anonymous Webbrowsing services to stalk their victims.

The widespread availability of anonymizing tools can increase the amount of cyberstalking and Internet deviance in general. Theoretically, deviance will result from the use of anonymizing tools because people will feel less restrained when not faced with the fear of detection by their victim or the police. The absence of a legally binding international body to regulate the Internet leaves little hope that the deployment of anonymizing tools will be stopped. Even if a country did succeed in banning the distribution of anonymizing tools, the global reach of the Internet would enable people to seek out such tools in countries that allow their use. Consequently, citizens must learn to survive on an Internet where people can act without accountability. In the absence of a regulatory solution to safeguard Internet users against those who employ anonymizing tools to harass, Internet service providers and related software companies should seek a technological solution aimed at blocking unwanted anonymous communication.

CONCLUSION

Because the Internet allows human interaction without physical barriers and with the perception of anonymity, it has become the ideal instrument for individuals who wish to intimidate, threaten, or harass. Federal and state legislation have emerged to criminalize such behavior. Legislatures aiming to criminalize cyberstalking should take an evolutionary approach toward defining the means of communication covered by the law to ensure protection against harassing communications sent using newly developed technologies.

An examination of all computer crimes investigated by the New York City Police Department from January 1996 through August 2000 found cyberstalking to be the most prevalent computer crime investigated by the department. Thus, police personnel administrating computer crime units should prioritize staffing and training initiatives that properly equip their units to deal with the cyberstalking problem. Additionally, because cyberstalkers use e-mail as the communication method of choice, computer crime unit administrators should prioritize technical training that provides investigators with the knowledge needed to perform e-mail-related forensics.

Out-of-date and missing account, subscriber, and user information, as well as anonymizing tools, presented problems for law enforcement during cyberstalking investigations. Working relationships between computer crime units in all agencies can minimize the negative effects that jurisdictional issues have on the investigation and prosecutorial processes. These relationships can help facilitate the execution of out-of-state subpoenas and search warrants and provide law enforcement with an open door to out-of-state Internet service providers.

Out-of-date and missing account, subscriber, and user information also have prevented law enforcement from establishing an electronic link between the suspect and the victim. To offset this negative effect, legislative action should establish data collection standards for Internet service providers that meet the needs of computer crime investigators.

Finally, the infrequent use of anonymous remailers by cyberstalkers should not pull attention from the negative effect that these tools can have on the law enforcement process. The increased availability and continued development of anonymizing Internet tools that are easier to use than previous versions likely will increase the use of these options by criminals. When used, anonymous remailers successfully prevented law enforcement from tracing e-mail messages back to the offender. A technological solution aimed at blocking anonymous communication will offset the threat to users posed by anonymous remailers.

Distribution of Cybercrimes Investigated by the New
York City Police
Department January 1996 through August 2000

Crime	#	%
Aggravated harassment	201	42.8
Grand larceny	102	21.7
Hacking (e.g., computer trespass)	46	9.8
Forgery	23	4.9
Petit larceny	22	4.7
Criminal impersonation	20	4.3
Child pornography	19	4.0
Crimes against children	14	3.0
Scheme to defraud	10	2.1
Other crimes	13	2.8
Total	470	100

RESOURCES

U.S. Department of Justice Cybercrime Web Site:
http://www.cybercrime.gov

High Technology Crime Investigation Association:
http.//www.htcia.org/

SEARCH—The National Consortium for Justice Information &
Statistics: http://www.search.orgi

National Center for Missing & Exploited Children:
http://www.ncmec.org!

International Association of Computer Investigative Specialists:
http://www.cops.orgi

Compuforensics: http://www.compuforensics.com!

National Law Enforcement & Corrections Technology Center:
http://www.nlectc.org!

National White-Collar Crime Center:
http://www.iir.com/nwccc/nwccc.htm

RELATED ARTICLE: Cyberstalking Methods

Cyberstalkers have employed various methods of Internet communication to harass their victims. Although not exhaustive, the following list describes some of the methods that cyberstalkers may use:

* E-mail: A method of communication that allows an individual to transfer text, picture, video, and audio files to another person's electronic mailbox. In using e-mail to harass, the cyberstalker creates a text-based, graphic-based, or audio-based message of a threatening, alarming, or otherwise harassing nature and sends it to the e-mail account of the intended victim.

* Newsgroups: A method of communication that amounts to an ongoing discussion about a particular topic. Internet users contribute to the ongoing discussion by posting their opinions, comments, or related experiences about a particular subject. These postings are linked together and can be retrieved by querying a database of newsgroup topics. Cyberstalkers can use these forums to post threatening or defamatory statements directed at a specific individual or group of individuals. In New York v. Munn (688 N.Y. S.2d 384; i999), the court found the defendant guilty of aggravated harassment for posting a message to an Internet newsgroup that instructed people to kill police officers from the NYPD.

* Message boards/guest books: A method of communication similar to a newsgroup in that its contents amount to comments about a particular topic. Internet sites often have guest books where visitors can enter their names and make comments about the site. The visitor's name and comments are subsequently available to be viewed by others visiting the Web site. A person who wants to threaten or harass the owner of a Web page easily can leave alarming messages in a guest book.

* Internet sites: A method of communication that involves posting information to a unique uniform resource locator (URL). Internet users later can retrieve this information by directing their Web browser to the corresponding URL. An Internet site becomes the method of harassment when a cyberstalker posts information on a Web page about an individual that causes them to become alarmed or frightened. For example, a cyberstalker could create an Internet site that advertises sexual services for hire and includes the victim's picture, phone number, and address. Subsequently, the victim is bombarded with telephone calls or personal visits from individuals inquiring about the advertised sexual services.

* Chat rooms: A method of communication that enables real-time text, audio, and video-based group interaction. Chat rooms, or chat channels, usually are organized around specific topics of conversation. Topics include, but are not limited to, such issues as politics, religion, relationships, and sex. When communicating in a chat room, a participant's messages are broadcast to everyone signed into the particular chat room. Several types of chat services have emerged since the development of the Internet. Chat services can be public or private. Public chat services are open to everyone with access to the Internet. For example, Internet relay chat (IRC) and I seek you (ICQ) chat are open to all Internet users. Both IRC and ICQ chat rooms have hundreds of chat channels that cover a diverse range of subjects and enable the transfer of files between active participants. Unlike public chat services, private services limit access to their chat channels and are hosted by specific on-line service providers. Chat rooms provide cyberstalkers with different options to harass their victims. A stalker can send alarming messages directly to the victim while conversing in a chat room. The message is delivered to the intended victim, as well as to all those users who currently are logged into the chat room. In addition, the cyberstalker can pose as the victim in a chat room and provide personal information to participants, thereby resulting in the intended victim being directly contacted in person, by e-mail, or by phone.

* Third-party instant messengers: A method of communication that enables real-time text, audio, and video-based interaction between two individuals over the Internet or a computer network. Users program their instant messenger software to notify them when designated individuals log on to the network. With instant messaging software, users have the ability to engage in real-time dialogue with a designated person as long as both parties are connected to the network. Stalkers with prior knowledge of a victim's screen name can use an instant messenger to send harassing messages in real time when both parties are logged onto the Internet.

* Commercial service user profiles: A method of communication that involves posting descriptive information about oneself to the membership directory of a commercial Internet service. Service subscribers can query this directory so that they may find other members who share similar hobbies, interests, or backgrounds. People who want to harass others may establish a false user profile that will direct unwanted communication toward their victim in the form of repeated telephone calls, e-mails, or in-person contact.

Footnotes deleted.

5

Computer Hackers, Crackers and Fraudsters

13

Inhibitors of Two Illegal Behaviors

Hacking and Shoplifting

Lixuan Zhang; Randall Young; Victor Prybutok

ABSTRACT

The means by which the United States justice system attempts to control illegal hacking are practiced under the assumption that illegal hacking is like any other illegal crime. This article evaluates this assumption by comparing illegal hacking to shoplifting. Three inhibitors of two illegal behaviors are examined: informal sanction, punishment severity, and punishment certainty. A survey of 136 undergraduate students attending a university and 54 illegal hackers attending the Defcon conference in 2003 was conducted. The results show that both groups perceive a higher level of punishment severity but a lower level of informal sanction for hacking than for shoplifting. The findings show that hackers perceive a lower level of punishment certainty for hacking than for shoplifting but that students perceive a higher level of punishment certainty for hacking than for shoplifting. The results add to the stream of information security research and provide significant implications for law makers and educators aiming to combat hacking.

L. Zhang, R. Young, and V. Prybutak, Inhibitors of two illegal behaviors: Hacking and shoplifting. *Journal of Organizational and End User Computing*, 19(3): 24-33, July-Sept 2007. Reprinted by permission of IGI Global.

INTRODUCTION

Interest in hacking has increased in popularity due to high-profile media coverage of system breaches. In April 2005, hackers gained access to personal records of 310,000 individuals from the LexisNexis database (Gagnier, 2005). In June 2005, the information belonging to 40 million credit card holders was hacked through a credit card processor (Bradner, 2005).

Companies are reluctant to publicize that they have experienced information security breaches because of the negative impact such incidents have on their public image leading to loss of market value. Cavusoglu, Mishra and Raghunathan (2004) estimate the loss in market value for organizations to be 2.1% within two days of reporting an Internet security breach which represents an average loss of 1.65 billion. In addition to the damages to public image and market value loss, security breaches also impact the value of an organization because of the actual cost required to address the issues.

The rise of computer and Internet use has coincided with an increase in ability of users to commit computer abuses (Loch et al., 1992; Straub & Nance, 1990) along with an increase in the number of unethical, yet attractive situations faced by computer users (Gattiker & Kelley, 1999). In a study where students were asked if they had engaged in any form of illegal computer use such as software piracy and hacking, almost half of the students admitted using the computer in an illegal manner (Forcht, 1991). Recently, Freestone and Mitchell (2004) examined the Internet ethics of Generation Y. They found that hacking is considered less wrong than other illegal Internet activities such as "selling counterfeit goods over the Internet." It is recognized that illegal hacking activities encompass a wide array of violations of varying degrees of seriousness. For this study, the interest is not in any specific type of illegal hacking but rather illegal hacking activities in general.

Hacking is one of the technologically-enabled crimes (Gordon, 2000). Originally the term hacker was a complimentary term that referred to the innovative programmers at MIT who wanted to explore mainframe computing and were motivated by intellectual curiosity and challenges (Chandler, 1996). However, the term became derogatory as computer intruders pursued purposefully destructive actions that caused serious damage for both corporations and individuals. American Heritage Dictionary (2000) defines a hacker as "one who uses programming skills to gain illegal access to a computer network or file".

Hacking is a relatively new crime and, as such, is potentially perceived differently from other crimes. Most recently, there has been demand for research that will aid in developing an understanding of how computer crimes differ from more traditional crimes (Rogers, 2001). Due to cost-effectiveness concerns, the chief avenue utilized by the United States government to deter illegal behavior is to increase the severity of punishment (Kahan, 1997). This approach is also used to deter illegal hacking behavior. However, this approach to control illegal hacking is practiced with the assumption that the factors affecting illegal hacking are similar to the factors that influence other types of crime. This assumption is set out to be evaluated by comparing illegal hacking activities to shoplifting. The decision to use shoplifting for comparison to illegal hacking was motivated by three reasons:

First, the act of shoplifting is in some ways similar to hacking in that both are acts of illegally obtaining something (i.e. illegal hacking is an act of acquiring access and/or information). Hackers, especially those that are motivated by greed and profit, commit a crime that is analogous to trespassing and taking others' property with the intention of keeping it or selling it. Both of these crimes increase an organization's security costs and overburden the courts. Secondly, the social stigma associated with shoplifting is not as extreme as for crimes like auto theft, burglary of a residence, and money laundering. And as such it is believed that there is a higher probability that the target population has heard discussion of shoplifting or knows someone that has engaged in the activity. Thirdly, many people who commit these two crimes are juveniles. According to the statistics of the National Association for Shoplifting Prevention, 25% of the shoplifters are young juveniles and 55% of shoplifters started shoplifting in their teens. Research on hackers also shows that most hackers are between 12 and 28 years old (Rogers, 2001). Therefore, it is relevant to examine the differences in perception between these two crimes.

College students have been identified as a high risk population for supporting hacking activities due to their computer literacy and the general openness of university systems (Hoffer & Straub, 1989). For example, two students at Oxford University hacked into the school computer system to access students' e-mail passwords and other personal information (McCue, 2004). In 2002 and 2003, a former student at the University of Texas named

Christopher Andrew Phillips stole more than 37,000 social security numbers that resulted in more than $100,000 worth of damage (Kreytak, 2005).

This accentuates the importance of the computer user in the computer and information security domain. However, several researchers have pointed out the lack of research on antecedents of illegal behavior in the information security domain (James, 1996; Stanton et al., 2003). Therefore, this study attempts to examine some of the factors affecting the act of illegal hacking by answering the following question: How do hackers and students perceive the inhibitors of hacking compared to shoplifting?

The chapter is organized as follows: First, the theoretical foundation is discussed and the relevant alternative hypotheses are presented. Next, the research instrument and data collection activities are outlined and results are analyzed and reported. Finally, the key findings are summarized, the implications are highlighted, the study's limitations are discussed, and future research directions are proposed.

THEORETICAL FOUNDATIONS

General deterrence theory is often used to examine crimes, including computer crimes (Straub & Welke, 1998; Peace et al., 2003). The principal components of the theory are certainty of punishment, severity of punishment, and a set of average socioeconomic forces. Among these three components, the first two—certainty and severity of punishment—are the core components of the deterrence theory (Becker, 1968). The theory assumes that criminals are rational individuals. They will not commit crimes if the expected cost is greater than the expected gain. Therefore, any increase in severity of punishment or certainty of punishment will increase the expected cost of committing a certain crime. Since punishment may deprive the criminals of their freedom and social status, individuals may not want to take the chance of being caught breaking the law. The theory posits that severity and certainty of punishment are factors that can serve the purpose of reducing and preventing crimes.

Besides the two components of the general deterrence theory, researchers find informal sanctions to be a significant factor influencing criminal decision-making. In fact, it is claimed that adding the informal sanction construct to the theory is perhaps the most important contribution to deterrence theory (Jacob et al., 2000). Some researchers even suggest that informal sanctions may be even more salient than formal sanctions (Kahan, 1997; Katyal, 1997;

Paternoster & Iovanni, 1986). Informal sanction is defined as social actions of others in response to crime. Some examples of informal sanctions are loss of respect from family and friends (Liu, 2003), social stigma (Grasmick & Scott, 1982), and shame and embarrassment (Blackwell, 2000).

Building on the previous theories, the study examines the three inhibitors of crime: informal sanction, punishment severity, and punishment certainty. It is assumed that any potential offender will consider the three inhibitors before he/she commits deviant behavior. Few studies have examined the perception of these three inhibitors in regards to hacking. In addition, few studies have compared the perception of these three inhibitors between two or more crimes. This study intends to fill the gap by examining these inhibitors with respect to hacking and then compare them to inhibitors associated with shoplifting.

HYPOTHESES DEVELOPMENT

Informal Sanction

Informal sanctions are the actual or perceived responses of others to deviant acts (Liu, 2003). These sanctions can serve to reinforce or weaken people's deviant behavior. Sanctions from close friends or family members are more potent than those from distant relationships (Kitts & Macy, 1999). Informal sanctions are not sufficient to deter crimes, but it puts social pressures on the individuals who intend to engage in deviant acts.

Social views suggest that hacking behavior is less frowned upon than other crimes (Coldwell, 1995). In fact, hackers are viewed by some as talented individuals, and there are incidences of gifted hackers being treated like celebrities. For example, Mark Abene received a one year prison term for his hacking activities, but after his release, a large party was thrown for him at an elite Manhattan club. Also, he was voted one of the top one hundred smartest people in New York by New York magazine. In addition, famous hackers are invited to conferences, and granted interviews along with writers, scientists and film stars (Skorodumova, 2004). Researchers also find that there is a strong sense of peer group support in hacker chat rooms and there is no fear of social disapproval (Freestone & Mitchell, 2004). However, when asked about the perception of shoplifting, both shoplifters and non-shoplifters were negative towards shoplifting believing that it is a somewhat serious offense and is not acceptable behavior (El-Dirghami, 1974). Therefore the following hypotheses is proposed:

* H1a: Hackers perceive less informal sanction for hacking than for shoplifting.

* H1b: Students perceive less informal sanction for hacking than for shoplifting.

Punishment Severity

Severity of punishment refers to the magnitude of the penalty if convicted. It is a core component of deterrence theory (Becker, 1968). Based on the assumption that people engage in criminal and deviant activities if they are not afraid of punishment, deterrence theory focuses on implementing laws and enforcement to make sure that these activities will receive punishment. Deterrence theory proposes that an individual makes the decision to exhibit or not exhibit deviant behavior based on an internal perception of the benefits and costs of the respective behavior. The idea that the cost of committing a crime must exceed the benefit to reduce crime is a staple in the United States (U. S.) criminal justice system (Kahan, 1997).

The U.S. government regards computer crimes as both traditional crimes using new methods and new crimes requiring new legal framework. The Computer Fraud and Abuse Act (CFAA) is the main statutory framework for many computer crimes (Sinrod & Reilly, 2000). According to CFAA, punishment depends upon the seriousness of the criminal activity and the extent of damage. Researchers have argued that the CFAA has been overly punitive (Skilbell, 2003). For example, Kevin Mitnick broke into the computer system of Sun Microsystems and downloaded the Solaris operating system code for which Sun had paid $80 million. He pleaded guilty and received a harsh punishment because he was charged with causing damage equal to the cost of the operating system. However, Mitnick had no intention of selling the code for profit. Kevin Mitnick received a prison sentence of 68 months followed by three years probation. Later Sun Microsystems made the code publicly available for just $100.

In the United States, shoplifting is classified as a misdemeanor crime committed against a retail establishment. Punishment for shoplifting varies from state to state. In Georgia, the law calls for misdemeanor punishment for shoplifting goods worth $300 or less. Shoplifting goods worth more than $300 is a felony which can result in punishment of up to 10 years in jail. In California, the punishment for shoplifting is more severe. A person entering the store with the intent to shoplift constitutes burglary regardless of the value of the goods that are shoplifted. Any accused shoplifter who has a prior theft conviction will be charged with a felony.

Nevertheless, in most states, shoplifting is not prosecuted heavily. For example, in Texas, the amount in controversy determines the severity of the offense and, therefore, the range of punishment. However, if a person intends to obtain a benefit by breaching computer security, he or she would commit a felony. In addition, researchers find that a large proportion of apprehended shoplifters are never formally changed. Shoplifters with no prior arrests or only one prior arrest are more likely to be dismissed (Adams & Cutshall, 1987). Therefore, the following hypotheses are proposed:

* H2a: Hackers perceive a higher level of punishment severity for hacking than for shoplifting.

* H2b: Students perceive a higher level of punishment severity for hacking than for shoplifting.

Punishment Certainty

Certainty of punishment measures the probability of an individual receiving a legally-imposed penalty. Severity of punishment has little or no effect when the likelihood of punishment is low (Von Hirsch et al., 1999). However, when individuals perceive that there is a greater likelihood that they will get caught in committing a crime, they are less likely to engage in the associated crime.

Because hacking is committed anonymously and from any place in the world, it is not easy to catch an offender. Besides, many hacking cases are not even revealed to the public or reported to the police. Corporations and government agencies being attacked by computer hackers are reluctant to report the breaches. An FBI survey finds that 90% of corporations and agencies detected computer security breaches in 2001 but only 34% reported those attacks to authorities (Anonymous, 2002). The reason for this may be the fear of losing consumers' confidence.

194

Shoplifters also have a low likelihood of getting punished. Researchers find that salesclerks and store security are not effective in deterring shoplifting (El-Dirghami, 1974). According to the statistics from National Association for Shoplifting Prevention, shoplifters are caught an average of only once in every 48 times they steal and they are turned over to police only 50% of the time when they are caught. Therefore, it is unlikely for a shoplifter to get caught and then reported to police. In a study using observation data, researchers estimated that around 2, 214, 000 incidents of shoplifting occurred in a single pharmacy in Atlanta in 2001. However, only 25, 721 of the shoplifting cases were officially reported to the police. (Dabney et al., 2004).

Although some hackers have limited computer hacking ability (script kiddies), the majority of hackers either have a sound level or a high level of computer knowledge (Chantler, 1996). The popular press has described the attitudes of the hackers attending the Defcon conference as: "There is a core of arrogance, of genuine belief that hackers are somehow above not only laws, but people around them, by sheer virtue of intellect" (Ellis & Walsh, 2004). Because they possess unique hacking skills and techniques, hackers may feel safer in conducting hacking than shoplifting. Therefore, the following hypothesis is proposed:

* H3a: Hackers perceive a lower level of punishment certainty for hacking than for shoplifting.

Prior work supports the contention that students do not believe that store security is an effective deterrent to shoplifting because of the low probability of punishment (El-Dirghami, 1974). However, there is a paucity of studies that examine how students perceive the likelihood of punishment for hacking. Some researchers indicated that students perceived a low level of punishment certainty for other computer crimes, such as software piracy (Peace et al., 2003; Higgins et al., 2005). Since hacking can be conducted anywhere behind a computer screen, the hypothesis is proposed:

* H3b: Students perceive a lower level of punishment certainty for hacking than for shoplifting.

METHOD

Instrument development

Most measures were developed by the authors through literature review. Grasmick and Bryjak (1980) discussed at length the various means of measuring punishment severity and certainty of punishment along with strengths and weaknesses. In accordance with their suggestions, survey items were chosen that ask for the respondent's estimate of punishment severity in general terms and asking about specific penalties (i.e. prison time, fines, etc.) were avoided. Specific penalties such as fines may be viewed as severe to a financially-insecure individual but viewed as inconsequential to a wealthy individual. The items measuring informal sanction are adapted from the measures in Liu's (2003) manuscript which includes disapproval from families and friends. The items were measured using a five point Likert scale with anchors ranging from five which represents "Strongly agree" to one which represents "Strongly disagree". Appendix 1 shows the items in the survey. The hackers and students first answered the questions about shoplifting and then about hacking.

Content Validity

Content validity is based on the extent to which a measurement reflects the specific intended domain of content (Carmine & Zeller, 1979). The constructs that were used are relatively newer constructs although references supported their development. To ensure that what is measured is what was intended to be measured, a literature review was conducted to identify, select, and phrase the items to measure these constructs. This activity was followed with a panel of subject-matter-experts that were asked to indicate whether or not an item in a set of measurement items is "essential" to the operationalization of a theoretical construct.

Specifically, two scholars who are familiar with research in criminology were interviewed and asked for input on the constructs, their measurement domains, and the appropriateness of the measures selected from the prior studies. As a result of this input, some items were modified to make them easier to understand.

Sample

Data was collected from 136 undergraduate students attending a
university located in the southern United States. All students were
enrolled in a lower level MIS course. The majority of the respondents
have a high degree of computer literacy. Correspondingly, it was
presumed that they are reasonably likely to understand hacking and
their responses confirmed this presumption. Table 1 shows the
profiles of the student sample.

Data was also collected through handout surveys distributed
to participants of the 2003 DefCon hacker convention in Las Vegas,
the largest annual computer hacker convention. The majority of the
attendees are hackers or people who have an interest in hacking
activities. Participation in the study was strictly voluntary. The
handout survey was considered, by the researchers, an ideal approach
to the study because of the adequacy of the respondents and the
higher response rates and satisfaction scores associated with handout
surveys compared to mail surveys (Gribble & Haupt, 2005).
Additionally, all responses were anonymous and for purposes of this
study all data are reported in aggregate. A total of 155 surveys were
collected during the three day conference. Twenty-eight surveys are
deemed unusable as the respondents either answered every question
the same or failed to answer the majority of the questions. Therefore,
the usable responses from Defcon were 127.

Table 1. Profile of the students

Gender
Male	66
Female	60
Missing	10

Marriage status
Single	90
Married	34
Divorced	1
Widowed	1
Missing	10

Current university classification
Freshman	1
Sophomore	2
Junior	57
Senior	65
Missing	11
Number of students who shoplifted last year	8
Number of students who hacked illegally last year	1

Table 2. Profile of the illegal hackers

Gender
Male   54
Female   0

Marriage status
Single   54
Married   0
Divorced   0
Widowed   0
Number of hackers who shoplifted last year   16

Table 3. Factor loadings of hackers' and students' perception on shoplifting and hacking

	HKinformal	SLcertainty	
SLinformal			
HKinformal2	0.855	-0.004	0.278
HKinformal1	0.823	0.106	0.320
SLcertainty2	0.077	0.883	0.149
SLcertainty3	-0.049	0.799	-0.218
SLinformal1	0.370	0.048	0.891
SLinformal2	0.340	-0.052	0.849
HKseverity1	0.047	0.100	0.181
HKseverity2	0.517	0.239	0.110
HKseverity3	0.506	0.355	0.172
SLseverity3	0.185	0.091	0.133
SLseverity2	0.286	0.173	0.198
SLseverity1	-0.106	0.104	0.271
HKcertainty3	0.027	0.323	0.024
HKcertainty2	0.216	0.305	0.203
Variance explained	31.51%	15.65%	12.04%
Cronbach's alpha	0.870	0.600	0.700

198

	HKseverity	SLseverity	
HKcertainty			
HKinformal2	0.285	0.264	-0.121
HKinformal1	0.175	0.286	-0.300
SLcertainty2	0.121	0.179	-0.401
SLcertainty3	0.222	-0.029	-0.323
SLinformal1	0.139	0.174	-0.264
SLinformal2	0.203	0.132	0.028
HKseverity1	0.879	0.054	-0.145
HKseverity2	0.798	0.333	0.001
HKseverity3	0.750	0.381	-0.081
SLseverity3	0.171	0.926	-0.135
SLseverity2	0.200	0.909	-0.090
SLseverity1	0.301	0.632	-0.507
HKcertainty3	0.071	0.102	-0.879
HKcertainty2	0.108	0.172	-0.757
Variance explained	10.15%	6.36%	5.29%
Cronbach's alpha	0.748	0.827	0.686

Note:

HKinformal: informal sanction for hacking
HKseverity: punishment severity for hacking
HKcertainty: punishment certainty for hacking
SLinformal: informal sanction for shoplifting
SLseverity: punishment severity for shoplifting
SLcertainty: punishment certainty for shoplifting

See Appendix for survey items

Since not all attendees of the Defcon conference are hackers, to ensure that only people that have committed illegal hacking acts were examined, the respondents were asked if they had participated in a hacking activity that would be considered outside the bounds of that allowed by the court system within the past year. The answer for the question is worded in a yes or no format. Fifty-four respondents answered yes for the question. Although it is a conservative estimate since it was only inquired about illegal hacking activity within the past year, it can be assured that the 54 respondents are truly active illegal hackers. Therefore, data from the 54 hackers were used for the following analysis. Table 2 shows the profile of the 54 hackers. All hackers are single males.

DATA ANALYSIS AND RESULTS

Principal components factor analysis with an oblique rotation was used to assess construct validity for items measuring perceptions of inhibitors of shoplifting and of hacking. SPSS was used to perform factor analysis on the instrument based on data from 54 hackers and from Defcon and 136 students. Factor analysis shows six factors. Factor loadings above 0.5 on one construct and no cross-loadings over 0.4 provide evidence of convergent and discriminant validity (Campbell & Fiske, 1959). Table 3 provides the factor loadings for shoplifting and for hacking. Internal reliability was assessed by using Cronbach's alpha. As shown in Table 3, it varied from 0.600 to 0.870. According to Hair et al. (1998), 0.60 is satisfactory for exploratory studies. Other IS researchers have similar reliability estimates in their exploratory studies (Ma et al., 2005). Table 4 shows the means of these constructs for hackers and students.

Repeated measures analysis of variance was used to test hypotheses H1a, H2a, and H3a using hacker data and the same statistical technique was used to test H1b, H2b and H3b using student data. Repeated analysis is appropriate when measurements are taken on the same unit of analysis. In that case, each individual answered questions about their perception of the consequences of shoplifting, and then again answered those about perception related to those of hacking. Therefore, multiple measurements are used on the same unit of analysis.

Hypothesis 1a proposed that hackers perceive less informal sanction from hacking than from shoplifting. Repeated measures ANOVA supported this proposition (within subject $F = 142.03$, $p<0.01$), showing that there is a significant difference regarding hackers' perception of informal sanctions associated with hacking and shoplifting. Since Table 4 shows that informal sanction for shoplifting is higher than that of hacking, H1a is supported.

Hypothesis 1b posited that students perceive less informal sanctions associated with being caught hacking than from shoplifting. Tests supported this proposition, showing that students did have a significantly different perception of informal sanctions regarding hacking and shoplifting (within subjects $F=19.489$, $p<0.01$). Table 4 shows that the informal sanction for shoplifting is higher than hacking. Therefore, the data supports H1b.

Hypothesis 2a stated that hackers perceive a higher level of punishment severity from hacking than from shoplifting. Table 4 shows that hackers perceive a higher level of punishment severity from hacking than from shoplifting. The repeated measures ANOVA test shows that the difference is significant (Within subject $F=78.51$, $p<0.01$) and confirms this hypothesis.

Hypothesis 2b proposed that students perceive a higher level of punishment severity for hacking than for shoplifting. Table 4 shows that the students indeed perceive a higher level of punishment severity for hacking when compared to shoplifting. The repeated measures ANOVA test shows that the difference is significant (Within subjects $F=23.446$, $p<0.01$). Therefore, the data supports H2b.

Hypothesis 3a proposed that hackers perceive punishment certainty from hacking will be lower than shoplifting. Table 4 shows that their estimated possibility of getting caught from hacking is indeed lower than shoplifting. The repeated measures ANOVA test shows that the difference is significant (within subject $F=190.06$, $p<0.01$) and confirms this hypothesis.

Hypothesis 3b stated that students perceive a lower punishment certainty for hacking than for shoplifting. From Table 4, it can be seen that students perceive a higher possibility of punishment for hacking than for shoplifting. The repeated measures ANOVA test shows that the difference is significant (Within subjects $F=18.95$, $p<0.01$). Therefore, hypothesis H3b is rejected. The results of the hypothesis testing are shown in Table 5.

DISCUSSION AND IMPLICATION

In summary, this study intends to address one important question: whether or not students and hackers have different perceptions of inhibitors against hacking compared to inhibitors against shoplifting. The results of the study show that both hackers and students have a lower informal sanction for hacking than for shoplifting. In other words, they believe that a greater social pressure is associated with shoplifting than hacking. Among the student group, although the respondents regard hacking as fairly unacceptable, it is still more acceptable than shoplifting.

Ultimately the success of an organization's information security program is dependent on the behavior of the users (Stanton et al., 2003). As this population (student and hacker) accepts corporate and government job responsibilities, it is imperative for the host organization to recognize the lack of social pressure working to discourage hacking activities. Research within the information systems domain, oftentimes, assumes that a single culture (organizational culture) impacts individual behavior effectively ignoring ethical and social factors (Straub et al., 2002). Research must evaluate the impact of these other factors on the organization's information security risk.

Many researchers in the criminology discipline suggest that the key deterrent effect lies in the threat to expose individuals to social disapproval (Kahan, 1997; Katyal, 1997). The academic community must do more to change the perception that illegal hacking is more socially acceptable than other crimes like shoplifting. Hacking is not only illegal but the penalties are far more severe. One conviction can have a severe impact on an individual's future career goals. There are indications that issues of ethics, trust, integrity, and responsibility will become more crucial to organizations striving to protect themselves from information security risks (Dhillon & Backhouse, 2000) and students with a circumspect past that include illegal hacking will likely face a difficult prospect when it comes to landing a job. The academic community, largely, has failed to address ethical issues associated with computer and information use (Couger et al., 1995). The academic community should be proactive toward shaping an ethical student population that will one day accept corporate and government job responsibilities. As the ethical standards increase, social pressure to conform may increase as well.

Both hackers and students perceive that hacking receives more severe punishment than shoplifting. Because of the fear and unknown doubt of high-tech crimes such as hacking, the U.S. government has aggressively prosecuted criminal hackers. According to the National Association of Criminal Defense Lawyers, computer crimes are punished more harshly compared to other crimes. These findings suggest that the U.S. government has been successful in communicating the serious negative consequence of hacking to the public.

The findings show that hackers and students have different perceptions about punishment certainty. Hackers perceive a lower punishment certainty for hacking, while students perceive a lower punishment certainty for shoplifting. One possible explanation for these differing perceptions is the students may have little understanding about how hacking activities are committed and how little monitoring is done on the Internet. Students are possibly biased due to media publications of potential government monitoring of network activities (i.e. Carnivore) while hackers understand the difficulty of monitoring the extreme volume of network activities that exist on the Internet or even a corporate LAN. Another possible reason is that hackers may be very confident of their hacking skills while students have much less computer skills.

The lower probability of punishment may work to diminish the effect of severe punishment. Researchers have found that the punishment certainty has far greater deterrent effect on crimes than punishment severity (Von Hirsch et al., 1999). A criminal is more likely to engage in criminal activity despite the threat of severe punishment when he or she believes that there is only a small or no chance of being caught. This suggests that security enforcers should make investments that will improve their ability to detect illegal hacking activities and assist in criminal prosecution. For example, the government may need to allocate more of the computer security budget to hiring competent security and law enforcement personnel, as well as to increase employee training in computer security monitoring and investigation.

LIMITATION AND FUTURE DIRECTION

One limitation of the study is the restriction imposed by the sample. While students enrolled in a lower-level MIS course represent those intending to major in any of the business disciplines, care must be taken in generalizing to students in other majors and young adults not attending college. Future research needs to investigate the generalizability of these measures to other majors, as well as non-students in a similar age group. Of particular interest is to examine the perception of students majoring in computer science. These students have a comparatively higher level of computer knowledge than other students and may be more likely to be hackers than other students. Another limitation of the research is that more valid measures need to be developed. Since this is an exploratory study, most of the items were developed by the authors.

Researchers have called for the need for more end-user oriented research examining IT security issues (Troutt, 2002). The present study offers important insights about hackers' and students' awareness of ethics and moral issues associated with computer technology in comparison with the traditional crime of shoplifting. This study advances the knowledge of hackers' and students' moral judgment of inhibitors relevant to hacking and shoplifting. These preliminary results suggest that law enforcement officials and educators should consider means that will strengthen informal sanctions associated with illegal hacking.

APPENDIX A.

Shoplifting

Informal Sanction

** SLinformal1: My friends would think less of me if I were caught shoplifting.

** SLinformal2: My family would think less of me if I were caught shoplifting.

Punishment Severity

** SLseverity1: The punishment for shoplifting is severe.

** SLseverity2: If you were caught shoplifting, your life would be severely disrupted.

** SLseverity3: If you were caught shoplifting, it would have a detrimental effect on your life.

Punishment Certainty

** SLcertainty1: People who shoplift are caught eventually.

** SLcertainty2: If you were to shoplifting, the chances of you being caught are small. *

** SLcertainty3: The chance that an average person being caught shoplifting is small. *

Hacking

Informal Sanction

** HKinformal1: My friends would think less of me if I were caught hacking illegally.

** HKinformal2: My family would think less of me if I were hacking illegally.

Punishment Severity

** HKseverity1: The punishment for being caught illegally hacking is severe.

** HKseverity2: If you were caught hacking illegally, your life would be severely disrupted.

** HKseverity3: If you were caught hacking illegally, it would have a detrimental effect on your future.

Punishment Certainty

** HKeertainty1: People who hack illegally would be caught eventually.

** HKcertainty2: If you were to hack illegally, the chances you would be caught are small. *

** HKcertainty3: If other people were to hack illegally, the chances they would be caught are small. *

* Items are reverse coded.

References deleted.

14

Preventing Computer Fraud

Greg Hanna

Enemies from without and within are constantly looking for ways to break into vulnerable computer systems. All it takes is one successful attack to bring down an entire system.

Computer fraud is a booming business. Only a small percentage of computer criminals are ever apprehended, and even when they are caught, the courts tend to treat them leniently. Maybe that's why there are so many hackers and crackers out there trying to break into or bring down computer systems. They don't fear being called to account.

Corporate America has shown a surprising reluctance to bring these criminals to justice. The 2004 Computer Crime and Security Survey by the Computer Security Institute and Federal Bureau of Investigation found that the percentage of organizations reporting computer intrusions to law enforcement is actually declining, with fewer than half reporting such intrusions. The key reason cited for not reporting intrusions is fear of negative publicity. Many of the computer crimes that are reported expose embarrassing breaches in computer security.

G. Hanna, Preventing computer fraud. *Strategic Finance*, March 2005, p. 30-35.
Reprinted by permission.

How big is the problem? Studies show that small companies are subject to several attacks every day and that giant corporations are under attack virtually every minute of the day. The vast majority of these are virus attacks, most of which are repelled.

Yet despite their numbers and persistence, these outside hackers and crackers are just a small part of the story. The greater danger comes from within. A widely quoted figure claims that 75% of computer crimes are committed by insiders.

Often it's difficult to spot the culprits. In one company, an assistant to the CFO lent her password to a colleague. That colleague subsequently used the assistant's computer to access the system and make unauthorized payments to two dummy corporations. Suspicion fell upon the CFO's assistant.

Fortunately for her, a thorough investigation uncovered the conspiracy and exposed the real thief. In this case, the company reported the crime to law enforcement, and the thief was tried and convicted of fraud.

The real failure lay with the company for not keeping a tighter grip on its password security. All too often, human failure, like giving your password to another person, creates the opportunity for fraud. Training can greatly reduce failings like this, but all it takes is one mistake to leave the system open to attack. In addition to training, then, companies need to build strong defenses around their systems. It's a lot cheaper to keep intruders out than to clean up after them.

GUARDING THE PERIMETER

Let's take a look at the first line of defenses. Firewalls. An effective security system protects a company's computer operations with a series of defenses, like the walls and breastworks around a fort. The intruder who slips past the first line of defenses runs into another and then another and another. Usually, they get frustrated and quit.

The initial perimeter defenses are the firewalls. A firewall is like a steel-reinforced concrete fence with a few well-chosen gates. A small company may have a single firewall. A giant corporation may have firewalls on every floor and around every department.

Some people think of firewalls as the toughest defenses. Actually, they may be among the weakest. Firewalls limit external access to designated gateways but do little to protect the network from people who are already inside—disgruntled employees, would-be thieves, vandals, and the like.

In setting up firewalls, administrators try to build barriers that are strong enough to keep out would-be intruders but not so impermeable as to make it difficult for legitimate users to move information over the system. To meet these conflicting demands, the administrators have to make some compromises. As a result, many firewalls have undetected vulnerabilities that hackers can exploit.

To protect system integrity, some companies use vulnerability-scanning tools that continuously examine the system for oversights and vulnerabilities. These tools can monitor for a wide range of irregularities, including unauthorized software, unauthorized accounts, unprotected logins, weak passwords, and inappropriate access permissions.

Authentication. Getting through the firewall and gaining access to the system typically requires authentication in the form of a login name and a password. Bad and poorly guarded passwords are the bane of most systems. Users typically use four- to six-letter passwords, often words or dates that are easy to remember. With current technology, a hacker can crack a four-letter lower-case password in less than a minute and a six-letter lower-case password in less than an hour. If the password is an everyday word, even a long one or one written backwards, a hacker can easily crack it with an "online dictionary" attack, which can run through an entire English or foreign language dictionary, backwards and forwards, in a matter of minutes.

To deter intruders from guessing passwords, a password should have at least eight characters, including numbers, symbols, and both upper- and lower-case letters. As an added precaution, the password should be changed at frequent intervals, with the system automatically alerting the user when it's time to change.

Unfortunately, many users make it easy for intruders to steal their passwords. Because complex passwords are hard to remember people often jot them down on a slip of paper and tuck it away under their keyboard or even post it to the frame of the computer. Also, users are often tricked out of their password. They get a phone call from "MIS" saying there's a problem with their access to the system. The voice asks, "What password are you using?" And the unsuspecting employee gives away the password and unwittingly opens the system to the hacker.

A more insidious approach is called "spoofing." The spoofer makes the user think that he or she is talking to the system and, in that way, steals the password or other security information. For example, the spoofer may display what looks like the system login prompt on a terminal to make that terminal look idle. When the unsuspecting user logs in, the spoofer gets both the login name and the password. After getting this information, the spoofer prompts the user to try again. The user then logs on again, never suspecting that he or she has been victimized.

A "secure attention key" can prevent this kind of spoofing. When a user hits the key, it kills any process running at the terminal and guarantees a trusted path to the system.

Fighting Viruses. In the course of an ordinary day, a large corporation's perimeter may be attacked by tens of thousands of scans, probes, pings, and viruses. The firewalls will deflect the vast majority of them, and most of those that sneak through will be stopped by anti-virus software. Because new viruses are constantly being unleashed, this anti-virus software must be updated regularly with the latest "signature" files telling the anti-virus software what to look for.

The final line of defense is the computer user, who should be trained to recognize and reject suspicious emails. Unfortunately, employees are all too often tricked into unleashing viruses. They receive an e-mail that seems to come from a colleague, client, or customer and promptly try to open the attachment, usually one with an .exe, .bat, .scr, .zip, or .pif file extension. The virus is then loosed into the system.

Rather than risk leaving it to employees to recognize and delete suspicious e-mail, many companies use antispam systems to capture or kill virus-infected spam before it can reach anyone's PC. That minimizes the human element from the risk equation.

PROTECTING THE CORE

Now let's go a little deeper.

Anti-Spyware. Spyware is tracking software that sneaks into the user's computer, often bundled with legitimate software, and then reports back to the "mother ship" on the user's computer activities. For example, it can monitor every keystroke and, in that way, enable crackers to steal credit card and other financial information. It can also hijack the company's system and use it for other purposes, such as storing and transmitting pornography.

A number of anti-spyware software products (Spy Sweeper, Spyware Eliminator, AntiSpy, SpySubtract) can identify spyware and other hidden programs, such as Trojan Horses, and remove them. A Trojan Horse is defined as a "malicious, security-breaking program that is disguised as something benign." For instance, the user may download what looks like a free game. Then when the user tries to run the "game," the program erases every file in the directory.

Network World recently reported on a piece of spyware that disabled the security controls on a forensic investigator's browser and took control of it. Every time the investigator tried to erase the programs and reboot the machine, the software reinstalled. Eventually he was able to remove it using a remediation kit.

This investigator's distress shows how sophisticated hackers and crackers are becoming. If they get a toehold, they can take over the entire system.

Making Wireless Safe. The popularity of wireless laptops, notebooks, and PDAs has created a whole new threat to corporate computer systems. The problem is that the wireless access ports transmit continuous radio signals. Armed with just a laptop, a wireless adapter, and wireless scanning software, a hacker can park near a company and pick up these radio signals. If the system isn't protected by a secure password, the hacker can break into the wireless unit and from there gain access to the company's computer system.

There are a relatively small number of vendors of wireless network adapters, each with a limited number of default user names. Since very few wireless users bother to change the default name to a secure code, most wireless access points are unprotected, leaving the corporate network vulnerable to attack or misuse. One solution is to have every wireless user change the default name to a secure code. But if just one person fails to take such a step, the system will be wide open. For this reason, many companies have installed Wireless VPN (Virtual Private Network) Access Points.

A Wireless VPN Access Point grants access to the system to wireless users only if they are properly authenticated by a "custom generated" encryption key. Scanners can still detect the presence of a wireless network but can't get into it without a verifiable encryption key for that specific unit and Wireless Access Point.

With VPNs, the password or software authentication code can be the weak link. For this reason, some companies give their employees "authentication tokens." One kind of token looks like a key fob with a string of LCD numbers. To get into the system, the user enters the number on the token. To make this approach almost unbreakable, every employee has a different number, and the individual numbers change every few minutes in synch with the master server at the company's office.

Server Locking. Despite all the precautions, most systems are still vulnerable. That's because systems in both large and small companies require administrator or super-user-level passwords for system maintenance, repair, and upgrades, and these passwords are bound to get out.

To deal with this threat, some companies use server-locking software that, in effect, builds an encasement around the operating system's kernel. The kernel is the essential center of a computer operating system, the core that provides basic services for all other parts of the system. Encasing the kernel doesn't affect everyday users at the outer periphery, but, via the keyboard directly attached to the servers, it does prevent anyone from gaining unauthorized access to the very core of the system.

To get past this encasement requires a password that is held by just one person and is changed regularly. Before an IT engineer can work on the kernel, the password holder has to grant access. Only then can the engineer log in, even as the server administrator.

AN OUNCE OF PREVENTION

Cleaning up after an intrusion can be incredibly expensive, so it's critical to prevent intruders from gaining access or, if they do slip in, to limit their range and the damage they can cause. In terms of preventing fraud, here are several points to keep in mind:

* Create a security policy that clearly spells out what to do in the event of attack and who has the authority to pull the plug on the system.

* Establish specific responses for dealing with different kinds of intrusion threats. The plan should be preapproved by the CEO because it will be too late during an attack to get such approval.

* Establish both internal and external communications guidelines. How and when do you notify vendors and customers that their systems may have been compromised? Do you report the intrusion to the police or FBI?

* Ensure that everyone knows how to contact MIS if they suspect a system has been compromised.

* Set policies regarding access, passwords, and authorization—and enforce them.

* Scan the system regularly for anomalies, weaknesses, unauthorized usage, and other signs of misuse.

If you follow these procedures, you will have an excellent chance of keeping your computer system safe.

HOW MUCH PREVENTION IS ENOUGH?

How much should a company invest in system security? It depends on the amount of risk. Small manufacturers with no valuable trade secrets might make do with inexpensive systems that protect such things as accounts receivable, payroll, purchasing, and supplier payments. But large financial institutions with billions of dollars under their care will need far more sophisticated security systems that, in effect, create layer upon layer of security.

Going overboard on security can waste money and hinder operations. For example, too complex a system can cut into employee productivity.

To find the right balance, a company can create fraud and theft scenarios and then develop a security system that will hold potential losses to an acceptable level rather than trying to eliminate losses altogether. In other words, there's a point at which the cost of additional security will outrun the potential losses.

INTRUSION DETECTION

Building a completely secure system isn't feasible. For this reason, many defense systems include intrusion detection. Detecting breaches in the system provides information for eliminating flaws and tracking down crooks. If a person tries to break through the firewall and into the system, a "trigger" is tripped, and now the system watches this person's activities, logging everything as that person moves through the network, like a fox chasing a rabbit. Because every Internet connection has an IP (Internet Protocol) address linked to it, forensics experts can use the intruder's trail to backtrack to his or her site.

One company allowed its salespeople to have FTP (file transfer protocol) capabilities. FTP is simply a method of transferring files over the Internet. A salesman who was planning to leave the company and join a competitor set up his home computer as an FTP server and then stole the company's entire database by transferring it to his home via FTP. Fortunately, the system kept a detailed log of everything he did, and forensics was quickly on top of him. In this case, the company made the serious mistake of giving employees capabilities, like FTP, that weren't necessary for their work.

15

Computer Fraud

What Can Be Done About It?

Marshall Romney

Computer crimes are costing Corporate America a substantial amount of money. One study found that computer crime results in annual losses amounting to $555,000,000 and that the average loss is $109,000. As evidenced by this statistics, computer fraud has indeed become a growth industry. There are many ways that fraud can be committed. Perpetrators may alter input, steal computer time, steal and alter software, steal or modify data files, and steal or misuse systems output. To discourage employees from committing such crimes, there are a variety of things that an employer can do. One is to make sure that applicants for positions are honest and trustworthy before hiring them. Another is to help disgruntled employees through grievance channels and employee counseling. Training on security can also be helpful in curbing computer crimes. Techniques on how to make a fraud-proof design system are provided.

More and more, we depend on computerized systems to meet our increasing needs for information. As the complexity of these systems and our dependence on them grows, companies risk having the security of their systems compromised by intentional acts—typically referred to as computer crimes.

Marshall Romney, Computer fraud: What can be done about it? *The CPA Journal* 65(5): 30-34, May 1995. Reprinted with permission from the New York State Society of Certified Public Accountants.

These can be acts of sabotage intended to destroy system components or acts of computer fraud, where the intent is to steal money, data, computer time, or services.

Computer fraud requires knowledge of computer technology for its perpetration, investigation, or prosecution. The resulting economic losses are staggering. An American Bar Association study found that half of the businesses and government institutions uncovered at least one fraud in the year of the study. The National Center for Computer Crime Data concluded that the cost of computer crime exceeds $555,000,000 a year and that the average computer fraud loss is $109,000. According to another study, up to 90% of companies have lost money to computer fraud. The Bank Administration Institute calculates that U.S. banks lose over a billion dollars a year because of information systems abuse.

Many computer frauds go undetected and unreported. The FBI estimates that only one percent of all computer crime is detected. Also, an estimated 80% to 90% of the frauds uncovered are not reported. The most common reason for not reporting computer fraud is that companies fear they will lose more money from the adverse publicity surrounding the disclosure than from the fraud itself.

As early as 1979, Time magazine labeled computer fraud a "growth industry." Among the reasons for growth—computers are more accessible and more people are computer literate. Another, is the ability to access remote computers through both public and private data networks. Also, many businesspeople don't believe it can or will happen to them.

COMPUTER FRAUD – WHAT IS IT?

There are a variety of ways that computer fraud is perpetrated. Altering Input. Altering input is the simplest and most common fraud. This doesn't require extensive computer skills; perpetrators only need to understand how the system operates to cover their tracks. To steal inventory, for example, they can enter data to show that stolen inventory has been scrapped. At a railroad on the East Coast, employees entered data to show that 200 railroad cars had been scrapped or destroyed. They then repainted and sold them.

Perpetrators can enter data to increase salaries, create fictitious employees, or leave terminated employees on the records and collect their salaries. In a cash receipts fraud the perpetrator can hide the theft of the cash by falsifying system input. For example, an Arizona Memorial Coliseum employee sold several tickets for full price, entered the sale as half-price tickets and pocketed the difference.

Theft of Computer Time. Theft of time means using a computer system for unauthorized purposes—for example, some employees use company computers to keep personal records, records for an outside business, or even a charity of their choosing.

Software Theft and Modifications. Making unauthorized or illegal copies, modifying software, or using software in an unauthorized manner, all constitute computer fraud. This might also include developing software to carry on unauthorized activities.

Altering or Stealing Data Files. In numerous cases, data files have been scrambled, altered, or destroyed by disgruntled employees.

Employees can also steal company data. The office manager of a Wall Street law firm found information about prospective mergers and acquisitions in the firm's word processing files. He sold this insider information to people who used it to make several million dollars trading securities. In Europe, an employee stole all of a company's data files. He then drove to the offsite storage location, removed the company's backup files, and demanded half a million dollars in return for the files. He was arrested while trying to exchange the tapes for the money.

Theft or Misuse of Systems Output. Many people share printers, and this output can be subject to unauthorized copying. Monitors can be read by anyone near the screen. Few people are aware of how easy it is to monitor system output. One Dutch engineer has shown that computers emit a television-like signal that can be intercepted, restructured with inexpensive electronic gear, and displayed on a standard TV screen two miles away. During one experiment this engineer set up his equipment in the basement of an apartment building and read the screen from a terminal on the eighth floor.

COMPUTER FRAUD TECHNIQUES

The following techniques are commonly used to commit computer crimes:

* A trojan horse is a set of unauthorized computer instructions in a program that performs some illegal act at a preappointed time or under a predetermined set of conditions. For example, one ambitious

computer programmer instructed the computer to ignore overdrafts on his account.

* The round down technique is used to take advantage of financial institutions that pay interest. In the typical scenario, the programmer instructs the computer to round down all interest calculations to two decimal places. The fraction of a cent that is rounded down on each calculation is then placed in the programmer's account.

* The salami technique is an approach used to steal money in small increments. For example, one disgruntled accountant used a computer to increase production costs by a fraction of a percent every few months. These increments were then placed in accounts of dummy customers and pocketed by the accountant.

* A trapdoor is a set of computer instructions that allows a user to bypass the system's normal controls. System developers place trapdoors in programs to allow them to modify the programs during systems development—these are "normally" removed before the system is put into operation.

* A software utility called SuperZap was developed by IBM to handle emergencies, such as restoring a system that has crashed. superzapping is the unauthorized use of special system programs such as SuperZap to bypass regular system controls and perform illegal acts.

* Software piracy is the unauthorized copying of software. It is estimated that for every legal copy of software, there are between one and five illegal copies. The software industry estimates that it loses between two and four billion dollars a year to software piracy.

* Data diddling involves deleting, changing. or adding data before, after, or during the time data is entered into the system.

For example, one brokerage clerk altered a transaction to record 1,700 shares of Loren Industries worth $2,500 as shares in Long Island Lighting worth $25,000.

* Data leakage is the unauthorized copying of data. Often there is no indication that data has been copied. One company claimed millions of dollars in losses when an employee copied the company's customer list and sold it to other companies.

* Piggybacking involves tapping into a telecommunications line and latching onto a legitimate user who is logging into a system. The legitimate user unknowingly carries the perpetrator with him or her as he or she is allowed into the system.

* Masquerading occurs when an unauthorized user uses a legitimate user's identification numbers and passwords in order to gain access to a system.

* Hacking is the unauthorized access and use of computer systems, usually by means of a PC and telecommunications networks. Most hackers are motivated by the challenge of breaking and entering and looking for things to copy and keep. In numerous cases, students have tapped into school computers and changed their grades. Hackers have also broken into computers belonging to government agencies and private companies. A case reported in The New York Times on February 16, 1995, tells of a superhacker tracked down by a cybersleuth (see sidebar). This is a tale of hacking at its "best."

* Scavenging is the unauthorized searching of records or data files to gain access to confidential information. Jerry Schneider rummaged through trash cans and discovered operating guides for Pacific Telephone's computers. His scavenging resulted in a technical library that allowed him to steal one million dollars worth of electronic equipment.

* Eavesdropping involves listening to transmissions intended for someone else. In one wiretapping fraud, perpetrators pulled critical information from telephone lines and made 5,500 fake ATM cards. The perpetrators intended to use the cards to withdraw money from banks all over the country. However, they were apprehended by authorities before they could use them.

REDUCING FRAUD LOSSES

Employee integrity can be a company's major strength or its greatest weakness with regard to internal control—up to 80% of computer frauds are insider jobs. To increase employee integrity and reduce the likelihood that employees with commit a fraud, companies should follow the steps below.

Hiring and Firing Practices. In employment interviews, candidates should be asked if they are honest and trustworthy. This signals to candidates that honesty is valued by the company. The company can also inform applicants that security checks will be run on their background and that fingerprints will be taken and checked against regulatory agency files.

Companies should require written applications, solicit resumes and letters of reference, and conduct background checks on all job applicants. Companies should be careful when dismissing employees; they should be immediately removed from all sensitive jobs and denied access to company computers, preventing any last moment sabotage to the company's system.

Managing Disgruntled Employees. Many fraud perpetrators are disgruntled employees who seek revenge. Companies need to identify these individuals and either help them resolve their feelings or remove them from jobs that allow them access to the computer system. One way to minimize the chances of having disgruntled employees is to provide grievance channels and employee counseling.

Employee Training. Fraud is less likely to occur when employees believe that security is everyone's business, when they are protective of company assets, and when they believe it is their responsibility to report fraud. To develop this culture, employees should be trained in security measures and security should be monitored and enforced. Employees also should be taught why people commit fraud and how to deter and detect it.

Companies should stress the importance of ethical behavior. Many business practices are neither definitely right nor definitely wrong. For example, many computer professionals see nothing wrong with gaining unauthorized access to databases and browsing through them. One programmer was shocked when he was arrested and prosecuted for unauthorized browsing. He felt that he had done nothing wrong; he believed what he had done was normal industry practice. To avoid confusion about ethics, acceptable and unacceptable practices should be defined for employees.

Employees should be informed of the consequences of acting unethically. It could be a Federal crime to use a computer to steal or commit fraud. Any employee who commits fraud should be dismissed. The company should display notices of program and data ownership and inform employees about the penalties of misuse.

Companies can educate their employees by conducting informal discussions and formal meetings, issuing periodic departmental memos, distributing written guidelines and codes of professional ethics, circulating reports of securities violations and the consequences of the violations, and by sponsoring security and fraud training programs.

DESIGN SYSTEM AGAINST FRAUD

Companies should design internal control systems to protect their assets. One way is to implement the following risk assessment strategy:

* Determine the threats, such as fraud, that a company may face.

* Estimate the risk, or probability, of each threat occurring.

* Estimate the exposure (monetary loss) from each threat.

* Identify controls to guard against each threat. Decide what objectives the controls must achieve, and then select the most efficient and cost-effective control to achieve the objectives.

* For each threat, determine if the potential loss is greater than the cost of control.

* Implement control procedures that are cost-beneficial, and ensure that controls are complied with and enforced.

Some important controls are discussed briefly below. Segregation of Duties. Good internal control demands that management allocate tasks among employees so that any one employee is not in a position to both perpetrate and conceal a fraud. Three functions—authorization. recording, and custody of assets- must be separated to achieve effective segregation of duties. In computer systems, procedures that might otherwise be performed by separate individuals may be combined within the computer processing function. Thus employees with unrestricted access could both perpetrate and conceal a fraud. To minimize this risk, an organization must segregate duties within the following systems functions: application systems analysis and programming, computer operations, systems programming, transaction authorization, file library maintenance, and data control

Enforced Vacations and Rotation of Duties. Many fraud schemes require the ongoing attention of the perpetrator. If mandatory vacations are coupled with a temporary rotation of duties, these ongoing fraud schemes often fail. In one case, when Federal investigators raided a gambling establishment, they found that Roswell Steffen, a man with an annual salary of $11,000, was betting $30,000 a day. Working with his employer, Union Dime Savings Bank, investigators discovered that Steffen had embezzled $1.5 million dollars over a three-year period. Steffen, a compulsive gambler, started by borrowing $5,000 to bet on a "sure thing" that did not pan out. It was later observed that the fraud could have been prevented by coupling a two week vacation period with a rotation of duties.

Restrict Access. Alarm systems, closed circuit TVs, security badges, and machine-readable access cards that restrict physical access to computer equipment can reduce the incidence of computer fraud. Access to data should be restricted by using passwords and other access codes.

Companies sometimes forget to cancel the passwords of former employees. It is important to ensure that all data used in restricting access is updated immediately when an employee leaves the company.

Another approach is to use biometric security systems, which measure unique physical traits such as speech patterns, eye and finger physiology, and signature dynamics. The system must be reliable and yet able to account for minor changes in physical characteristics such as a cut finger or a hoarse voice. This system requires the user to be present to access the system.

Encrypt Data and Programs. Data encryption involves converting data into a scrambled format either for storage purposes or before transmitting the data. The data can then be converted back into meaningful form for authorized usage. Data encryption is particularly important when confidential data are being transmitted across great distances, because data bans mission lines can be electronically monitored without the user's knowledge. Companies can now attach an electronic lock and key to their telephone lines. When one such device was tested, researchers concluded that it would take up to 188 days working nonstop to break the one trillion combinations.

Control of Sensitive Data. Confidential documents should be shredded before being discarded. Data files should be controlled to prevent or discourage their being copied. Employees should be informed of the consequences of using illegal copies of software, and the company should ensure that illegal copies are not used. Local area networks can use dedicated servers that allow data to be downloaded but never uploaded. Closed circuit televisions can monitor areas where sensitive data or easily stolen assets are handled.

Some organizations are installing diskless PCs. In these companies, data are stored centrally in a network and users download the data they need. At the end of the day, data that is to be kept is stored in the network. Since users cannot alter or delete stored data, the system is protected from abuses a user might intentionally or unintentionally cause. Without disks, employees cannot copy or remove company data on diskettes.

Conduct Frequent Audits. Auditors should periodically test system controls and search the company's data files for suspicious activities. Informing employees that company auditors will conduct random surveillance not only ensures that employees' privacy rights are not violated, but it deters computer fraud. One financial institution that implemented this strategy uncovered a number of abuses, resulting in the termination of one employee and the reprimand of another.

Consider a Computer Security Officer. Hiring a computer security officer who is responsible for fraud can significantly reduce the incidence of computer frauds. The security officer can monitor the system and disseminate information about improper uses of the system and consequences of violations.

What About a Fraud Hotline? People who witness fraud often have conflicting feelings: They feel obligated to report fraudulent behavior, but they hesitate to inform on others. When employees are able to report fraudulent behavior anonymously, it is easier for them to resolve this conflict. The insurance industry set up a hotline to control $17 billion dollars a year in fraudulent claims. The first month they received 2,250 calls. Between 10% and 15% of the calls resulted in investigative action. The disadvantage of the hotlines is that many calls are not worthy of investigation.

Use Computer Consultants. Many companies hire computer consultants to find weaknesses in their internal control systems. The consultants will probably attempt to breach the security of a system. Each means of breaching the system that is uncovered is closely evaluated, and protective measures are taken to prevent further occurrences. Some companies do not use this approach because of the risk of demonstrating that the system has weaknesses and the message it sends to employees.

OTHER OPTIONS FOR LOSS REDUCTION

No matter how hard a company tries to deter or prevent fraud, it may still occur. One way to minimize losses is to buy adequate insurance. Another is to keep a current backup copy of all program and data files in a secure off-site location. A third approach is to develop a contingency plan to handle fraud incidences. A fourth is to use software that monitors system activity and helps companies recover from frauds, by identifying the corrupted files.

16

Quieting the Virtual Prison Riot

Why the Internet's spirit of "Sharing" Must be Broken

Albert Z. Kovacs

It's amazing what you can do when you don't have to look at yourself in the mirror anymore.

HOLLOW MAN

To demand equality of rights ... as the socialists of the subject caste do, is never an emanation of justice but of greed. — If one holds up bleeding chunks of meat to an animal and takes them away again until it finally roars: do you think this roaring has anything to do with justice?

Friedrich Nietzsche

Thou shalt not steal.

Exodus 20:15

Albert Z. Kovacs, Quieting the virtual prison riot: why the Internet's spirit of "sharing" must be broken. *Duke Law Journal* 51 (2): 753-786. Reprinted by permission of the author.

INTRODUCTION

The Internet has changed much about everyday life. The way people shop. The way they communicate. The way they conduct business. The way they buy airline tickets and get driving directions. The Internet promises freedom from many of the delays and limitations of the physical world. But in doing so, could the Internet also distance people from the rules and moral conceptions that bind them in the "real world"?

Because in cyberspace people can exist independent of their names, identities, faces, and personalities, they often transcend the real world's moral and legal boundaries. Although the Internet allows them to transcend or violate these boundaries more easily, it generally has not changed moral and ethical concepts—notions of what it means to "do wrong." However, these notions are under attack. The ease with which content on the Internet can be (often erroneously) categorized as mere "information" threatens to erode legal conceptions of intellectual property protection and our ethical definition of theft.

Using Michel Foucault's historical analysis of punishment and the development of disciplinary surveillance, I argue that the "spirit of sharing" that has developed on the Internet is effectively a revolt against the "prison" erected by copyright law. To assert their proprietary rights effectively, successfully, and with both legal and moral authority, the recording industry (and other content-based industries) must break that "spirit of sharing" by making a visible display of power in cyberspace. By publicly "torturing" Napster and similar file-exchange services, the content industries are taking a first step toward quelling the virtual rebellion against copyright.

I. THE PROBLEMATIC MORALITY OF THE INTERNET

Through its decentralized architecture, which promises free communication, the Internet has modified concepts of property and information, seducing an entire generation into associating copyright infringement and theft of intellectual property with "discourse" and "sharing."

A. The Original Structure of the Internet

The Internet was designed as a communications system that could survive a nuclear war; communication on the network depends not on any single path of information flow or central server, but on a "distributed" architecture that can circumvent system failures or blockages. An oft-quoted comment by Electronic Frontier Foundation cofounder John Gilmore sums up the original, and to some extent current, popular conception of the Internet: "The Net interprets censorship as damage and routes around it."

The Internet's capacity to circumvent obstacles to data flow has created a new means of communication that seems to eliminate the possibility of censorship or centralized authoritarian monitoring, control, or supervision. This unsupervised realm promises to be a paradise island for those who yearn for a truly free and seemingly infinite exchange of ideas, restricted neither by physical location nor by social or political convention or stigmatization. "In the utopian vision, a worldwide digital network transcends national borders and promotes open dialogue, cooperation, and self-regulation. It is a vision of free and robust scientific, artistic, educational, and political interaction. It is a model of `any-to-any,' a two-way street where all recipients are also producers of information."

This "utopian vision" of discourse on the Internet seems to realize what long has been a political ideal: the free exchange of ideas from one person to another, without interference from the state. In the "real world" (at least in the "real" United States), the Constitution limits with words the power of the government to control the intellectual interaction of the citizenry. In the virtual world, freedom from state supervision and intervention promises that ideal intellectual exchange can be completely realized. The Internet can transform "politics by making true dialogue and free debate available to everyone," allowing its users the freedom to disseminate their thoughts and to access the thoughts of others, with peer criticism and commentary the only possible forms of censorship. The anonymity and metaphysicality of the Internet promises to free its users from the burdens of both their location in the physical world and the socioeconomic strata that define it. By shedding names, bodies, and faces—and thus to a large degree their real-world identities—people can interact (and be judged) in a realm of ideas as ideas themselves.

B. Digital Anonymity and Moral Independence

The anonymity and freedom from physical restriction that the Internet provides generally has not changed our value systems or ethical mores. However, in the area of copyright and intellectual property, they encourage a systematic mutation of our concepts of property and "sharing."

The structure and design of the Internet promise the development of a freer and more expansive exchange of knowledge and an explosive increase in political and cross-cultural discourse. In that sense, the anonymity and metaphysicality of the system allow people to escape the restrictions of the real world that would inhibit communication. But the very features of the Internet that hold its greatest promise also permit users of the system to shed some of the beneficially restrictive norms, laws, and moral structures that govern behavior in the real world.

When one enters cyberspace, one can abandon almost all things "real" about one's self; name, face, gender, age, nationality, and religion all can be erased, hidden, or changed. The inhibitions and restrictions that accompany one's place and identity in the real world can vanish in the virtual one. In a realm of imagination and ideas, the very notion of reality falls away. What would be impossible or impracticable in the real world—for example, a face-to-face, real-time conversation among students located at different corners of the globe—becomes possible and even commonplace on the Internet. Similarly, activities and behavior that are rendered impossible or impracticable by law, moral edict, or social pressure become possible once the contextual reality that gives those commands their authoritative force fades away. In the real world, one's conduct is governed largely by one's location in space, which creates physical limitations on behavior and helps to determine applicable law, and cultural context, which defines social behavioral expectations and norms. The virtual world for many seems different from the real world in a moral sense, and that difference has varying degrees of impact.

In a statement regarding the protection of intellectual property on the Internet, United States Attorney General Janet Reno recounted the following anecdote:

A man once told me, a man well-versed [in computer crimes]: "You know, my 13-year-old daughter knows that she can't open other people's physical mail and read it. She doesn't go into her sister's bedroom when the door is closed. She doesn't rumble through her drawers without permission. But she doesn't know how to act on line. She doesn't know what to do with other people's email."

This is one of the more harmless examples of the moral confusion that results from the physical "depersonalization" of the Internet. It shows that the simple personal courtesies extended to others, and the privacy boundaries almost instinctively respected can be confused, neglected, or simply ignored on the Internet. It is easier—and thus more tempting—to snoop in cyberspace because it is easier to avoid detection.

The moral dilemma that results from the libertarian structure of much of the Internet stems from what can be seen as the dual citizenship of the "netizen." When one inhabits cyberspace, one is still physically present in the real world, but one also exists on another metaphysical plane. The Internet provides a vehicle by which people can escape the restrictions of the real world without having to sacrifice the security and benefits it holds for them. In this sense, one can view the Internet as a fantasy world or escape from reality, where one can harmlessly transcend moral restrictions without paying any "real" penalty. Professor Lawrence Lessig describes an example of such an escapist, a college student named Jake who published stories on a USENET group called alt.sex.stories: "Jake was a character in his own stories, yet who he was in his stories was quite different from who he was in 'real' life.... Jake wrote stories about violence—about sex as well, but mainly about violence. They seethed with hatred, especially of women."

In Jake's stories, he could display his own brand of despicable "bravery" and become a hero to those who admired his work. These were expressive possibilities and outlets that Jake never would have had save for the Internet. He may have been able to publish his work in the real world, but his audience would have been much smaller and the rewards less significant. In the real world, Jake was unable, or simply unwilling, to express the depravity that lurked within his imagination. But on the Internet, his depravity found an outlet and more—an eager, (blood) thirsty audience more than willing to receive, applaud, and demand more of the same. In the real world, Jake was someone bound by morals, norms, and social convention. "On the Net he was someone else."

The previous examples represent two possible manifestations of the Internet's unrestricted nature: first, a simple transgression of common courtesy, and second, a slicing expression of socially unwelcome fantasy. While each of these may be morally troubling to some, they pose little threat of harm to the real world. What is most troubling is when the freedom and libertarianism of the Internet threatens the moral and legal constructs of the real world, permitting people to cultivate their repressed desires and instincts by facilitating acts in cyberspace that would be illegal and far less practicable in the real world.

Perhaps the clearest and most disturbing example of this phenomenon is that of a pedophile soliciting minors online. In many instances, adults have solicited children (or law enforcement officers posing as children) for explicit sexual conversations online, and have attempted to make real-world contact with them, either by arranging meetings for actual sexual intercourse or by exchanging photographs or other media involving sexual activities. "Surreptitious and anonymous predators can disguise their identities and prey on young people or others who [sic] they simply trust when they meet them online."As Professor Lessig points out, the anonymity of the Internet, coupled with its severance from the physical world, allows this type of criminal to be more effective than he could be in the real world: "Without this technology, it would be relatively hard for the same adults to engage in such conversations with kids (thirty-five year old men roaming playgrounds are usually easily noticed); with the technology, this criminal activity is increased." The anonymity and metaphysicality of the Internet again produce an escape from some of the limitations of real-world morality and its normative structures. But even this example of the Internet's facilitation of moral failure does not represent a change in society's moral and ethical systems.

Although the Internet might facilitate the occasional invasion of personal privacy (the child's reading someone else's e-mail), encourage the production of deviant fantasies in the mind of a repressed libertine (Jake's telling violent sex stories), or perhaps make it easier for certain particularly vile criminals to approach their victims (the sex offender's stalking children), can the Internet be blamed for any actual degradation of real-world moral norms? The architecture of the Internet might facilitate these transgressions, but can that architecture really carry the blame for the moral attitudes of its users? In the above examples, the answer is no.

The young girl reading her sister's e-mail is probably doing nothing more than she would do had she a similar opportunity in the real world—namely invading the privacy of another when the chance of detection is slight. The Internet just makes it easier for her to avoid the consequences of her moral choice. The sexually and socially underdeveloped author who shares his demented fantasies with like-minded individuals is doing no more than digitizing the ideas that would occupy his mind regardless; the Internet merely provides the vent through which that repressed energy can dissipate. And many child molesters will seek out victims with or without a computer. The Internet might make it slightly easier for the perpetrator to escape detection, but the decision to violate society's sexual taboos is made long before he enters any Internet chat room.

It would then seem that the Internet, while facilitating moral transgressions, has done nothing to affect the moral values and ethical systems people transgress. To put it simply, although the Internet may in some instances make it easier to "be bad," it has not changed what it means to "be bad." If the architecture of the Internet is not responsible for the moral values that lead to virtual transgressions, then it is unlikely that changing that architecture will have any real reformatory effect. But there is one area in which the architecture and structure of the Internet appear to be degrading the legal, moral, and normative constructs of the real world—namely the theft of intellectual property.

The supposedly uncontrolled (and at least formerly uncontrollable) nature of the Internet produces a free flow of information, an exchange of ideas with perhaps only infinitesimal recognition of the restrictions and limitations of the real world. This unrestricted flow of information results in a mutation and misunderstanding of property rights and has seduced a generation into equating stealing with "sharing." The architecture of the Internet appears to be largely, if not entirely, responsible for the moral values that have spawned the virtual spirit of sharing. Thus, a change in that architecture not only might control actual transgressions, but also might reform the confused ethical constructs that are responsible for them.

C. Intangibility, the Myth of Free Information, and the Free-For-All Ethic of Cyberspace

The Internet's architecture allows users to exist in a digital plane where information and other data travel with few restrictions. This architecture tempts users to identify all content as "information" once it is separated from a physical storage or transfer medium. It is this alluring misconception that distorts legal concepts of property and ethical prohibitions against theft.

Intellectual property law cannot be patched, retrofitted, or expanded to contain the gasses of digitized expression any more than real estate law might be revised to cover the allocation of broadcasting spectrum.... Digital technology is detaching information from the physical plane, where property law of all sorts has always found definition.

232

In his article Selling Wine Without Bottles, John Perry Barlow describes his vision for the future of copyrighted materials in the Information Age. He adopts the widely known maxim of writer Stuart Brand that "[i]nformation wants to be free." Barlow thus directly rejects the notion of information as a thing, especially on the Internet, where information is freed from its containers—the pages, books, tapes, film, and compact discs in which it formerly resided. When information ceases to be attached to any tangible medium, it becomes free to flow naturally as an "activity," a "life form," and a "relationship." Barlow suggests that current business models in the music industry fail to recognize the true nature of information on the Internet, and that copyright as it is currently known will not be able to adapt to the new "dematerialized information economy," in which there is no "final cut," and works remain "liquid" without being "fixed by a point of publication."

Professor Margaret Jane Radin also comments on the increasingly fluid nature of formerly "fixed" works. In her view, copyright protection "perpetuates the notion that property attaches to objects .... `Objects' in cyberspace, however—collections of bits that are apprehended as works—are ceasing to be fixed and tangible. They are becoming moving, dynamic, and malleable.... Works and the medium that embodies them are ceasing to be objects, and becoming processes." These commentaries suggest that information is liberated-made free—by its removal from any kind of tangible or physical medium. Barlow's conception of information naturally engulfs the realm of copyrighted music: "No longer will we mistake music for a noun, as its containers have tempted us to do for a century. We will realize once more that music is a verb, a relationship, a constantly evolving life form."

Barlow's analysis of information and its dissemination on the Internet appears at first glance to be a fair one. If one understands "information" to mean ideas, concepts, and facts, and "free" to mean open and available to a wide audience, then it would seem obvious that "[i]nformation wants to be free." Once an idea is made accessible on the web, it is generally available to all who can find it, and it will more than likely be shared, lauded, criticized, manipulated, edited, revised, and ultimately adopted, incorporated, or rejected.

The expansive view of free information that Barlow suggests contains two fundamental errors. First, it seems to define "information" so broadly as to include all data that has been or can be digitized and made accessible on the Internet. Second, it understands "free" in a way that suggests that all information should not only be widely accessible, but accessible to everyone at no cost whatsoever.

By labeling all content on the Internet "information," Barlow would seem to allow the inhabitants of cyberspace to lay claim to all materials available online, regardless of whether they enjoyed a traditionally protected status in the real world. This type of logic essentially would require that any data made available on the Internet be relegated to the public domain. In Barlow's vision, copyright used to make at least some sense because musical "information" was stored in tangible media that had to be transferred or copied physically. But now that quality reproductions can be made at almost no cost and can be transferred without the exchange of any physical object, he seems to argue, copyright protection and intellectual property rights should fall away as an outdated and unwelcome reminder of a pre-digital, primitive understanding of property. Ideas, facts, concepts, and theories formerly could be distinguished as unprotectable "information," as opposed to the protected "property-things" of copyright. Under Barlow's system, the Internet removes that copyrighted content from the physical world (apparently ignoring the fact that the content simply has moved to computer hard drives from vinyl records or compact discs) and permits a blurring of the line between, on the one hand, the ideas and "information" that all rightfully share and, on the other hand, the creative expression that is deserving of respect, protection, and reward.

Ambiguity as to what counts as "information" is compounded by ambiguity as to what kind of "freedom" the information (apparently) demands and the Internet (apparently) promises. In an online article, Nicholas Petreley, a self-avowed "open source, free software, and free speech advocate," comments: "Take this mantra: `Information wants to be free.' Horsehockey. Information doesn't want anything. People want information to be free. But face it: people want corned beef sandwiches on rye to be free, too. That doesn't mean we are entitled to them." There is a difference between stating that all information (whatever that might be) wants to be free and stating that all information should be available free of charge. What file-"sharing" and free-source advocates should not do "is license or buy existing information that is not free and then cut it loose without permission. That's just plain wrong, and people who do it are demonstrating that what they are interested in is ... getting stuff without having to pay for it."

These two fundamental misunderstandings—the expansive redefinitions of the words "information" and "free"—are causing a shift in moral expectations and claims of entitlement with respect to formerly protected materials. Perhaps a clearer translation of "information wants to be free" is "ideas should not be property." This formulation is perhaps less catchy, but it is conceptually neater and less subject to popular manipulation and misunderstanding. It also expresses nothing new, at least with respect to copyright protection. (39) The more expansive and more popular articulation of this sentiment, however, results in the development of three new "truths," which, if left uncorrected, could easily become moral axioms of the digital world (if they have not been established as such already).

First, digitalization becomes equated with liberation. Anything that one might copy onto a hard drive or post to an Internet server becomes classified as "information," regardless of whether that label would have been appropriate when the material was in its real-world, or tangible, form. Second, availability is identified with entitlement, meaning that if it is technologically possible for one to access something in a digital form (or to make it available in such a form), one has a right to do so, since that is merely the natural realization of information's true state of being. Third, stealing becomes known as "sharing." If information is truly free, then it belongs to no one. No matter how one obtains information, it is rightfully in one's possession and, in turn, one is free to share it with anyone. Any restriction of that freedom to "share" could then be construed as a restriction of the individual's right to "interact" and "associate" freely with Internet peers.

Some of these new digital "axioms" already have been reflected in the comments that formerly were exchanged on Napster's message boards: "File sharing advocates and distributors are victims not thieves.... Our choice to exchange whatever information or data ... with whom we chose [sic], for no commercial gain, and without restrictions [is the] embodiment of our right to freely associate and exchange information." That same Napster user also states that the rights to "freely communicate [and] exchange information are basic and fundamental," and that lawsuits such as those brought against Napster "are designed to effectively eliminate and restrict file sharing technology and are designed to restrict and limit the nature and scope of each individuals [sic] ability to interact with each other and to participate in an entire category of interaction, communication, and association."

Clearly, these concepts do not translate into the real world. It is highly unlikely that even the most adamant Napster user would suggest that one should be allowed to enter a record store, make copies of whatever one chooses, then make those copies available to anyone who might want them, not only without payment by the recipient, but also without financial reward to the artist. Even less plausible would be a defense of that kind of activity that involved a claim of freedom of association or interaction. Nor would one claim that just because one has purchased a compact disc, one should be entitled to take another copy from any record store one finds convenient. The physicality of the real world prevents this logic from taking hold. In the above scenarios, one would be stealing things, objects that are tangible, tactile, visible, and thus value-able. In cyberspace, however, the physicality of things falls away, and the notion of transferring to millions of anonymous listeners the music one either has purchased or has taken from somewhere else does not seem so wrong, since no thing is transferred. Often the only physical act required to effect the transfer is the simple click of a computer mouse. The digitized content that is transferred cannot easily be located in the physical world, so it is classified as "information," which demands to naturally and "freely" flow from one user to another. Thus, while music pirates exchanging compact discs hardly could claim freedom of association as a defense (without being greeted by hearty laughter from judges), it seems more feasible for Internet music pirates to do just that. For if music (once stripped of its physicality) is merely information, then what is being stifled by copyright holders is not illicit commerce or thievery, but discourse.

Although many Napster users adopt this type of libertarian, discursive philosophy, many others do not feel the need to embrace the notion that "information wants to be free." Some members of the file-sharing community view free music downloads as an entitlement stemming from previous expenditures by music fans for "overpriced" recordings. "A lot of people are like, `Why should I feel guilty for downloading MP3s—I've seen all their concerts, I own all the CDs, I've bought T-shirts—they've got my money already....'" "Artists have been ripping us off for years! ... We only like one or two [of their songs, but if] we want to listen to the few, we have to buy them all.... Personally, I feel the artists owe the public alot [sic] of free downloads!"

Others see the free exchange of copyrighted materials as an attack on a supposedly corrupt system which degrades music as an art form by considering its development and promotion as a business: "[Y]ou guys have RUINED music by turning it into a business and these `artist' [sic] are not trying to make music they're trying to make money. So we are bringing back the soul [sic] reason as to why music is what it is." Music, once freed from the surface of a tangible medium, apparently regains a lost intrinsic and artistic value: "You lower your ... prices and make music less hyped by superficial people like Brinty [sic] Spears and Back Street boys [sic] and bring back what its [sic] all about or we are going to do it on our own!"

The music industry should be alarmed by both the "noble" libertarian Napsterites and their more boisterous and revolutionary cousins (for reasons more significant than poor grammar and bad spelling). From the recording industry's perspective, Napster users, as well as the members of other file-sharing communities, regardless of their underlying ideology, have been seduced into believing that they are entitled to free music on the Internet. Contrary to the claim that Napster and its many clones reveal the true meaning and value of music by removing it from a commercialized context, the Recording Industry Association of America argues that "Napster is devaluing music itself, teaching an entire generation that music is free and has no value." The feeling of entitlement is something created and fostered by the "free"-for-all ethic of the Internet and must be addressed quickly before it becomes engrained as a popular truth. "Once consumers become accustomed to obtaining something for free, they resist paying for it.... If the perception of music as a free good becomes pervasive, it may be difficult to reverse."

The lawsuit against Napster is but one of several in the past few years aimed at controlling unauthorized "sharing" of copyrighted materials. Whether one views these suits as attempts by the industry to eliminate peer-to-peer file-sharing technology altogether or merely to use its legal leverage to take control of that technology, the focus of the music industry's counterattack to the ethic surrounding the myth of free information is the technology itself. It is this technological structure and architecture that has fostered the free-for-all mentality of the Internet, and it is that same architecture that promises to re-educate the confused cyberlibertarian while at the same time quieting the revolt of copyright's virtual prisoners.

II. "BUILDING" A SOLUTION: DISCIPLINARY ARCHITECTURE

The philosophy of Michel Foucault provides a historical analysis of the development of the modern prison system from its origins in public spectacles of torture. The features Foucault attributes to modern disciplinary surveillance—automatic, supervisory, invisible—all can be analogized to the architectural controls which can be established on the Internet to control the flow of information as well as to observe those who access it.

A. Foucault and the Historical Development of Disciplinary Surveillance

In Discipline and Punish, Michel Foucault examines the structures of disciplinary power and their historical development as a reform of public torture. Through this reform, power becomes vested in a web of societal supervision and training rather than in the person of the sovereign. An inversion occurs in which the sovereign, who forged his superior individuality by tormenting the bodies of those who would dare challenge his status by asserting their own wills, fades away into obscurity, while the subject of punishment becomes individualized as the object of disciplinary surveillance, punishment, and study.

Early in Discipline and Punish, Foucault shows how the ritualistic display of torture is a response to what could be understood as a direct attack upon the power of the sovereign. "[B]y breaking the law, the offender has touched the very person of the prince; and it is the prince—or at least those to whom he has delegated his force— who seizes upon the body of the condemned man and displays it marked, beaten, [and] broken." By transgressing the law, the criminal in this primitive system dares to raise himself to the level of the prince, declaring himself an equal or superior in power by defying the will of the sovereign. The criminal, through his misdeeds, attempts to individualize himself, singling himself out from the herd within the sovereign's power. The sovereign, through a terrible display of physical strength and political authority, destroys this individuality, reestablishing himself as the solitary figure of independence, freedom, and power. It is the strong, swift hand of the prince that crushes dissent, reaffirming his position above the faceless, nameless crowd that swarms beneath his scepter.

The inversion of this open, visible display of the sovereign's power occurs with the abolition of public torture and the rise of supervisory structures and disciplinary punishment. In this inversion, the criminal—the object of discipline and training, as well as punishment—is the one who must at all times remain visible. In the former system, the object of the mechanisms of power could "remain in the shade.... Disciplinary power, on the other hand, [was] exercised through its invisibility; at the same time it impose[d] on those whom it subject[ed] a principle of compulsory visibility." In modern systems of punishment and correction, it is the criminal—the object of the mechanisms of power—who is individualized, isolated, recognized, and identified—made a visible subject. At the same time, the machinery of power remains anonymous and invisible, as the mechanism itself takes control. The principal example of this system of observational discipline in the real world is the Panopticon, which establishes an almost automatic exercise of anonymous power. The prisoners are individualized, each in a separate cell, always in plain view of the central tower, the occupants of which are hidden from the prisoners' view. This central tower enforces a silent, automatic rule of discipline, for the prisoners have no idea when they are being observed, or if they are being observed at all. Thus, the mere possibility of being observed—the potential for the discovery of misbehavior—imposes upon the prisoner a kind of self-discipline, where the authority—the faceless remnant of the sovereign—disappears further into the machinery of power. The theoretical result is a disciplinary and supervisory system in which power functions automatically, without maintenance and at a low cost. The structures of power Foucault describes—automatic, supervisory, invisible, decentralized-all seem analogous to the architectural codes of the Internet, which can silently and without outward signal control the behavior of the inhabitants of cyberspace

The Panopticon also individualizes the criminal by making him the subject of experimental observation and study: "The Panopticon is a privileged place for experiments on men, and for analysing with complete certainty the transformations that may be obtained from them." Similarly, the "trusted systems" that are (or soon will be) established on the Internet could track a wide variety of information about those who access or manipulate online works. The architectural code becomes both an exercise and a form of institutional power. "[W]e must ask of every exercise of power: Why? ... `Power,' in this account, is just another word for constraints that humans can do something about.... [T]he architecture of cyberspace is power in this sense; how it is could be different."

But how should the architecture be established, and who should make the important decisions involved in that determination? Who can claim the right to determine the boundaries of possibility on the Internet, and how will accountability be maintained? It has been argued that these questions should be answered through privatized efforts. (66) In the case of online music swapping, that would mean that the music industry should seek to develop systems that would protect its interests.

From the content industries' perspective, the promise of a digital Panopticon should seem like a most wonderful solution to what at first glance looks like a daunting problem. Upon the anarchical system of the Internet, the industry quietly could impose a structure that would protect its rights, while providing detailed consumer information that would allow for targeted market research and advertising. Indeed, whoever controls the architectural code of the Internet will hold the virtual scepter of power in cyberspace.

B. The Rise of the Internet Panopticon

The computer architecture of the various spaces that comprise the Internet determines the possible spectrum of online conduct and behavior. The original architecture, as discussed in this Note, promised a type of freedom and interaction that seemed impossible in the real world. What accompanied that promise of freedom was a loss of control and regimentation. "The Internet changed the balance of protection afforded by law, by enabling behaviors that weaken the protections of a legal regime." While this weakening of governmental influence was apparent on many fronts, Professor Lessig suggests that the greatest threat lay in the area of copyright protection. The original architecture of the Internet permitted perfect digital copying at negligible (if any) cost and permitted equally costless distribution. Lessig argues that while the early architecture of the Internet posed a threat to copyright protection, developments in code have the potential to create an era of almost perfect copyright protection on the Internet—a level of protection that could surpass anything possible in the real world.

[C]yberspace does not guarantee its own freedom but instead carries an extraordinary potential for control.... Too many believe liberty will take care of itself. Too many miss how different architectures embed different values, and that only by selecting these different architectures—these different codes—can we establish and promote our values.... Architecture is a kind of law: it determines what people can and cannot do.

The idea of using a coded system to protect legal copyrights by making it technically difficult to infringe upon them is not unique to the Internet. A less perfect system of architectural copyright protection was established in response to what was considered by many to be a similar, real-world threat to copyright—Digital Audio Tape (DAT). The eventual response to the threat of a machine that could produce perfect, digital copies of compact discs was a change in the architecture of that machine itself. The technology was changed to degrade deliberately the quality of each successive recording, thus wiring into the machine a protection against infinite, perfect copying. The previous technology's physical limitations were programmed into the new technology to maintain the previous level of protection. On the Internet, however, developments in code would permit copyright holders not only to maintain the level of protection against impermissible copying and distribution that exists in the real world, but also actually to surpass it.

Lessig refers to these developments in code as "trusted systems." With these systems, copyright holders could use software to perfect control over their works, without resort to legal action, governmental intervention, or social normative reform. "Trusted systems" could control when and how a copyrighted work is accessed, manipulated, edited, and transferred. "The technology, in other words, would give the copyright holder a kind of power over the user of copyrighted material that the copyright holder has never before had."

Copyright orders others to respect the rights of the copyright holder before using his property. Trusted systems give access only if rights are respected in the first place. The controls needed to regulate this access are built into the systems, and no users (except hackers) have a choice about whether to obey these controls. The code displaces law by codifying the rules, making them more efficient than they were just as rules.

Thus, the architecture of the Internet, which originally had suggested that copyright protection would be profoundly difficult or impossible in the digital realm, could be modified to create a space of almost perfect copyright protection, where users would have even less power to access, manipulate, and duplicate works than they have in the real world. Technologies like Secure Digital Music Initiative (SDMI) and digital watermarks offer copyright holders the potential to restrict copying of protected materials and to track the uses of those copies that are permitted. These new technologies also might be used to track information about how their protected works are used and who is using them. "Documents will keep track of how many times they are read and may complain if they are read too much or by the wrong person.... [These will be] texts that 'rat' on you." This information would be part of a system in which individual (and perhaps individualized) fees could be charged for every infinitesimal use— even those that would have been considered free or "fair" in the real world.

Such ultraprotective architectural codes would offer protection for copyrights unparalleled by any protection available in the real world. Digital technology, which once promised to be a scalpel, severing works from the protection of copyright, very soon could coil its sharp edges into a barbed wire, guarding against anyone who wishes to gain access. The digital fences that could be, and already have been, erected could create a virtual Panopticon that would prevent unauthorized use of protected works and permit the works themselves to keep vigilant watch over those with access to them.

III. A DISPLAY OF SOVEREIGNTY: THE "TORTURE" OF NAPSTER AS PUBLIC SPECTACLE

To institute a system of digital surveillance and automatic power on the Internet, the content industries first must make a public display of that power. Although certainly not the only example, the lawsuit against Napster has provided the music recording industry the opportunity to make a very public example of what is (or at least was at the time of the suit's initiation) the largest of the Internet's file-sharing communities. To efficiently and legitimately establish a regime of copyright protection on the Internet, the recording industry effectively must "torture" Napster in full public view, reasserting its property rights in cyberspace against the rebellious challenge made in the name of free discourse and "sharing."

A. The Internet as Prison Riot

Foucault's analysis of disciplinary power shows that the Panoptical system not only applies to prisons, but also is found in many of the structures that define who people are and what they become: "The practice of placing individuals under `observation' is a natural extension of a justice imbued with disciplinary methods and examination procedures.... Is it surprising that prisons resemble factories, schools, barracks, hospitals, which all resemble prisons?" If the structures of power have become so pervasive in society that one cannot escape them—in fact, if one is defined by them—then would not the Internet be a revolt from that disciplinary system? Is the Internet not then essentially a prison revolt?

The Internet originally was designed to avoid the restrictions, observations, and controls that burdened the real world. Recall the manifesto Professor Lessig cites: "We reject: kings, presidents and voting." The Internet can be viewed as a rebellion against the disciplinary surveillance of modern society. The Internet has created a space in which one can shed the name, identity, and social status handed down and created by the structures of disciplinary power. One can abandon the traditional norms and rules of society that are taught in schools and enforced in prisons. And most importantly, one can do it anonymously and invisibly. The Internet seems to be the one place the prying eye of discipline cannot see, or, if it can see, the one place it cannot see very well.

If the Internet is a rebellion against the disciplinary structures of the real world, then the rebellion must be crushed to establish "real" order and stability. In this respect, the last vestiges of the invisible sovereign must rear up, reveal themselves once again momentarily, and, in a transitory display of force, establish in this new world the order of the old system that the Internet subverted. It is the rarest of prison riots that can be quashed by invisible surveillance. Once the system of observation has broken down, it takes a show of force to restore and stabilize things once again. When the prisoners smash all the video cameras and take control of the central observation tower, it may take just the sound of one gunshot and the sight of one dead inmate to restore the sanity of ordered control. Perhaps it will take the execution of Napster—arguably the ringleader in the revolt—to make Internet users realize that in fleeing reality by entering cyberspace, they have not escaped society's prison, but have, ironically, merely encapsulated themselves in a different cell.

B. The Benefits of Public "Torture"

The most significant and immediate benefits of shutting down Napster and its progeny will be to the content industries, which will have sealed off an avenue of copyright infringement and media piracy. The exercise of sovereign power extends legitimacy to whatever surveillance system is established. Also, the visibility of that power might help disrupt the popularized notion of "free information."

1. Legitimacy. By "torturing" Napster in public view, the recording industry makes a claim of right or authority to establish the supervisory system it likely will establish. Instead of merely establishing a system of digital fences, watermarks, or other new copyright-protective technologies in secret, the music industry also needs to make an open, unabashed, and honest claim about its rights and power in cyberspace. If Lessig is right that "the space is sovereign," then a show of individual power must be made to change the space. Without this open show of power as a claim of legitimate authority, the imposition of a new architecture—especially one that significantly restricts the formerly unchecked flow of information— might seem arbitrary and unjustifiable. By vigorously pursuing its lawsuits against Napster, the music industry can obtain what is in effect the grant of a legal right to exercise its power in cyberspace. By openly claiming this right (and displaying it by shutting down

Napster's infringing activities), the legitimacy of the forthcoming architectural imposition is preserved against claims that the music industry is acting without moral or legal authority.

2. Visibility. The spectacle of public violence confronts those who witness it with a show of power, might, and authority. By establishing its system, Napster openly and directly has challenged the legitimacy of copyright protection on the Internet (if not everywhere). In this sense, it has "touched the very person of the prince," flaunting any claim of authority that the music industry might have in cyberspace. By obtaining a very public condemnation of Napster's activities, and by effectively destroying Napster (through a permanent injunction and a significant damage award), the music industry can stake its claim to power and right on the Internet. At the same time, this display of destructive power might awaken or startle those who witness it (especially Napster users) from the illusion of free information. By executing Robin Hood publicly, the sovereign might remind a few of the merry thieves that stealing is wrong and will be punished, no matter how praiseworthy the perpetrator or villainous the victim.

But the benefits of the public torture of Napster will not be limited to the content industries. Despite the "harm" suffered by advocates of free information, there are some latent advantages to Internet users from this type of public display of authority.

First, the visibility of a public spectacle like the Napster lawsuit ensures that users know who established the disciplinary system under which they live. The music industry must identify itself as a major impetus for the erection of digital fences and similar impediments to the flow of information. The industry cannot hide behind claims of market forces or other invisible hands. Those who will have their wrists bound with digital cuffs, and who will be tagged and observed as they navigate cyberspace, will thus be aware of these restrictions. When the restrictions are hidden in the architecture of the space itself, it is paramount that people be made aware of their existence and of their contingency, since otherwise they might consider those structural restrictions to be "just the way things are."

Second, this type of a showing of sovereign power establishes a focus or center from which the disciplinary system can be said to originate, thus resulting in some accountability for those who establish it. The visibility of the destructive force of the music industry as effected upon Napster would identify the music industry as the author of the disciplinary system that likely would replace current file-sharing technologies. In this respect, "the way things are" would be revealed not as the result of anonymous evolution or the unfolding of inevitable technological fate, but rather as the direct result of an imposition by an authority. Thus, "the way things are" becomes "the way things have been made to be." If the controls and restrictions become oppressive, unreasonable, impracticable, or unconstitutional, Internet users will know at whom to direct their accusations.

C. Why Settlement Is No Option

Why has the music industry apparently chosen to eliminate Napster completely? Why did it not use the leverage of the lawsuit and impending legal judgment against Napster to force a settlement that would have allowed the content industries to acquire file-sharing technologies and utilize them for their own gain?

Settlement would have tended to discredit the legitimacy of the music industry's claim of sovereign right. This air of illegitimacy could have taken two forms, both of which relate to the adequacy of the industry's claims against Napster. Settlement could have weakened the apparent strength of the music industry's claims, giving the appearance that Napster's defenses carried such weight and strength that the industry had to give in, rather than risk the embarrassment of a legal defeat. Also, failure to see the lawsuit through to a final judgment could have left open the important question of whether Napster's activity was definitively illegal or improper. The lack of a final resolution would have allowed those who believe file sharing to be a protected right akin to expression or association to persist in that belief. And those who view free online music to be an entitlement premised on the music industry's abuse of its copyrights would have been able to claim that Napster's demise was not the result of legal or moral culpability, but was merely the result of the music industry's formidable leverage and financial strength. Either way, any subsequent limitations on music downloads imposed by a deal between Napster and the music companies would have lacked the legitimacy the limitations will have if Napster is defeated and disabled.

Settlement not only would have legitimized Napster's defenses, it also would have made Napster appear in the eyes of some of its more idealistic supporters to be a traitor to its revolutionary founding principles. While settling with Napster would have ingrained even more deeply the idea that file sharing is a legitimate activity being unfairly suppressed by an evil and greedy music industry, it also would have undermined file sharers' loyalty to the Napster service. Thus, the settlement agreement would have been self-defeating from a business perspective as well. Robin Hood would lose the support of his followers if they learned he had replaced his rebellious ideals and activities with the title of "tax collector" and a paycheck from the king.

One plaintiff in the Napster lawsuit, Bertelsmann, reached a settlement agreement with the servicer. The response of Napster users was hardly optimistic or relieved. "Initially, Napster.com depicted itself as a challenger to the present system of intellectual copyright," one user wrote. "It was to be a community ... of free file sharing; akin to having several thousand people in your basement sharing and appreciating a diverse range of music." A settlement or licensing agreement with record companies merely would make Napster an extension of the corporate machinery that free information advocates rebel against. "It appears Napster.com was never about a `free' community committed to sharing but about putting Napster into `play' with the major record labels.... How else does Napster explain the secretive and relatively unexpected announcement of a `partnership' with BMG? ... [T]he revolution was always for sale."

Napster users easily could have become disenchanted with a service they viewed as having "sold them out." If Napster users envisioned themselves as fighting the status quo together with the creators of the Napster service, they would have felt betrayed if the service secretly stopped the rebellion by hopping into bed with the enemy. One user complained that Napster, by "having taken money from a large record label has sold us out.... Your storage space, internet connection, collection of MP3s has been handed over to a record label. They now talk of using our resources to sell MP3s to me and you. ... WE HAVE BEEN SOLD OUT."

Settlement also would not have prevented the departure of users from Napster to another, decentralized file-sharing service like Gnutella. Users who refuse to pay even a nominal fee are being lured by the cost-free nature of substitute services that offer the same file-sharing capabilities as Napster. Those who feel betrayed by Napster's "selling out" will prefer the even more decentralized (and thus more rebellious) systems. Within days of the settlement announcement with Bertelsmann, some Napster users began jumping ship.

Fans are turning to alternatives. "We'd been getting a few hundred new members each day, but that increased to several

246

thousand" Wednesday [the day after the Bertelsmann agreement was announced], says Gavin Hall, 20,co-founder of Napster clone Songspy.com. Online for a month, Songspy, with 30,000 members, vows to stick with a policy of free music. "We don't want to betray our users like Napster did," Hall says. "Charging dues is not in the spirit of sharing."

This exodus has continued, especially during Napster's recent self-imposed, and temporarily court-mandated, shut-down. "Other programs used to exchange music.... have emerged ... [not only] as users have become accustomed to obtaining music online but [also] as a vacuum was created by the demise of Napster...."

It is clear that merely eliminating Napster will not end the misconception of "free information" and the culture of entitlement that accompanies it completely. Some ardent rebels will seek new sources of free music, moving away from the servers of Napster to more elusive, decentralized systems like Gnutella. These services might pose an even greater threat to the content industries than did Napster, since the newest generation of file-swapping technologies is easier to use than ever. These new technologies are "becoming increasingly more difficult to police, possibly forcing record companies to sue individual users, a daunting, if not impossible task." It is possible that the display of power necessarily might extend beyond Napster and other Internet services to the users of those services themselves, perhaps by seeking criminal prosecution of the most egregious and flamboyant (and perhaps the proudest) advocates of file sharing. A prime target for such prosecution would be someone like the "law office manager in Tampa, Fla., and former Napster user who has moved to MusicCity.com," who has said that "he had downloaded more than 120 full albums in the last year from the Internet, first from Napster, then from MusicCity, and he said he had not bought a single album during that time."

The music industry cannot hope to counter the true threat to copyright on the Internet—the "spirit" of "sharing information"— without a visible and definite display of power, first against services like Napster, and perhaps later against the individuals who use them. Without some way to reform the ethic of "free information" and the sense of entitlement that accompanies it, technological advances meant to protect copyright in cyberspace will lack legitimacy and will be resisted perpetually. The music industry need not achieve support for its position. Internet users need not become ardent supporters of copyright law. But the "spirit of sharing" must be broken if copyright is to survive. The wild horse must be broken before it can be trusted alone in its stable.

CONCLUSION

The metaphysicality of the Internet allows people to shed the moral limitations and social stigmas that inhibit transgression of social norms in the real world. In most instances, this merely permits people to conduct themselves in the same way they would in the real world could they avoid detection. However, the formless freedom of the Internet, as well as its lack of physicality, results in an additional moral shift with respect to the infringement of copyrighted materials. The widespread, unauthorized, and free distribution of digital media on the Internet allows people to take advantage of their virtual invisibility by appropriating music with great ease, minimal (if any) social stigma, and very little chance of detection. The structure of the Internet also confuses them into thinking that they are entitled to the things they steal. Free-flowing, non-restrictive "sharing" technologies like Napster have been developed, effectively cutting the lock to the candy store door. Unfortunately, the children who have been stealing candy feel they have a right to complain when the store owner contemplates buying a new security system.

This situation represents a revolutionary departure from the moral and legal restrictions of the real world. The proper response (from the perspective of the music and other content industries) is a show of sovereign power, which quiets what is in effect a revolt from the "prison" of ordered, real-world society. By vigorously pursuing its suits against Napster and other similar file-sharing services, the music industry can make that show of power.

Through this public display, the music industries can momentarily centralize and visualize the power structures that will guide the future of the Internet. This moment will be followed by a quiet retreat into silent observation, where the centralized power exerted on the Internet by the content industries can diffuse into an architectural power incorporated into the very architecture of the Internet, which will exercise control from within. The moment of visualization is necessary to make the subsequent architectural power structures more legitimate and effective. By urging the music industry to seek complete victory over Napster, I do not mean to endorse completely the industry's claims or the likely results that would follow from their legal success against Napster and other file-sharing services. I intend merely to suggest that making the display of power over Napster public and complete will be the most legitimate, efficient, and successful means by which the industry can establish a true system of copyright enforcement in cyberspace.

248

Those who support Napster and the relaxation of copyright laws to permit music "sharing" on the Internet should not necessarily decry my call for a display of authority. If the music industry takes a public and visible approach to asserting its claimed property rights, it necessarily will make itself accountable for its actions. The music industry also will expose itself to criticism for the approach it takes and for the institutional and architectural changes it imposes on the Internet. The music industry will not be able to shirk responsibility for the imposition of architectural controls that most certainly will come to encapsulate digitized copyrighted materials. "The way things are" will not be considered the result of happenstance or an accident of history, but rather will be the direct consequence of an affirmative, public action taken by an identifiable sovereign. The king, before dissolving into the secret mechanisms of power, must stand triumphantly over the broken body of the defeated rebel. But in doing so, he lets potential assassins know precisely where to take aim.

Footnotes deleted.

6

Combating Cybercrime

17

Countering the Cyber-crime Threat

Debra Wong Yang and Brian M. Hoffstadt

I n these early years of the 21st century, we continue to live in the
Information Age—an age when our economy's greatest assets
are not steel and coal, but ideas and their practical applications.
We have been able to exploit this intellectual capital more effectively
in large part due to the widespread use of computers, which has
enabled businesses to manipulate their intellectual property with
greater ease and to buy and sell physical products with greater
efficiency over the Internet. Our economy's reliance on computers
has created a concomitant vulnerability, however. A person seeking
to harm a business in this day and age does not aim his attacks at the
company's physical assets; instead, he takes aim at its computers.

Not surprisingly, criminal and other harmful acts aimed at
computers—so-called "cyber-crimes"—are on the rise. Recent
surveys indicate that anywhere from 25% to 50% of American
businesses have detected some sort of security breach in their
computer networks in the past year. The losses caused by these
breaches are more pernicious and far reaching than one might
initially think. The damage caused by a single computer intrusion
typically entails more than the cost of repairing the compromised
data or system, as news of the intrusion may adversely affect the
company's "market capitalization or consumer confidence." This is
one of the reasons why companies routinely fail to report cyber
intrusions, including to the authorities. Despite the absence of precise
data, however, most observers agree that "computer crime causes
enormous damage to the United States economy."

D. Wong-Yang and B.M. Hoffstadt, Countering the cyber crime threat. *American
Criminal Law Review* 43 (2): 201-216, Spring 2006. Reprinted by permission of the
authors.

252

The prevalence and increasing prominence of cyber-crime has not escaped the notice of the President or the Congress. In 2003, the White House released its National Strategy to Secure Cyberspace. In 2004, the United States Department of Justice Task Force on Intellectual Property issued its Report, and detailed the Justice Department's roadmap for combating crimes involving trade secrets and other intellectual property often stolen or distributed over computer networks, the "increasing threat of malicious attacks" through computer intrusions. Congress also enacted the Family Entertainment and Copyright Act of 2005, which made it a felony to use a computer to upload previously unreleased movies, games and software onto the Internet.

The Federal Bureau of Investigation has made cyber-crime a top priority. More recently, the House of Representatives passed a resolution acknowledging Among other bills, Congress is currently considering legislation that would make it a crime to use a computer to obtain personal information (such as names, social security numbers or credit card information) and legislation that would make it a crime to place software on a computer with the intent to use that computer to commit further crimes.

Despite this much-needed attention, however, and as we discuss in Part I of this Essay, the threat of cyber-crime is still likely to grow in the coming years because of two factors. First, we are seeing an increase in the number of American businesses that are potential victims of cyber-crime. Second, we are beginning to see an upsurge in the number of potential perpetrators. A brief sampling of the cyber-crimes the Justice Department is currently prosecuting demonstrates that this threat is real.

At this time, the debate about how to address this growing threat is still in its infancy. No consensus has yet emerged. Although, as noted above, the federal government has increased its efforts to combat cyber-crime, market forces have remained the primary impetus for sorting out where the burdens and costs of cyber-crime fall. Thus far, they have fallen largely on the victims of cyber-crime—that is, American businesses—which have been forced to absorb the burden of preventing cyber-crime and any subsequent losses stemming from their failure to do so. It is yet to be seen whether this current arrangement is the best for our economy. Fortunately, this arrangement is not permanent. It is now—at this early stage in the debate—when we should ask the twin questions: Where should the onus of fighting cyber-crime and absorbing its costs lie, and what role should the various players play in this calculus?

In this Essay, we address these two questions and, in so doing, examine the possibilities of leaving the burdens of cybercrime on victim companies, of placing it upon the software and hardware manufacturers, of expanding the role of governmental regulation, and of a combination of all three options. We also propose the considerations that policymakers should examine in choosing among these options. In the end, we postulate that the ultimate response to cyber-crime is likely to be a three-way synergy of all these options.

I. THE GROWING CYBER-CRIME THREAT

In the coming years, two demographic trends are likely to increase the potential number of cyber-crimes perpetrated against American businesses. First, there is likely to be a greater proliferation in the number and types of businesses that will be potential victims of cyber-crimes. Until the past few years, cyber-criminals typically targeted one of three types of businesses: information brokers, manufacturers and distributors of digital media, and businesses who offered products or services for sale over the Internet. Information brokers, such as credit reporting agencies and data aggregators like ChoicePoint or LexisNexis, are ripe targets for cyber-crime because their databases contain information that provides a treasure trove for identity thieves. Indeed, several states have already acknowledged the prevalence of this more traditional form of cyber-crime by statutorily requiring these database aggregators to report the compromise of information to potential individual victims. The manufacturers and distributors of digital media—most notably, the motion picture, recording, and software industries—have also long been the victims of cyber-crime, typically through the illegal copying and online distribution of their copyrighted content. Each of these industries has resorted to civil lawsuits against downloaders, uploaders, and those who facilitate the distribution and to lobbying Congress for more stringent criminal copyright laws to stave off the billions of dollars in losses attributed to digital piracy every year. The final category of more traditional targets of cyber-crime are businesses who offer their wares for sale over the Internet, and more particularly, on the World Wide Web, where their websites can be defaced or "knocked offline" by a flood of malicious Internet traffic.
    Cyber-crime is no longer confined to targets in these industries, however. No matter what its core product or service, nearly every business in today's economy relies upon computers and computer networks to conduct its daily affairs. It is likely that many of a company's assets—including its trade secrets—are archived on these computer systems. If the company's computer network is

254

accessible to the Internet (or, for that matter, to disgruntled or enterprising but disloyal employees), those assets are subject to cyber-theft. Similarly, companies often store their customers' names, contact information, and payment information in order to facilitate electronic transactions (so-called "e-commerce"). This data is also likely to be stored electronically and, as such, is likely vulnerable to theft or destruction. As a consequence, as the trend toward increased reliance on computers continues, nearly every business will become a potential target of cyber-criminals.

The second reason why the threat of cyber-crime may loom larger in the coming years is that the number of persons capable of committing or directing others to commit these crimes is likely to increase. Traditionally, the universe of cybercriminals has been limited to persons with the technical knowledge—mastery of computer languages, computer programming, or network architecture—capable of orchestrating what are technically complex crimes. That universe is expanding along two axes. On one axis, the number of technically savvy individuals capable of committing cyber-crimes continues to grow as computers are integrated into our business culture and personal lives. On the other axis, we are beginning to see "enablers"—persons who use their technical expertise to create and then sell to others easy-to-use tools that make it possible for non-technically savvy people to engage in cyber-crime. This secondary market in "cyber-crime tools" is just beginning to emerge.

The threat of cyber-crime is not an idle one, as the Justice Department's recent experience in prosecuting cyber criminals demonstrates. As anticipated, the victims of cyber-crimes are increasingly diverse—ranging from manufacturers of computer network products to companies that research floods to online search engine companies. This is largely because company insiders familiar with the company's computer networks and the intellectual property assets stored within them are the perpetrators. Employees and former employees of victim—businesses have launched malicious and harmful computer programs on their employer's systems (a so-called "employee hack back"), have stolen the company's trade secrets, or have engaged in extortionate acts by holding the company's network hostage. Although cyber-crime attacks from skilled outsiders continue to plague American businesses, this past year the Department prosecuted the first-ever cyber-criminal who infected thousands of computers with a malicious computer program, effectively turned the infected computers into "zombie" computers capable of responding to any commands, and then sold that "army" of "zombie" computers—which could be used to attack and harm the computer systems of others—to the highest bidder. Thus, the secondary market in cyber-crime tools is just beginning to surface.

As this informal survey indicates, cyber-criminals have already proven themselves to be resourceful and innovative as they have continued to invent and perpetrate new and ever-evolving forms of attacks aimed at computers and the data they contain. Consequently, it is advisable as a policy matter to contemplate-sooner rather than later—how best to allocate the burdens of fighting malicious conduct aimed at computers and how best to distribute the losses associated with such conduct.

II. ALLOCATING THE BURDENS AND COSTS OF CYBER-CRIME

Because cyber-crime is unlikely to disappear and will likely continue to inflict substantial losses upon the American economy, it is important to consider who should be responsible for protecting American industry against cyber-attacks and, when they nevertheless occur, who should bear the losses associated with such attacks. Because this burden can, in a very general sense, be allocated among three different groups—the American businesses who are victimized by cyber-attacks, the American businesses who manufacture the computer hardware and software aimed at resisting such attacks, and the government—it is also critical to ask what role government should play in fighting and addressing how losses from cyber-attacks should be allocated. In this Part, we briefly consider the policy outcomes of placing the onus of fighting cyber-attacks on each of these three groups independently.

A. Placing the Burden upon Victim-Businesses

In this first scenario, the American companies who may be victimized by cyber-attacks would be responsible for protecting themselves from such attacks and for suffering the consequences if their efforts are not entirely successful. The consequences of inadequate computer security would likely be two-fold in this situation. First, a victim-company would be forced to absorb the losses attributable to any computer intrusion or loss of intellectual property, thereby cutting into its net profitability. As noted above, this cost is likely to go beyond the simple cost of replacing any lost data and re-securing its systems; the losses would ostensibly have a ripple effect that might entail lost opportunities for capitalization and loss of consumer confidence in the company and its computer security. Second, the company might incur additional monetary losses if it is sued civilly for failing to secure its intellectual property and computer systems. We are already seeing such lawsuits, and law professors and other legal commentators do not all oppose the expansion of the civil law into this realm. Such lawsuits generally seek relief under one of two theories: a tort theory involving the breach of a duty of care to maintain a secure network; or a breach of fiduciary duty to keep data secure. This type of legal liability is arguably aided by the notification laws that require victim-companies to notify potential plaintiffs of the company's failure to adequately secure the individual plaintiffs' information in the company's database.

The twin consequences of direct losses and exposure to third-party lawsuits would ostensibly spur businesses who run the risk of being potential victims of cyber-attacks into taking efforts to protect against these outcomes. Because the most certain way to avoid consequential losses associated with a cyber-attack is to prevent the attack in the first place, a system that places the burdens of protecting against cyber-attacks squarely on the victim-businesses would likely result in businesses allocating more resources toward securing their networks: purchasing anti-virus software, installing firewalls around their networks, running computer programs that monitor and log computer usage, limiting remote access to the companies' networks, encrypting data stored on the computer network, and educating employees about the importance of changing passwords and vigilant computer security. Additionally, some insurance companies are now offering "hacker insurance" that shifts the losses associated with computer intrusions onto insurance companies; at this time, however, only about 25% of businesses rely on such insurance and opt instead to rely solely on "self-insurance"—that is, taking steps to prevent intrusions in the first place. Victim-companies also have some limited statutory redress against the cyber-attacker, although remedy by way of lawsuit is largely illusory unless the hacker can be positively identified (which is not always easy to do over cyberspace) and is also not "judgment proof." All of these potential avenues of redress, however, presuppose that the victim company has sufficient assets to devote to network security or obtaining indemnification via insurance or litigation for any attacks; businesses that do not would be forced to run the risk of an attack that could potentially cripple it entirely. As this Essay suggests, this scenario is largely the one that has emerged by default and remains in operation today.

B. Placing the Burden upon Hardware and Software Manufacturers

Were the burden of preventing cyber-crime placed upon the manufacturers of computer hardware and software, that particular subset of American industry would be held accountable for flaws in their products later exploited by cyber-criminals and other attackers who subsequently inflict damage upon victim-businesses using that hardware or software. This is not the law today. Currently, hardware and software manufacturers and distributors typically insulate themselves from liability under contract theories by conditioning use of a product upon acceptance of a licensing agreement that absolves them of most forms of liability for any design or application defects that may result in future vulnerabilities in users' computer systems. Hardware and software users are left to wait for software "patches" that eliminate subsequently discovered product vulnerabilities, with little or no recourse for damage or losses incurred in the interim.

A policy regime that held software and hardware manufacturers liable for a subclass of defects in the design of their products would significantly alter the current allocation of the burdens of cyber-crime. Adhesion contracts negating liability would no longer be enforceable. Courts would entertain lawsuits based on tort theories, as some commentators are currently advocating that they should. Arguably, this new liability would prompt most manufacturers to replace the current pattern of "release now and patch later" with a system that favored more extensive "Beta testing" prior to a product's release to guard against vulnerabilities. To be sure, this type of system would likely mean that new products would be released less frequently. But this delay may be ameliorated if some relief from liability were granted for products that complied with published standards for computer security.

C. Placing the Burden upon Government

Under this policy, the government would further expand its current role in regulating cyber-security and prosecuting cyber-criminals. Presently, Congress has taken a measured and conservative approach to federal involvement using the civil laws. Congress has tasked federal agencies with developing security guidelines for certain records stored in computerized databases, but only with respect to the discrete areas of medical records and records maintained by financial institutions. The Federal Trade Commission ("FTC") is also empowered to investigate and seek civil redress against certain types of unlawful activity occurring over the Internet and computer systems. Additionally, and as noted above, Congress has opened the federal courts and empowered certain victims of cyber-crimes to bring civil lawsuits against the perpetrators of cyber-crime.

The government's involvement in criminal prosecution of cyber-crime has also been steadily increasing. Over the past few decades, Congress has engaged in a pattern of expanding the ambit of federal criminal jurisdiction over cyber-crimes, thereby granting prosecutors the tools to investigate and prosecute such acts. The Computer Fraud and Abuse Act creates several federal felonies involving unauthorized access or exceeding authorized access to "protected computers"—that is, computers "used in interstate or foreign commerce or communication." Currently, the broadest basis for federal jurisdiction—that the victim company suffered a "loss" of at least $5,000 within a one-year period—has on occasion stymied the government's ability to bring cases and, more troubling, to obtain convictions of cyber-criminals who readily admit that they otherwise committed the crimes of computer intrusion contained in the Act. Similarly, the Electronic Espionage Act of 1996 makes it a crime, among other things, to "download," "upload," or otherwise "transmit" or "convey" trade secrets. Title III of the Omnibus Crime Control Act of 1968 criminalizes the act of intercepting electronic mail messages ("e-mail") and potentially use of a "keystroke logger" to capture data entered into a computer. The CAN-SPAM Act makes it a crime to send more than a threshold number of unsolicited, commercial e-mail in a given period of time. The Justice Department has taken these new tools and made cyber-crime a priority. Since 1990, the Department has established units comprised of specialized federal prosecutors trained in the law and technology necessary to bring cyber-criminals to justice in 18 different United States Attorney's Office scattered throughout the country, as well as creating a specialized unit at Main Justice tasked with coordinating multi-jurisdictional investigations and advising the Department on policy matters relevant to cyber-crime. In a similar vein, the two most recent Attorneys General have made protection of intellectual property a top priority, including those crimes committed using computers. Additionally, the number of federal prosecutions of cyber-criminals continues to increase.

Despite this greater involvement, the government cannot carry the full responsibility of addressing the cyber-crime threat. Requiring more and more businesses to comply with civil regulations may help guard against further intrusions within the regulated industries, but the costs of monitoring and enforcing compliance may be too great a burden to impose on the subset of regulated businesses and may thus be passed along as an assimilated cost to all businesses. Civil enforcement actions against cyber-crime perpetrators, like all civil actions, is only useful if the defendant can be identified and is not judgment proof or, with respect to injunctions, recalcitrant. Likewise, criminal prosecutions are limited by the willingness of victim-businesses to report an incident, to cooperate with investigations, and, if necessary, to testify at trial or sentencing. Prosecutions are also fundamentally constrained by the reach of jurisdictional statutes and by the need to prioritize the use of finite prosecutorial resources also tasked with investigating complex organized crime syndicates and fraud schemes, counter-terrorist threats, narcotics trafficking, and a panoply of other criminal offenses.

In this Part, we have attempted only to provide a brief sketch of how the legal and economic landscape might look depending on who is tasked with the burdens of fighting and absorbing the losses from cyber-crime. We next provide a few thoughts on how to evaluate which incentive structure should be adopted.

III. CRITERIA FOR EVALUATING CYBER-CRIME POLICY

Thus far, we have highlighted two trends that are likely to result in a continued and arguably greater threat from cyber-crime in the coming years, and have outlined three possible options for where policymakers might place the burdens of addressing that mounting threat—on the businesses who are potential victims of cyber-crime, on the manufactures of software and hardware relied upon by business to protect against cyber-crime, and on government institutions. A comprehensive analysis of which of these three options, or which combination thereof, is most optimal as a matter of public policy is beyond the scope of this Essay. It may nevertheless be useful to consider how policymakers should evaluate the various policy options by suggesting the criteria upon which such evaluations should be based.

The first and perhaps most directly relevant consideration is whether the policy to be adopted will be effective in stemming the tide of cyber-crime. In this instance, effectiveness refers both to the policy's ability to deter cyber-crime in the first place and, relatedly, to its ability to minimize the losses to the American economy as a consequence of undeterred cyber-crime.

Take, for example, the third option outlined above, which relies upon the government—including prosecutors—to carry a larger burden in fighting cyber-crime. In examining the efficacy of this option, policymakers should consider several factors, including both its deterrence-inducing and loss-avoiding aspects. With respect to deterrence, it is important to ask several questions. First, are there any "gaps" in the criminal statutes that fail to reach conduct that should be criminal? For instance, the Criminal Fraud and Abuse Act, as noted above, contains a $5,000 threshold loss requirement. Given the absence of such a requirement in many other federal criminal statutes and the contentiousness of this element in cases in which the criminally culpable conduct itself is conceded, policymakers could increase the deterrent effect of the criminal law by eliminating this requirement and thereby closing the "gap" it inadvertently created. Second, is the risk of non-detection sufficiently high that cyber-criminals do not fear being identified and prosecuted? Many activities conducted over the Internet are logged and, as such, may be later tied to a physical location; however, new technologies are emerging that enable Internet users to surf anonymously and to confound efforts at re-constructing the trail of cyber-criminals—even when law enforcement has obtained proper legal process. In addressing these new technologies, policymakers need to balance any First Amendment advantages of this "perfect anonymity" with the need for law enforcement to effectively identify and prosecute cyber-criminals. Third, are the consequences of prosecution and conviction, including the stigma of conviction and any possible sentence, sufficiently stringent to deter cyber-criminals? Fourth, to the extent such data exists, do empirical studies indicate that the existence of these criminal laws and their use by prosecutors actually deter cyber-criminals? With respect to the loss avoidance, policymakers should ask whether criminals are required by statute to pay restitution to victims of their crimes and, as a practical matter, whether the restitution actually paid offsets the losses sustained as a result of the criminal conduct.

Aside from the effectiveness of a particular option, a second factor policymakers should consider is whether the sector of the society burdened by the option has the resources to carry that burden. If, for example, policymakers seek to place a greater responsibility upon the manufacturers of software and hardware to better ensure that their product is not vulnerable to cyber-attacks, it would be important to assess whether those manufacturers have the wherewithal to undertake this burden—either by passing along the additional cost to their customers or through protection from liability should their products comply with published cyber-security standards. Similarly, policymakers contemplating a greater role for governmental rule-making and prosecution would need to address whether there are sufficient regulators and prosecutors to handle any additional duties placed upon them.

A third consideration is whether the adopted policy is consistent with the general population's views about cyber-crime, or whether any gap between the policy and public opinion is likely to be reduced by the new policy. If, for example, the public views certain types of cyber-crimes (such as defacing a company's website) as little more than cyber-vandalism and therefore as harmless, policymakers will need to consider whether efforts to prosecute more such cases will result in verdicts of acquittal based on jury nullification. Policymakers need to be mindful that members of the public, and the businesses that they operate, will need to be supportive of any new policy. Although societal norms can be shaped by legislative action, the gap between the current norms and desire norms should not be too great.

A fourth, and closely related, factor is whether there exists the "political will" to enact and enforce whatever new policy is deemed the most advantageous in light of the three broad policy criteria set forth above. No matter how theoretically sound a policy might be, if it is not feasible politically, it is of little value.

IV. CONCLUSION

Despite the unique technologies that make the Internet and the Information Age a reality, policymakers do not write on a blank slate. Crime is a persistent problem, and policymakers have fashioned policies to combat it and reduce its costs to society for centuries. It may accordingly be helpful to look to non-cyber analogies in determining the proper ingredients to be combined together in a thoughtful policy against cyber-crime.

For example, policymakers could look to public policy regarding fire damage as a possible analogy. As with cyber-crimes, businesses can be victimized by fires—both inadvertent and intentional—and can suffer losses as a result. Moreover, fire is similar to Internet viruses and other malicious software insofar as neither is easily contained and may spread from one location to another unless halted. Right now, the burden of preventing fires and reducing the business losses attributable to fire does not rest solely on the potential victims of fire damage. Instead, it is divided among the business owners who are responsible for taking actions to minimize the risk of fire (and the insurers who insist upon such measures before insuring against fire damage); the manufacturers of smoke detectors, fire extinguishers, and alarms designed to alert the authorities; and governmental fire marshals who conduct regular inspections and prosecutors who investigate and prosecute arsonists. Policymakers might consider how a sharing of burdens in a similar fashion would translate into the realm of protecting against cyber-crime.

We believe that the optimal policy solution to combating the ballooning cyber-crime trend is likely to involve a collaborative effort of American business, software and hardware manufacturers, and government. Government involvement is essential to coordinate and assist with the international aspects of cyber-crime, to facilitate standardized security protocols and unfair practices over the Internet, and to prosecute persons who commit the acts legislatures deem harmful enough to make criminal. Private industry would likely share the remaining burden-divided, as policymakers see fit, between the software and hardware industries who are in a centralized position to improve the effectiveness of products aimed at security, and the potential victim-businesses who are able to monitor and update those products and train and monitor their employees regarding cyber-security.

Whatever balance is ultimately struck will depend in large part upon the input of industry representatives, large and small businesses, computer experts, government regulators, prosecutors and defense lawyers, and members of the general public. As the cyber-crime threat continues to grow, so too will the impetus and need for further policymaking. Participating in this debate sooner rather than later will enable policymakers to reach the optimal result and, one can hope, ensure the vitality of the American and world economies in the face of cyber-crime.

Footnotes deleted.

18

Ten Tips to Combat Cybercrime

James F. Leon

Despite the increased efforts to strengthen Internet security in recent years, cybercrime has jumped enormously, as shown in the annual 2007 cybercrime survey conducted by the Computer Security Institute (www.goesicom/press/20070913.jhtml). According to the survey, the average loss per cybercrime in 2007 for U.S. companies escalated to $350,000 from $168,000 the previous year.

Data breaches, credit card fraud, fraudulent websites, eavesdropping, and identity theft all fall under the umbrella term cybercrime. To execute these crimes, hackers and con artists use tools such as fraudulent e-mails, network sniffers, Internet cookies, scripting languages, software vulnerabilities, and wireless networks. Below are 10 practical tips that accountants can implement to minimize security threats, plus detailed explanations of several tools that computer criminals commonly use.

J.F. Leon, Ten tips to combat cybercrime. *The CPA Journal* 78 (5): 6-11, May 2008. Reprinted with permission from the New York State Society of Certified Public Accountants.

1. IDENTIFY SUSPICIOUS EMAILS

E-mails often come from a different source than the company or entity they appear to be sent from. Although the sender of an e-mail may appear trustworthy, recipients should be aware that the sender's name in the header can be construed (spoofed) by a con artist. Individuals should also note to whom the e-mail is addressed in the first line of text. Con artists often send fraudulent e-mails stating, "Dear Customer," "Dear Patron," or "Dear Member," because they do not know the recipient's name. An e-mail with an individual's correct name in the first line of text can still be a hoax. Names can easily be acquired through many sources, including compromised company databases that contain personal information.

Fraudulent e-mails tend to have catchy openings intended to play on the recipient's propensity for fear or greed. An e-mail eliciting fear may claim that an individual's personal information has already been compromised, such as an account number, credit rating, or stolen password. An e-mail enticing greed may claim, "You have won the contest" or "You are entitled to a large tax refund." In all cases, fraudulent e-mails will require the recipient to click on a link.

Exhibit 1 shows an example of a fraudulent e-mail allegedly from the IRS. The hacker wants the individual to follow the "click here" link, but hovering the mouse over the link exposes a spoofed website:, www.criticalsecret.org/abcd.html. Navigating to this site gives the hackers access to the recipient's computer, making it vulnerable to attacks. Hackers are also increasingly sending pictures, banners, and other graphic forms in fraudulent e-mails, asking potential victims to click on these graphics (see section 2.2.2 in www.ngssoftware.com/papers/NISR -WP-Phishing.pdf).

EXHIBIT 1

Fraudulent Email

After the last annual calculations of your fiscal activity, we have determined that you are eligible to receive a tax refund of $709.30. Please submit the tax refund request and allow us 6-9 days in order to process it.

A refund can be delayed for a variety of reasons. For example, submitting invalid records or applying after the deadline.

To access the form for your tax refund, please click here

[Dangerous link to] http://www.criticalsecret.org/abcd.html

Regards,
Internal Revenue Service

2. Create a Link Homepage

In addition to avoiding links in potentially fraudulent e-mails, individuals should not follow links in foreign webpages (third-party URLs that can possibly be deemed untrust worthy). A tip is to create a "link home-page", which is an HTML page that lists the links of one's favorite sites.

A link homepage is an actual page on the Internet created through one's Internet service provider (ISP) that can be accessed from any computer in the world. For example, if Jane Doe's ISP is Comcast, she could set up a hypothetical page with Comcast named www.comcast.net/jane-doelink.html. Exhibit 2 shows an example of Jane Doe's sample link homepage at Comcast. The link homepage has a list of the correct URLs of Jane's most commonly visited sites and is deemed trust-worthy because Jane herself typed in the trusted links when she created her page. All she has to do is remember the URL of her link homepage at any computer in the world with Internet access. Using a link homepage will significantly reduce the possibility of clicking a harmful link, and Jane will be able to visit her favorite websites from any computer in the world within seconds.

EXHIBIT 2

Sample Link Homepage

JANE DOE LINK HOMEPAGE

http y/www. cpajournal,com

httpy/www. aicpa.org

http://www.irs.gov

http://www.fdic.gov

http://www.fdic.gov/regulations/laws /rules

The link homepage should not be confused with a person's "favorites" list that is bookmarked in a web browser. Bookmarks can be accessed only from the computer on which they were saved, whereas a link homepage can be accessed from any computer with an Internet connection. A user's bookmarks are the ideal links to be copied over to a link homepage, assuming the links are trustworthy.

3. ENCRYPT AND DIGITALLY SIGN EMAIL WITH CLIENTS

Unencrypted e-mail sent to clients can be easily viewed (sniffed) by a hacker along the path of communication between the sender and recipient. The most obvious party sniffing one's e-mails could be the ISP, which can handle upwards of thousands of e-mails per day (see www.computer.howstuffworks.com/carnivore2.html). Most ISPs will eventually archive all e-mail they handle, and even deleted e-mail can still be accessed by the ISP later in time.

To address these concerns, all confidential e-mail should be encrypted with an e-mail encryption program. In a typical encryption system between a CPA and a client, each party will have a public and a private key, used to encrypt messages. To send an encrypted e-mail to a client, the CPA will encrypt the message with the client's public key. The client will decrypt the e-mail with her private key to read the message. To reply back to the CPA with an encrypted e-mail, the client will encrypt the message with the CPA's public key; the CAP will subsequently decrypt the client's e-mail with his private key. As long as private keys are not lost or stolen, it is virtually impossible for a network sniffer to decrypt the message.

Most e-mail encryption programs also allow the use of digital signatures, the electronic equivalent of a CPA's written signature. It is legal proof that an e-mail sent from a CPA to a client is indeed authentic and not fraudulent.

Several vendors specialize in the use of encrypted e-mail and digital signatures, either free or for a fee. Companies specializing in e-mail security include Pretty Good Privacy (www.pgp.com), Zixcorp (www.zixcorp.com), Hushmail (www.hushmail.com), Encryptomafic (www.encryptomatic.com), Tryten (www.tryten.com), and CryptoMail (www.cryptomail.org).

4. DISALLOW PERMANENT COOKIES IN WEB BROWSERS

A cookie is a small text file from a website that is saved on a user's computer during interaction with that website. A cookie can contain nonsensitive information, such as a user's favorite actor, at a movie database, or favorite author, at a bookseller's website. A cookie can contain sensitive information as well, such as a user's password to a site, credit card number, or account number.

There are two types of cookies: session or permanent. Session cookies are temporarily stored on a computer and present limited risks. Permanent cookies are text files that are stored long-term on a computer and can persist for up to several years. Hackers try to steal permanent cookies through a variety of methods, hoping the permanent cookies contain user's confidential information. Users should enable the option on their web browsers to block permanent cookies, eliminating the risks they pose.

5. DISABLE SCRIPTS IN WEB BROWSERS

By clicking links on the Internet, users receive pages of hypertext markup language (HTML). The HTML may contain a small program called a script. The script is written in a scripting language, which then executes on one's computer. Like cookies, some scripts pose no threat to a user's computer. Many scripts, however, come from hackers and are malicious. These malicious scripts can steal data (cookies) and even change the operating system's settings. Users should disable scripts on their browsers, rendering them unable to execute. To disable scripts, go to the security preferences in a browser and "check" the disabling of scripts. An article (with screenshots) explaining the steps involved in blocking cookies and scripts can be found at www.aicpa.org/pubs/jofa/apr2007/leon.htm.

6. UNDERSTAND SOFTWARE VULNERABILITIES

Many software programs can unknowingly lead to security vulnerabilities. An example is the Google desktop search bar often installed for convenience. Users may not realize that when certain options are enabled in the Google desktop, documents opened on their computer are automatically sent to Google servers. A highly confidential file may unknowingly be sent to a Google server.

Users must be aware of the vulnerabilities that installed software may contain. A suggested site to learn more about common software vulnerabilities is Carnegie Mellon's Center for Internet

Security (CERT, www.uscert.gov/cas/techalerts). This site is updated daily with software vulnerabilities that have been found.

Another valuable site for software vulnerabilities is the System Administration, Audit, Network, Security Institute (SANS). This institute is highly respected for its vast resources on security topics, shared through training, conferences, and research. SANS maintains a yearly list of software vulnerabilities called the "SANS Top 20 Security Risks" (see www.sans.org/top20), as well as a reading room of papers written on software vulnerabilities (see www.sans.org/reading_room/).

As a security precaution, users should be vigilant in updating their software. Older versions of Microsoft products, such as Internet Explorer, Outlook E-mail, MS Office, SQL Server, and IIS Web Server, have many known vulnerabilities that can be easily exploited.

7. INSTALL A FIREWALL

All communications performed over the Internet involve exchanging packets with other computers. These packets may contain e-mail messages, instant messenger chats, or HTML pages. Unfortunately, packets can contain harmful software or malware sent from a hacker. A firewall is a mechanism that screens and filters packets sent to a computer and exists as either a software or hardware firewall. Exhibit 3 shows the difference between a software firewall and a hardware firewall.

A software firewall (sometimes referred to as a personal firewall) is a packet screening program that is installed on a computer. Some operating systems (such as Windows) have built-in software firewalls but could benefit from the installation of additional software firewalls, such as the Norton firewall (www.symantec.com). In a software firewall, the packet sent to a computer is filtered upon entry into the computer. The drawback is that the software firewall must be individually installed on each computer, which could pose a problem for an office with multiple computers.

A hardware firewall (sometimes referred to as an enterprise firewall) is a separate physical device, that performs packet screening before the packet reaches a personal computer. The Juniper Netscreen-204 from Juniper Networks (www.juniper.net/products_and_services/firewall_slash_ipsec_vpn/netscreen_204_slash_netscreen_208/) is an example of a hardware firewall. The hardware firewall device is connected to the computer and filters malicious packets, based on specific screening criteria. Sample criteria that can be screened by a firewall include the sender of a packet or the contents inside the packet.

A packet that is deemed unauthorized or dangerous to a computer is discarded (dropped) and never physically received inside the computer. Although hardware firewalls tend to be more expensive than software firewalls, one of them can protect a whole network of computers.

8. CONDUCT FINANCIAL TRANSACTIONS AT SECURE WEBSITES ONLY

A secure website is one that has received a certificate of authentication from a certificate authority (CA). Businesses set up secure websites to assure their customers that the site is not fraudulent. CA companies such as Verisign, Ensure, and Thawte are designed to set up such certificates for businesses. A company can acquire different levels of certification and assurance with its certificate from a CA, as can be seen on Thawte's website (www.thawte .com/comparison/comparison.html).

The CA is the trusted third party that will vouch for the identity of a secure website. The business entity must prove its legitimacy to the CA during its registration process. Once the business proves its identity, the CA establishes the domain name (URL) that will be used for the secure website.

Users should look for two indicators when browsing a secure site. The first is a "lock" image displayed on the webpage. Exhibit 4 shows the lock in the URL area. The second item, also shown in the exhibit, is that "https" will begin the URL instead of the typical "http." To inspect the site's certificate, users can click on the lock and the certificate will appear (see Exhibit 5).

A benefit of a secure website is that all Internet transactions will be encrypted using secure socket layer protocal (SSL), which is created by Netscape. An unsecured website poses the risk of being spoofed, or of a hacker sniffing the financial transaction (because communication will not be encrypted).

9. SECURE WIRELESS NETWORKS

In addition to having secure login passwords, wireless networks should also be encrypted. Wired encryption privacy (WEP), used for security in wireless networks, is not a secure protocol because it can be easily hacked. In choosing a wireless encryption protocal because it can be easily hacked. In chossing a wireless encryption protocol on a wireless router, users should opt for Wi-fi protected access (WPA), either WPAI or WPA2.

Most wireless access points have an option to hide the service set identifier (SSID) broadcast stream from the wireless router or access point. When this option is turned on, hackers attempting to access wireless networks will be unable to see the hidden SSID access point in the list of wireless networks that are broadcasting.The broadcast is still occuring, but hackers will need more sophisticated equipment and knowledge to gain entry on the wireless network.

10. INSTALL PASSWORD MANAGEMENT SOFTWARE

Password management software programs securely manage all website and network passwords by making them randomized and encrypted. These programs also securely maintain all passwords internally so users no longer have to write down or recall their passwords to the websites they frequent. Using password management products drastically minimizes password theft. Vendors specializing in password management products include Password Safe (passwordsafe sourceforge.net/), AES Software (www.aespasswordmanager.com), and RoboForm (www.roboform.com).

STAY ON THE DEFENSIVE

An accountant should be aware of cyber crime and the tools of cybercriminals. When using the Internet to conduct business, it is best to be defensive. By taking some or all of the appropriate action presented above, accountants can minimize potential disasters and stay one step ahead of cybercriminals.

19

Watching the Web

Thoughts on Expanding Police Surveillance Opportunities under the Cyber-crime Convention

Laura Huey and Richard S. Rosenberg

O n 23 November 2001, the Council of Europe and non-member states Canada, Japan, South Africa, and the United States signed the Convention on Cybercrime (CC), an agreement that requires participating nations to enact legislation that facilitates investigation and prosecution of crimes committed through the Internet. Among the measures mandated is legislation that grants new powers of search and seizure to law enforcement authorities, including the power to compel Internet service providers (ISPs) to provide intercept technology to ensure "lawful access" to data transmissions, to provide assistance to police in the storage and search of data traffic generated by an investigation target, and to release to police general information (i.e., names and addresses) regarding a service's customers.

Laura Huey and Richard S. Rosenberg, Watching the web: Thoughts on expanding police surveillance opportunities under the cyber-crime convention. *Canadian Journal of Criminology and Criminal Justice* 46 (5): 597-607, 2004. Reprinted by permission of University of Toronto Press Incorporated. Article available at www.http://www.ccja-acjp.ca/.

The CC places obligations upon ISPs that, in effect, convert service providers into integral cogs in the apparatus of online law enforcement. We see this as part of a larger trend in the field of policing as a whole. Western states have begun to recognize the limitations of public police services in effecting crime control in various areas, including the field of telecommunications. To this end, law enforcement and other state agencies have been extending the reach of the state by establishing "policing" networks with elements of the private sector (from local community watch programs to private security companies and insurance agencies) that have the tools and capacity to achieve desired results beyond the state (Ericson and Haggerty 1997; Garland 2000). Both in isolation and in the context of the larger shift towards extending surveillance and policing functions throughout civil society, we see the CC's requirements as representing a substantial threat to Internet users' online privacy while placing onerous obligations on private businesses.

THE CONVENTTION ON CYBERCRIME

In this section we would like to explore in further detail those articles of the convention that bear most directly on issues relating to the role of service providers in facilitating Internet data surveillance and the search and seizure of customers' records.

The bulk of the concerns addressed here arise in Articles 16 through 21. Article 16 specifies that signatories will adopt legislation or regulatory mechanisms to permit authorities to order the preservation (up to 90 days, though renewable) of computer data, including traffic data, relevant to an investigation. Article 16 also calls for measures to be enacted that lead to the "preservation of specified computer data." As the convention fails to define "preservation," the result has been concerns by users, ISPs, and civil libertarians as to whether governments will actually be seeking to trap the traffic of a targeted user (data preservation) or the network traffic of all users of a service (data retention). These worries appear to be justified: both the United Kingdom (Millar 2002) and Finland (EFFI 2002) have attempted to institute data retention schemes.

Article 18 increases privacy concerns: it obliges signatories to adopt legislation or regulations that permit authorities to order computer data from a repository of those data, as well as ISP service subscriber information, including the identity and location of subscribers, their telephone number or other access method, billing and payment information, the type of service used, and the length of service. Article 20 further mandates the adoption of legislation to compel ISPs to provide access capability to law enforcement to monitor real-time traffic data or to assist law enforcement in collecting and recording real-time traffic. This would permit authorities to track the means by which targeted data are travelling. Article 21 calls for legal means to be established through which ISPs could be compelled to intercept and store content data such as e-mail messages, or to assist law enforcement in doing so.

Each of the articles described, in effect, casts ISPs in the role of police agents, either by compelling them to function as officially sanctioned surveillants—searching for, collecting, analysing, and turning over data to agents of the state—or by ordering them to assist police in these same activities. The benefits of this move are readily apparent with respect to states' interests. Police are granted the opportunity to penetrate beyond the traditional veil of privacy shrouding personal communications, and to do so in a manner that far exceeds the scope of traditional law enforcement techniques used for similar purposes. Further, the CC itself provides no safeguards against abuses of users' privacy rights; all law enforcement actions performed in furtherance of the convention's aims are subject to domestic laws only.

The problems created by this lack of safeguards are already apparent in Canada. The Canadian government recently released a consultation paper entitled "Lawful Access" (Department of Justice Canada, Industry Canada, and Solicitor General of Canada 2002) in response to their obligations under the CC. The paper proposes, among other dubious recommendations, the collection of data by ISPs at the request of law enforcement, without prior judicial authorization, in exigent circumstances.

The convention poses few problems for lawmakers in the United States, however. Under the PATRIOT Act (2001), law enforcement agencies already have expanded surveillance capabilities, including the right to obtain certain forms of non-content data from ISPs with only a subpoena (and without judicial review) (Rosenberg 2002). Further, the act permits the FBI to override state and federal privacy laws to compel disclosure of records under claims that said records are connected to an intelligence investigation (Rosenberg 2002).

THE POLICING NETWORK

As we noted previously, we see the CC's requirement that ISPs provide knowledge, expertise, and technical support for law enforcement activities as part of a larger move by governments to establish policing networks "beyond the state." We would like to discuss this claim more fully through an examination of recent literature on "governance" and policing.

Loader (2000) contends that Western societies are witnessing a major transformation with respect to the provision of security and order, a shift that involves both the fragmentation and the diversification of policing services. This shift can be understood, in part, within the context of the commodification of policing: traditional policing services now form the core of a new market in which professional and personal safety services are bought and sold in the form of security guards, surveillance cameras, alarm systems, and crime prevention through environmental design, among others (Ericson and Haggerty 1997; Loader 1999). It is not simply that the private sector has embraced the rhetoric of policing to sell products, but also that the rhetoric of consumerism is shaping public police services and their delivery. Loader explains that there is "a discursive re-presentation of the police as deliverers of a professional service (rather than a force) and of 'the public' as 'consumers' of that service" (1999: 376).

This shift to increased police presence beyond that of the state can also be explained with reference to what Garland (1996) terms a "responsibilization strategy." Garland, following O'Malley (1996), notes that recognition of the resource and capacity limits of states has led to a willingness by several Western governments to divest themselves of some of their former responsibilities. With respect to crime, citizens and private-sector entities are encouraged directly and indirectly, through government programs and other initiatives, to take "responsibility" for crime prevention and safety of their person, home, car, family, neighbourhood, business, and so on. An underlying motivational factor for private actors is a similar recognition of the limits "of the state's powers to regulate conduct and prohibit deviance" (Garland 1996: 447).

The coupling of the rhetoric of consumerism with strategies of "responsibilization" leads to a central paradox for the public police (Huey, Ericson, and Haggerty 2004; Loader 1999). The promotion of the public police as service providers to a consumer citizenry is occurring simultaneously with a push by police and other state agencies to reduce the number of public services performed. This paradox is neatly resolved, however, through increased investment in public-private policing networks. As Loader explains,

What we might call a shift from police to policing has seen the sovereign state—hitherto considered focal to both provision and accountability in this field—reconfigured as but one node of a broader, more diverse "network of power" (Castells 1997: 304). Sure enough, this network continues to encompass the direct provision and supervision of policing by institutions of national and local government. But it now also extends ... to private policing forms secured through government; to transnational police arrangements taking place above government; to markets in policing and security services unfolding beyond government; and to policing activities engaged in by citizens below government. We inhabit a world of plural, networked policing. (2000: 323-324)

Of the five types of policing arrangements within this new constellation of policing services, the most relevant to this discussion is that which Loader (2000) terms "policing through government." These are policing services provided by the private sector at the request of government agencies, including private security services and hardware purchased for the protection of government sites and the purchase of expertise or services from private-sector agents or consultants (Loader 2000). We could also add to this category arrangements formalized through law, regulation, or custom through which policing services are provided to law enforcement by ISPs.

EXPANDING SURVEILLANCE OPPORTUNITIES

The net effect of states' efforts at redistributing and expanding policing functions with, and through, the private sector is to increase opportunities not only for crime prevention and arrest, but also for surveillance. The use of ISPs and other private-sector interests to assist law enforcement agencies in gathering and analysing data on individuals and groups online is but one means by which both the state and private interests monitor selected targets for their purposes.

The recent proliferation of surveillance tools in the private sector alone has been staggering. Discount shopping cards and bank debit and credit cards track customer purchases. Cameras owned and operated by individual citizens, retailers, and private business groups are mounted in stores, in workplaces, outside homes, and on public streets outside businesses (Whitaker 1999). In Britain alone it has been estimated that there are some 500,000 surveillance cameras operating in both public and private spaces (Haggerty and Ericson 2000); "the minute you arrive in England, from the ferry port to the train station to the city centres, you're being CCTV'd," states the manager of a British surveillance firm cited by Freeman (1999: 14). Security has become a commodity that can be purchased in local malls by merchants retailing "Nannycams," and other home

276

surveillance devices, next to shops selling hair care products and newspapers. Private-sector businesses maintain large data banks of personal information on consumers, some of which are interconnected so that data about individuals and aggregates can be shared. Online, we are tracked through [cookies.sup.3] and other monitoring technologies. And these are only a few of the very many examples that we could point to.

Government agencies are also increasingly dependent on information-gathering tools to "govern" populations. Indeed, public police forces are major users and beneficiaries of surveillance and other information-gathering technologies. Video surveillance cameras are becoming an integral part of policing technology; cameras are used by police to record protests and police-citizen interactions and as a crime deterrent in public spaces (Whitaker 1999). Online, law enforcement agencies employ programs to monitor activities on the Internet. A notable example is the FBI's use of an online surveillance system called Carnivore to monitor, intercept, and store e-mail and other electronic communications of targeted individuals (Barrett 2002). Some states, such as Australia, the Netherlands, and Germany, have established databases for law enforcement and national security agencies to obtain, without court order, Internet subscriber and service provider information; a similar scheme has been proposed in Canada (Department of Justice Canada et al. 2002).

Police agencies also benefit enormously from information networks with private sector sources and other state agencies. As private security expands in retail and business districts, police in some cities are networked through computerized paging systems to private security firms, from whom they receive information derived from surveillance of targets, or are provided access to private security databases (Huey et al. 2004). State and local police organizations also receive access to non-police databases, including those of insurance companies and financial institutions (Haggerty and Ericson 2000). Individual citizens are also increasingly serving as police informants. "Tip lines," through which individuals can supply information on crimes known and unknown to police, are used in several Western nations. Marx (1989) notes several of these found in the United States, including TIP ("turn in a pusher") and "Drop-a-Dime" for drugs. Canada, Britain, and the United States also rely heavily on Crime Stoppers and Neighbourhood Watch programs, both of which encourage citizens to be aware of what their neighbours are doing and to report any legal infractions to authorities. Increasingly, policing agencies are sharing information transnationally. Recently, Canada and the United States signed an expanded information-sharing agreement that would permit police databank information to be shared not only at but across the border (Canadian Embassy, Washington, DC 2002). Following the events of September 11, we anticipate significant further expansions with respect to such cross-border information sharing.

The cumulative effect of the astounding growth of surveillance is the construction of what Haggerty and Ericson (2000) term the "surveillant assemblage." These authors rightly note that surveillance in contemporary society is "multiple, unstable and lacks discernible boundaries or responsible governmental departments," crossing as it does both the public and private sectors (2000: 610). They are careful to note that these processes can only be understood as multiples that work in concert by default, rather than by design (2000: 610). This does not mean, however, that the assemblage itself is not cause for serious concern.

We note that one of the central points made by Haggerty and Ericson is that focusing on any one technology as a cause for privacy concerns—and this would include the implementation of legislation, policies, and practices surrounding the use of ISPs as surveillants for law enforcement agencies—is problematic because, in the face of multiple connections across myriad technologies and practices, struggles against particular manifestations of surveillance, as important as they might be, are akin to efforts to keep the ocean's tide back with a broom—a frantic focus on a particular unpalatable technology or practice while the general tide of surveillance washes over us all. (2000: 614)

With respect to the central concern of this commentary, we agree with these authors to the extent that we situate the Convention on Cybercrime's requirements within the wider spectrum of contemporary surveillance and within the larger shift to policing beyond the state. We do so because we see the convention as part of a larger threat to privacy. However, we also believe that this convention poses a significant danger above and beyond other current forms of surveillance, and thus remains an appropriate target of both concern and resistance. Unlike other dangers to privacy that exist in both public and private sectors, the CC's requirements hold the potential to expand the state's capacity for surveillance of private citizens far beyond the parameters of the current form that the

278

surveillant assemblage takes; these mandates are more penetrative of privacy than having one's picture taken on a public street or at a bank machine, as frustrating and offensive as we may find these latter activities. The Internet provides not one but multiple spaces in which we engage in personal activities, including meeting people, sharing our personal thoughts, visiting online doctors and health sites, shopping, engaging in business transactions, indulging in fantasies, and exploring our world. All of these activities represent unique portals into the interior of our personal lives. As such, they ought to be respected as private territory, to be breached by the state only in the rarest and most serious of circumstances, subject always to judicial review. The CC's articles, however, demand that signatories enact and use legislation that permits public policing agencies to co-opt Internet service providers into being willing or unwilling informants against us, in some situations without prior judicial review. This is clearly an abuse of the trust that we place in the Internet as a medium and in those service providers that we contract with.

Footnotes and references deleted.

20

Virtual Neighborhood Watch

Open Source Software and Community Policing Against Cybercrime

Benjamin R. Jones

Cybercrime—crime committed through the use of a computer—is a real and growing problem that costs governments, businesses, and individual computer users millions of dollars annually and that facilitates many of the same crimes committed in realspace, such as identity theft and the trafficking of child pornography, only on a larger scale. However, the current strategies deployed by law enforcement to combat cybercrime have proven ineffective. Borne out of traditional notions of criminal behavior, these strategies and tactics are often ill-suited to prevent or punish cybercrime, which often defies the traditional notions of criminal behavior bounded by the corporeal world such as scale and proximity. This Comment argues that a more effective methodology in the fight against cybercrime is to develop a model of community policing, in which the power to deter and prevent cybercrime is divested into the hands of individual computer users.

B.R. Jones, Virtual neighborhood watch: Open source software and community policing against cybercrime. *The Journal of Criminal Law and Criminology*, 97 (2): 601-629, 2007. Reprinted by special permission of Northwestern University School of Law, The Journal of Criminal Law and Criminology.

One such strategy for achieving effective community policing against cybercrime is through the increased use of open-source software, software in which users are given access to the underlying source code and may make modifications to that source code in order to ameliorate vulnerabilities that may enable cybercrime. This Comment looks at the development of traditional community policing strategies and argues that the increased use of open source software—spurned by greater involvement by government and corporations—may be a more effective technique in the fight against cybercrime.

I. INTRODUCTION

One of the few constants of the Internet age is the recognition that technology and the law are not always the best dance partners. From the effect of Internet file-sharing technologies on copyright law to the impact of e-commerce on notions of jurisdiction, there is often a fundamental disconnect between laws written to govern the corporeal world of "realspace" (the tangible, real world, as distinguished from the virtual world of cyberspace) and technological advances, which enable the almost instantaneous flow of information across the globe. From the time of the framing of the Constitution to the present, the development of new technologies has created challenges and opportunities beyond the conceptual scope of legislators and courts. Modern policymakers have struggled to close the gap between the technological world and the legal world.

Perhaps the most fundamental change wrought by the development of the Internet is the way in which information now moves. A user sitting in front of a computer connected to the Internet can access a virtually boundless stream of information—from the price of gold on the Tokyo currency exchange to the home movies of a Muscovite, back from a first vacation in Las Vegas—moving at nearly the speed of light. These changes in the flow of information have impacted almost every facet of society—from commerce to communication to government, reshaping many of the ways in which we interact.

Not surprisingly, the impact of this revolution in the flow of information extends to the criminal world as well. Criminals and potential criminals have seized upon the power of the Internet to enable the commission of a host of crimes—from the sale of illegal drugs to the trafficking of child pornography—and to expand the criminal enterprise into the commission of an entirely new breed of crime, possible only in the virtual world of computer technology. A quick scan of newspaper headlines over the past five years reveals the breadth and impact of cybercrime. Indeed, the spread of cybercrime has reshaped the modern lexicon to include new definitions for words such as "identity theft," "worm," and "Trojan Horse."

Like the relationship between law and technology, the strategies and tactics of modern law enforcement also lag in responding to the new challenges posed by cybercrime. Importantly, the reactive model of law enforcement—developed over centuries in response to traditional, realspace crime—is ill-equipped to combat the challenge of cybercrime, unbounded by the constraints of the physical world. As one commentator notes, "Like the common law, the traditional model of law enforcement is a compilation of past practices that have been deemed effective in dealing with the phenomena it confronts. The model's general strategy, the reactive approach, is one that has been in use since antiquity."

This reactive approach, focused on identifying a crime, apprehending the perpetrator, and meting out some punishment through the justice system, emerged as a response to crimes in the real world, constrained by the simple laws of physics. Important among those limits are notions of proximity and scale. For most crimes, the perpetrator must actually be physically proximate to his victim. A pickpocket in nineteenth century London could not remove the wallet of a gentleman across town; he would have to get within close proximity of his unwitting victim, risking detection or failure. The scale of most crimes was also one-to-one; a single perpetrator targeted a single victim before he could move onto the next crime. That same pickpocket could not simultaneously remove the wallets of a thousand Londoners. The limits of proximity and scope made it relatively easy to identify the perpetrator and the specific instances of crime, and law enforcement officers could focus on capturing the individual perpetrator.

It is increasingly clear, however, that those same constraints of proximity and scale do not bind criminals operating in the virtual world of cyberspace. The Internet, which connects millions of computers (and computer users), allows criminals to commit crimes anonymously against victims thousands of miles away. Importantly as well, those crimes are far from one-to-one in scale. Our old friend the pickpocket, operating in twenty-first century London, could unleash a "worm" that affects computers around the world and causes millions of dollars in damage or that gains access to the computer system of a bank in Seattle and loots the accounts of hundreds of customers at the same time. The fundamental difference between cybercrime and crime in realspace means that the current strategies designed to combat realspace crime, particularly those predicated upon the reactive approach, are ill suited to combat the increasing problem of cybercrime.

This Comment explores the notion that current strategies designed to prevent and punish cybercrimes are ineffective and argues that the community policing model may provide an alternative for more effectively deterring and punishing cybercrimes. Section II provides an introduction to the growing problem of cybercrime and its various forms. Section III illustrates how current strategies focused on punishing perpetrators of cybercrime are ineffective. Section IV describes the community policing model and demonstrates how this model can be applied to create effective deterrents to cybercrime. Finally, Section V argues that the increased use of open source software—especially in the operating system and Internet browser markets—is an important tool in making the community policing model a success.

II. WHAT IS CYBERCRIME?

At the outset, it is helpful to describe exactly what is meant by the term cybercrime, as it is a label applied to acts ranging from the propagation of computer viruses to cyberstalking. At the broadest level, cybercrime can be described as any crime committed through the use of a computer or computer technology, but a more specific taxonomy helps classify the different types of offenses. Although specific definitions will vary, cybercrimes can be placed in four broad categories—unauthorized access to computer programs and files, unauthorized disruption, theft of identity, and carrying out of traditional offenses, such as distribution of child pornography, using a computer.

a. Unauthorized Access

Unauthorized access occurs whenever "an actor achieves entry into a target's files or programs without permission." This access can be achieved either remotely—by gaining access to the target computer from another computer connected over a network—or physically, by using the target computer. Interestingly, the crime of unauthorized access—however it is defined under federal or state criminal codes— is the unique crime of invading another's private workspace, in and of itself. Malicious acts such as "causing harm to the files or programs or using the data improperly" are classified as separate crimes of their own.

The targets of unauthorized access are most commonly the government, corporations, or private individuals. The government is an obvious target because its vast computer files contain a myriad of sensitive information, ranging from the Department of Defense plans for military contingencies to law enforcement information on individuals and criminal organizations. Access to a corporation's computers places at risk information ranging from proprietary business documents and trade secrets to private customer information like credit card account numbers and social security numbers. The unauthorized use of personal computers may reveal the same personal financial information as described above, but also risks harms to individual privacy. Computer files may contain private information "as personal as love letters, as banal as grocery lists, or as tragic as unfinished drafts of law review articles," the loss of which creates a feeling of lost privacy in addition to any quantifiable economic harm.

B. Unauthorized Disruption

Unauthorized disruption, by comparison, occurs when an individual interferes with the operation of a computer system, whether by gaining unauthorized access or through some other means. Such acts are at "the heart of what most people consider cybercrime." These crimes occur when an actor—human or machine—interferes with computer hardware or software, without permission. The different types of authorized disruption attacks—including viruses, worms, and Trojan horses—are now a familiar part of the lexicon, but again it is helpful to describe the unique features of each.

1. Viruses

In its simplest form, "[a] virus is a program that modifies other computer programs." The modifications ensure that the healthy computer will replicate the virus. Once the now-infected computer is connected to another computer—via the Internet, a direct computer-to-computer connection, or a shared storage disk—the virus can be transferred onto the new computer. Interestingly, viruses are not, in and of themselves, harmful. Their harmful nature depends upon the additional elements, beyond the instructions for self-replication, written into their code. Indeed, there are some viruses which have a benign or merely annoying effect on the computers they infect. Others, however, have caused widespread damage.

2. Worms

A worm is a stand-alone program that is able to replicate itself over a network without any action by the user, unlike a virus, which requires some human action, such as downloading an infected file or placing an infected disk in the computer. Like viruses, the destructive nature of worm programs depends on the additional instructions

284

inserted into the program code beyond the basic instructions for replication. Perhaps the most noteworthy worm is the ILoveYou bug, which infected over a million computers and spread nine times faster than the "Melissa" virus. The infection caused major corporations such as Ford Motor Company and AT&T to shut down their e-mail systems, resulting in lost time and productivity, and also reached the computer systems of government agencies including the Department of Defense, the Central Intelligence Agency, and NASA.

3. Trojan Horses

A Trojan horse is a program that appears to perform some useful function, but which also may contain hidden malicious code. The Trojan horse may act as a delivery vehicle for a virus or worm or permit unauthorized access by another. Often, the Trojan horse program will contain spying software or "backdoor" functions that allow a remote user to gain information about the computer or to actually control the computer via the network, creating a "zombie computer."

4. Distributed Denial of Service Attacks

A final type of unauthorized disruption is known as a Distributed Denial of Service (DDoS) attack. These attacks overwhelm websites with network traffic and disrupt their ability to communicate with legitimate users. A DDoS attack begins when:

[A]n individual obtains unauthorized access to a computer system and places software code on it that renders that system a "Master." The individual also breaks into other networks to place code that turns those systems into agents (known as "zombies" or "slaves")…. The Masters are activated either remotely or by internal programming (such as a command to begin an attack at a prescribed time) and are used to send information to the agents. After receiving this information, the agents make repeated requests to connect with the attack's ultimate target, typically using a fictitious or "spoofed" [Interact Protocol] address, so that the recipient of the request cannot learn its true source. Acting in unison, the agents generate a high volume of traffic from several sources….[T]he destination computer becomes overwhelmed….[and] loses all or most of its ability to serve legitimate customers….

DDoS attacks can have a tremendous impact on the flooded target computers, resulting in millions of dollars in lost productivity.

C. Identity Theft

A third category of cybercrime is identity theft. In its most familiar form, identity theft occurs when an individual—via unauthorized access to digital information—steals the personal information of another, such as the victim's credit card numbers or social security number. Now able to disguise himself as the target individual, the criminal can access the individual's bank accounts, make purchases using the stolen credit card numbers, obtain credit cards in the victim's name, or commit other malicious acts.

There are also other forms of identity theft via computer that do not have a clear realspace analog because they involve the unique properties of computer systems, particularly those linked over the Internet. "Cross-site scripting" occurs when malicious code is inserted into a website, forcing the website to send out information not authorized by its owners. "Page-jacking" involves the reprogramming of an Internet address to take the unwitting user to an alternate site. If a user clicks on a GMC Truck ad atop the ESPN.com website and is instead redirected to an Interact gambling website, the page has been "jacked." Finally, "IP spoofing" occurs when a perpetrator uses software to disguise his Interact Protocol (IP) address to match that of a "trusted" user and is able to gain unauthorized access to a secured computer or website. A criminal with IP spoofing software could mimic the IP address of a corporate employee's home computer to gain remote access to the corporation's computer systems.

D. Use of Computers to Carry Out Traditional Crime

A final broad category is the use of computers to carry out traditional criminal offenses. These offenses can range from the distribution of child pornography to the sale of illegal firearms to so-called cyberstalking. While the nature of these offenses does not differ merely because of the use of computer technology, "[e]ach reveals the advantages, from the criminals' perspective, of cybercrime— widespread, quick distribution, and cost minimization."

In short, the range of cybercrime is quite broad. The different categories, however, are neither co-extensive nor mutually exclusive; a cybercriminal may choose to carry out only a DDoS attack or gain unauthorized access to a computer network in order to plant a virus and steal the identities of network users. Each of these different types of crime has the power to cause tremendous damage, whether it is economic loss or more intangible harms, such as in the case of the sale of child pornography or the unauthorized access of personal data.

III. WHY CURRENT STRATEGIES ARE INEFFECTIVE

Each of the different types of cybercrimes share one salient feature—the use of computer technology. This technology fundamentally alters the nature of cybercrimes from those committed in the real, corporeal world. Crimes committed in realspace without the use of technology—from murder to pickpocketing—share two significant characteristics: proximity and scale.

A. Proximity

The first of those common elements is proximity. Given the constraints imposed by space and time, a perpetrator of realspace crime must actually be physically proximate to the victim. Of course, there are examples of realspace crime that do not require the perpetrator to be near his victim—for example, securities fraud or the sending of poison through the mail. However, the vast majority of realspace crimes require such proximity. In turn, the notion of proximity has created a presumed dynamic in the model of traditional law enforcement—"victim-perpetrator presence in the same general locale; victim-perpetrator proximity and consequent victimization; perpetrator efforts to flee the crime scene and otherwise evade apprehension; investigation; identification; and apprehension of the perpetrator." Even as modern cities have moved beyond the parochial world where victims and perpetrators tended to live in the same small communities, law enforcement still relies heavily on the spatial limitations of crime. Importantly, "the real-world model still assumes that the investigation of a crime should focus on the physical scene of the crime."

Unlike crime in realspace, however, cybercrime does not require any degree of proximity between the attacker and victim—"[i]t can be committed by someone who is located anywhere in the world against a victim who is in another city, another state, another country." The blessing of the Internet—the simultaneous connection of computer users all over the world—is also a curse when viewed through the lens of cybercrime. An attacker merely needs a computer connected to the Internet in order to gain access to millions of other computers. Having gained that access, he can inflict harm upon others—either directly upon their computer or by accessing information that will allow him to commit future crimes.

The physical separation between attacker and victim also has important consequences for the investigation of cybercrimes. In a virtual world comprised of ones and zeroes transmitted over cables and wires, there is often no "crime scene" for investigators to comb for clues. And, where there is such a crime scene, it can be found in hundreds, if not thousands, of computers and servers owned by corporations and individuals around the world.

Two important advantages conferred upon cybercriminals by the use of computer technology further erode the notion of proximity—anonymity and encryption. As Katyal points out, "Computers ... confer massive efficiencies on the criminal by hiding the perpetrator's identity and covering data streams." Perpetrators of cybercrime are often identified only by a pseudonymous e-mail address, linked to an IP address, which appears as a seemingly random string of numbers. Without the cooperation of the Internet service provider that maintains the e-mail address, there is almost no way to connect the e-mail pseudonym with the realspace identity and location of the attacker. Moreover, a host of technologies exist that allow users to mask their true identity, leaving them essentially invisible to detection over the Internet. This anonymity further insulates the criminal from his victim, and shields the criminal from law enforcement authorities responding to an attack. Such anonymity confers a great advantage upon computer criminals as "[e]ven masked or otherwise disguised criminals in realspace may unwittingly indicate their height, race, voice, and now their DNA."

Further adding to the anonymity conferred on computer criminals is the use of encryption technologies. Encryption involves the use of algorithms or other mathematical formulas to encode data into a pattern that is indecipherable except to those who have the password or key to decipher it. While methods for encoding messages predate the computer by millennia, "computers have for the first time put encryption into broad use." From the perspective of criminal law, encryption is uniquely "Janus-faced"—it can be used both by criminals to mask their true identity and to render communications unreadable by law enforcement authorities, but it also can be employed to prevent cybercrimes by protecting confidential data and communications from unauthorized access. The debate over the benign and malign effects of encryption technology could fill volumes far longer than this Comment. Yet the fact remains that such technologies can be employed by cybercriminals both to mask their own identity and to communicate beyond the prying eyes and ears of law enforcement officials.

288

B. Scale

The second characteristic of traditional crime is its scale. Real-world crime tends to consist of a single event with one perpetrator and one victim:

The "crime" commences when the victimization of the target is begun and ends when it has concluded; during the event the perpetrator focuses all of his or her attention on the consummation of that "crime." When the "crime" is complete, the perpetrator is free to move to another victim and another "crime."

The one-to-one nature of real-world crime is a generality, more than an absolute. One can think of many examples—especially with the advent of organized crime and gang violence—where multiple perpetrators commit the same crime against one victim. However, the opposite—the perpetration of crimes against many individuals by one criminal—is rare without the use of technology. There are certain criminal acts—ranging from terrorism and genocide to corporate fraud and environmental pollution—that defy this traditional notion of scale and involve the commission of a single criminal act that impacts a large number of victims. However, as in the case of realspace crimes that do not require proximity, such crimes represent only a small number of the total crimes committed in realspace, and—perhaps more importantly—they have not had a profound effect on the development of traditional law enforcement techniques.

Cybercrime reverses the traditional notion of the one-to-one scale of crime in realspace. Particularly, the use of technology acts as a force multiplier that "vastly increases the number of 'crimes' an individual can commit and the speed with which she can do so." The cumulative scale of cybercrime is particularly troublesome for traditional law enforcement efforts; police are accustomed to responding to and investigating single-victim, single-perpetrator crimes. Cybercrime, by contrast, is committed on a far greater scale and represents an entirely new set of offenses that must be investigated along with the spate of traditional crimes.

Cybercrime, unlike terrestrial crime, is also automated; a criminal can set in motion a series of repeated attacks by uploading a single virus or worm or initiating a single DDoS attack. Automation "allows a perpetrator to commit thousands of crimes quickly and with little effort, making one-to-many victimization a realistic default assumption for cybercrime." The ILoveYou worm provides a staggering example of how widely and quickly one act of cybercrime can spread among millions of computer users across the world. And, the speed and reach of cybercrime can only be expected to increase in lockstep with the increase in the number of computer users, particularly those who rely on computers connected to the Internet.

The automated nature of cybercrime is particularly troubling for law enforcement officials. After the commission of a real-world crime, officers react by investigating and, hopefully, identifying and apprehending the perpetrator. Cybercrime frustrates this traditional response. Though cybercrime—like real-world crime—is carried out by only a relatively small fraction of the population, "this relatively small group can commit crimes on a scale far surpassing what is possible in the real-world, where one-to-one victimization and serial crimes are the norm. As a result, the absolute scale of cybercrime, in terms of incidence of discrete crimes, exponentially exceeds that of real-world crime."

The traditional notion of crime control is, by and large, monolithic. It has emerged over the centuries as a response to crimes that, except for a few examples at the margins, share two salient characteristics: proximity and scope. Cybercrime, however, turns the notions of both proximity and scope upside down as computer criminals can take advantage of technology to perpetrate crimes against victims from across great distances and against large numbers of victims in a single act. The differences in the fundamental aspects of cybercrime demand a change in the strategies designed to combat that crime if we are to be successful in fighting such crime in the future.

IV. THE COMMUNITY POLICING MODEL

Given the shortcomings of the traditional law enforcement model to combat cybercrime, we must look for alternatives. As Brenner succinctly recommends, "We do need a new approach, particularly for cybercrime, because the traditional model is not ... a workable solution for online crime." Reworking the law enforcement model to stem the tide of cybercrime must begin with our understandings of the fundamentally different nature of cybercrime and the shortcomings of the reactive nature of traditional police work. This Comment suggests that the best way to combat the problem of cybercrime is to shift the focus from reacting to cybercrimes ex post, to preventing those crimes ex ante, before they occur. As this Comment suggests, one creative approach to achieving such prevention is to decentralize the responsibility for policing the Internet among the community of computer users, enabling changes at the code level that create effective deterrents against the commission of cybercrime.

This notion of community policing is neither new nor unique to the virtual space of the Internet. The concept of community policing arose in the 1970s and 1980s as scholars and policymakers looked to devise new solutions to the problems of crime and poverty plaguing America's inner cities. A growing consensus realized that relationships between police officers and citizens in these communities had become untenable. Many police departments and individual officers on the streets had embraced the so-called "warrior model," in which they saw themselves as doing battle with an ever-present adversary among the citizens in the community. This notion, in turn, led officers to believe that the public saw them in an equally hostile fashion. At the same time, criminological research began to reveal the inadequacy of police tactics of the day, which led to increasing the number of patrol officers, random saturation patrols, and rapid response to 911 calls. In sum, "the research undermined many of policing's core assumptions, thereby creating an opening for reformers to offer new approaches."

Central to the paradigm shift away from the warrior model was the recognition that, despite police perceptions about citizens' hostilities, inner-city residents actually held a favorable impression of the police. "Even more profoundly, it meant understanding that even those who were critical did not want less policing—they generally wanted more, and better, protection." This understanding of community support for the police was buttressed by a notion that even high crime communities are composed of a majority of law-abiding citizens. "Community policing was built upon the import of these findings, and its challenge was to replace the warrior model with one premised on the notion that the police and the community could become co-producers of public safety, rather than hostile antagonists."

The community policing model not only sought to improve the relationship between citizens and police officers, but also to give citizens an active role in "policing" their communities:

At its core, community policing is not a set of tactics, but instead is an organizational strategy for running a [police] department. In its most promising form, this strategy has two essential elements. First, it requires that citizens, at the neighborhood level, meet regularly with police to jointly define neighborhood crime problems and set police priorities.... The second critical element is that citizens, again at the local level, take responsibility for helping to address the problems that they have identified.

This set of tactics includes having officers physically walk through neighborhoods, rather than patrolling in cars, and hosting community building events such as prayer vigils and midnight basketball leagues. But, perhaps more importantly, it is premised upon a fundamental reconceptualization of the role of citizens in the policing process.

The community policing model has significant advantages over the traditional model of reactive, "warrior-style" policing:

First, a main drawback of conventional policing, as the individual-self-help proponents have observed, is that it trades off with private methods of controlling and reacting to crime. Community-based solutions sidestep this by incorporating private actors directly into the process of controlling crime. As such, the signal is sent that crime prevention depends not only on the government, but also on the community. Put differently, community strategies emphasize stewardship, in that it "calls on citizens to view themselves as responsible for the welfare of the larger community." Second, community-based solutions do a better job of promoting values of order and safety than the public model. When law enforcement is solely responsible for policing, a backlash can develop among residents. Such "top-down" solutions are not particularly effective ways of generating norms. Instead, "when a community responds to a criminal incident, it seeks not merely to restore credibility to the community's conception of the moral order ... but also to symbolically affirm community norms for others who have not disobeyed them."

The community based policing model not only reduces the antagonism between police officers and citizens, but involves citizens directly in crafting solutions to prevent crimes in their communities and affirming community norms against crime.

The need for community policing against cybercrime arises not because of the antagonistic relationship between law enforcement and computer users, but rather from an understanding that the model can be applied to take advantage of the strengths of third-party actors to prevent cybercrime. Given the fundamental differences between cybercrime and crimes in realspace and the shortcomings of the reactive model of law enforcement, prevention is a crucial element in reducing cybercrime. The emphasis on preventing cybercrime is borne out of the recognition that the traditional reactive model of law enforcement is simply ill-equipped, both normatively and practically, to combat cybercrime.

This is not to say that we would rather prevent cybercrimes, while allowing crimes in realspace to happen and focusing on arresting perpetrators, ex post. In an ideal world, we would prevent all crimes before they occurred; the question of punishment, ex post, would be moot. Such a goal is obviously unattainable. However, the preventative model is particularly applicable to the problem of crime for two reasons. First, there is a fundamental difference between cybercrime and traditional realspace crime that frustrates the application of traditional models of policing. Second, there is the realization that deterrent strategies may be particularly effective in preventing cybercrimes, vis-a-vis traditional crimes. Increasing the "cost" of committing cybercrime—including measures such as improving software so that it is less vulnerable to attack—has a powerful effect on preventing potential cybercriminals from attempting crimes in the first place.

At first blush, the lack of a tangible, physical location in cyberspace seems to suggest the absence of communities to engage in such self-help remedies. In fact, the opposite may be true:

[T]he fact that "place" is unfettered online cuts both ways, since it means that opportunities for self-help expand, too. The community in cyberspace may revolve around a number of things, such as a virtual place (eBay); a place in realspace (Georgetown); a concept (Maoism); or even a sport (windsurfing). The proliferation of such communities, and the ease of transacting in each one, suggest a robust potential for community solutions.

Indeed, there is a host of community policing methods already in place in the realm of cyberspace, such as the user rating systems on e-commerce websites like eBay and Craigslist. There is, nonetheless, much work to be done, particularly in the prevention of cybercrimes.

V. OPEN SOURCE SOFTWARE AS A TOOL FOR COMMUNITY POLICING

One important tool that will allow computer users to "patrol" the virtual neighborhoods of the digital world in the attempt to prevent cybercrime is the increased use of open source software. Open source—in the broadest sense—refers to software whose underlying source code is made available to the public, so, in turn, users are able to alter that code and re-publish it. This stands in contrast to closed or proprietary software, in which, generally, the source code is not available to the user.

A. The Development and Use of Open Source Software

Perhaps the best known example of open source software is the Linux operating system developed by Finnish computer science student Linus Torvalds in 1991. The Linux operating system is currently used by over seven million users and is available either as free, open source software or as a commercial software package that includes support and other features. Among its many users are the popular websites Amazon.com and Google, which rely exclusively on Linux. The software is also used to power TiVo digital video recorders, cellphones, and some of the world's most powerful supercomputers. The open source version of Linux is distributed using the Free Software Foundation's GNU General Public License (GPL). A program distributed under the GPL must contain all of its source code. Any user can modify and re-distribute the program; however, any redistribution must also be done according to the terms of the GPL. The GPL license is unique among software licensing schemes—"[w]hile most licenses serve to limit the copies that a licensee may make, the GPL serves to limit the restrictions on copying that a licensee can make." Anyone is free to use and modify software distributed under the license, "as long as, in the words of the license preamble, 'you ... give the recipients all the rights that you have. You must make sure that they, too, receive or can get the source code.'" The effect is a viral propagation of open software—if a user is to take advantage of the openness of the code, he must send along any improvements he makes with the same openness, giving other users the ability to access and modify the source code. A licensee under the GPL cannot simply free-ride on the backs of the previous developers and "close" the code by making the software proprietary. Other prominent examples of open source software include Apache, the most widely used Web server, and Sendmail, which is used to route most email.

The success of open source as a means of community policing against cybercrime lies in the way in which the software distributes the power to identify and correct potential security flaws to the entire community of software users. A key element to developing effective preventative measures against cybercrime is to eliminate the software security flaws that allow criminals to gain access to computer systems and to propagate destructive programs such as viruses, worms, and Trojan horses. To remedy such problems in proprietary closed-source software, the security flaws must be found—by the company that develops the software, by users who discover these flaws and report them to the company, or by cybercriminals who exploit the security flaws to launch an attack. The company must then develop a patch to remedy that problem and release that patch to all users of the software. (140) By contrast, when open source software is released, and again upon the release of each subsequent user-modified version, users are continually scouring the source code for ways to make the software safe from attack.

This continuous search for security flaws and almost-instantaneous release of patches to remedy those flaws means that "[c]omputer platforms such as Linux ... will have major security advantages ... [over] closed platforms, such as Windows.... Because more people can see the code, the likelihood that security vulnerabilities will be quickly discovered and patched rises." Particularly, "if a program is ubiquitous, like a computer operating system, the open source proponents are fight that the multitude of users will examine the code[,] reveal its flaws" and help to craft ways to fix those flaws. AS President Clinton's Technical Advisory Panel pointed out, "[A]ccess by developers to source code allows for a thorough examination that decreases the potential for embedded trap doors and/or Trojan horses." Tellingly, in 2001, Microsoft's closed source web server—IIS—was the most frequently targeted server by hackers, despite the fact that there were a far larger number of Apache web servers in use.

The use of open source software to combat cybercrime also brings with it the same normative values as community policing, namely the erosion of the traditional barrier between law enforcement and citizens:

Open-source programs involve the user in the process of security, instead of relegating it to someone else. Closed-source software creates the same type of "we/they syndrome" as conventional policing does. There is just not much impetus to try to come up with solutions to Windows XP's security flaws when one cannot even access the code. The closure of code sends a signal, and that signal is that Microsoft will take care of your security problems. Such centralized solutions are no doubt successful under certain conditions, but, as the self-help proponents rightly point out, they can also be efficient. In this way, the Linux community, often viewed as a bunch of anti-market sympathizers, have much in common with the market-based economists who emphasize self-help on efficiency grounds.

Just as community policing initiatives empower residents to take responsibility for the security of their communities, open source software empowers computer users to proactively take charge of identifying and correcting security breaches, rather than relying on the distributors of proprietary software.

B. Going Forward

Open source software is not, however, a panacea that can be easily and seamlessly deployed to stem the tide of cybercrime. Important questions must be answered about the organizational structure of a potential open source community policing effort. First, will individuals be motivated to contribute to open source projects? Second, will software corporations be willing to abandon the proprietary software model in order to devote more resources to open source software? And finally, what is the proper role of government, if any, in promoting the increased use of open source software? The answers to each of these questions reveal not only a promising future for effective preventative measures against cybercrime, but also an alternative to firm and market driven economies that dominate the landscape of modern industry.

1. Individual Users

Looking first to individuals, there is persuasive evidence that individual users can and will invest their time and resources in creating and updating open source software programs to protect against cybercrime. First, the emergence of the model of peer production (of which open source software is one example) is tied to the emergence of the networked, information age. In essence, the interconnectivity of millions of computer users, which contributes to the scope and power of cybercrime, is a powerful tool for allowing individuals to collaboratively work on open source software projects. As one scholar points out, "[U]biquitous computer communications networks are bringing about a dramatic change in the scope, scale, and efficacy of peer production." In short, programmers, connected via the Internet, are able to freely and cheaply exchange information. This exchange of information allows users to quickly and easily identify areas of production (including security flaws in software that create avenues for cybercrime) and contribute their productive efforts to the overall open source project.

The second important characteristic is the size, or granularity, of the tasks performed by each user in an open source community. Given the number of users collaborating on an open source project, the size of the individual tasks that each user must perform is quite small. Thus the motivation necessary to compel each user to complete that task is correspondingly small. When a project "is broken into little pieces, each of which can be performed by an individual in a short amount of time, the motivation to get any given individual to contribute need only be very small." If the creation of an operating system requires fifty thousand man hours of production, and the community of users numbers ten thousand, it is far easier to motivate each one to contribute five hours of her time than it would be—absent a firm-based command notion or a market-based structure—to motivate fifty individuals to perform one thousand hours of work each. This is particularly true of users in the open source community who are often motivated to improve and distribute software for non-pecuniary interests such as increased reputation in the programming community.

296

At this point, it is important to understand the nature of open source software itself. A common misconception regarding open source is that the software is only designed for savvy computer users or those who are "in the know" about a range of products beyond those in common use (particularly those offered by the dominant players in the software market such as Microsoft). At its simplest, this assumption is false. Open source programs, including the Linux operating system and functionality software such as the Firefox browser and the OpenOffice suite, are no more difficult to use for even the novice computer user and—importantly—are often available for free. Yet, it reveals an important challenge for a model of community policing built upon increasing the use of open source: not only making that software more accessible to the public, but increasing the public use of that software.

However, in recent years, open source software such as Linux and Firefox have gained increasing use among both savvy and novice computer users. These developments provide an important glimpse into the efficiency and "user-friendliness" of open source projects and illustrate the power of large numbers of individuals, each completing small scale tasks, to produce powerful results, despite the absence of command behavior from a firm or state organization. It is helpful to look at a few of the most prominent examples of peer-produced projects to see not only the capacity for organization and collaboration among a large group of individuals, but also the accessibility of these programs to even the most novice computer user.

a.   Wikipedia – The Collaborative Encyclopedia

The first example is the Wikipedia project, an ambitious attempt to create an Internet-based encyclopedia whose content is continually written and edited by its users. The project uses a collaborative software, Wiki, that is a markup language similar to HTML and allows multiple people to edit a single document and to link it to other, related documents. Begun in 2000 with a small number of volunteers, the site now features over a million entries in languages ranging from English to Luxembourgish to Tagalog. All users of the site are free to add articles and to update or edit existing articles. If a user feels that there should be an entry on the pygmy hippopotamus, she is free to add that content to the site. The unique feature of Wikipedia, vis-a-vis traditional encyclopedias, is that there is no central editor who reads the content added by users checking for misinformation. Instead, users themselves must be alert for mistakes in articles and are encouraged to correct those mistakes as they encounter them. Just as the power to correct bugs in open source software is spread among all of the users who access the source code, the editing power of the encyclopedia is distributed over the entire base of users of the site.

b. Firefox – A Better Browser?

The second example of the power of open source collaboration is the development of the Mozilla Firefox web browser, which stands as a shining example of the potential to create open source software solutions to the problem of cybercrime. The Firefox browser is the product of the Mozilla Foundation, spun off from America Online in 2003 as one of the last vestiges of Netscape, the Internet browser that dominated the competitive landscape before the introduction of Microsoft's internet Explorer. The browser is built upon an open source architecture where programmers and developers are given access to the source code, not only to search for security flaws, but also so that they may write additional plug-ins and extensions that increase the browser's functionality. While its market share still pales in comparison to the near-ubiquitous internet Explorer, Firefox has captured an increasingly large segment of the market, driving Microsoft's share below 90%. The software is touted for its security features and its resistance to viruses and other forms of unauthorized disruption.

Given the nature of the software market and the enabling characteristics of the internet, peer-produced projects such as open source software systems may emerge as a viable alternative to the traditional firm-based theory of economic behavior. The emergence of open source software projects, shaped not by the top-down leadership of a dominant firm, but by the collaboration of many peer contributors has forced a rethinking of Coase's firm-based theory of production, one of the bedrock principles of modern business operation. Open source programmers do not choose to participate in a project because their boss instructed them to do so, nor do they rely on the presence of a market price for their work which provides the prospect of either present or future monetary returns. As Benkler suggests, the peer production of open source software projects may in fact have a unique advantage over traditional, firm-based theories of production, allowing programmers to "scour larger groups of resources in search of materials, projects, collaborations, and combinations than is possible for firms or individuals who function in markets."

There is also a responsibility incumbent upon the developers and users of open source software to create programs that can be used by a greater number of computer users (users, here, in the traditional sense of the term, including those who only make use of the software for its intended purpose). For many, open source programs such as Linux are seen as more complicated and risky than traditional proprietary programs, such as the Microsoft Windows operating system. This perception is part myth and part truth. In the future, this perception may even cease to be true: if open source developers work to create more programs—like Firefox—that are accessible to even the most unsophisticated computer users, the demand for such products and the use of products better equipped to prevent cybercrime will only increase.

2. Corporations

The question of how to motivate users to participate in the improvement and expand the use of open source software is not the only dilemma. The next step is how to encourage corporations—still the producers of most software programs—to embrace open source. For software companies, proprietary software is an extremely profitable enterprise. It would be folly to suggest that distributors of proprietary software abandon their business model to embrace open source. By "giving away" the source code to software, companies lose the very profit-generating benefits that flow from closed-code, proprietary software. However, there may be feasible solutions that allow for the greater introduction of open source software. One such solution could be for Microsoft—the dominant producer of operating system and productivity software for end users—to give programmers and developers greater access to the source code for Internet Explorer, which is currently bundled with its Windows operating system. Without revealing the source code for Windows—the lifeblood of Microsoft's revenue stream—the company could give greater transparency to its Internet browser, allowing developers to scour the source code for security flaws before they were exploited by potential criminals. This raises the question of whether making the source code for Internet Explorer open to all would not only benefit those who seek to prevent cybercrime, but also those who perpetrate cybercrime. Would we, in effect, be letting the fox into the henhouse? Of course, making the source code available to all could increase the ability of cybercriminals to exploit potential weaknesses, but it would also vastly increase the ability and the motivation of users to test and update the source code in order to fix security flaws.

Indeed, drawing on the success of companies such as RedHat (a for-profit distributor of Linux software and technical support) and IBM (which has also become involved in the distribution of Linux platform), an increasing number of firms are realizing the potential of the open source market. Venture capital firms invested over $400 million into open source companies over an eighteen month period dating from 2004 to 2005, a sum that seems even larger given the capital-efficient nature of open source firms, which do not require massive armies of salespeople or developers. The key is to further develop this notion that the open source model is not an anathema to traditional notions of sales and profit. Instead, drawing on the experience of Linux distribution, software companies can and should move toward the open source model.

3. Government

A final question concerns the role of government in promoting community policing through the use of open source. Unlike most policy choices, the increased use of open source software is one that must begin in the private sphere—among software distributors and, more importantly, those who write and use open source software. However, the government can and should take a role in furthering this end.

A potential first step is the subsidy of open source software developers. Given the obvious deleterious effects of cybercrime—both in terms of monetary losses and the diversion of law enforcement resources away from other forms of crime—government agencies (both federal and state) have a vested interest in promoting the spread of open source software as a defense against cybercrime. Government subsidies would give open source developers additional capital to expand the range and capabilities of platforms such as Linux and Firefox. Further, by encouraging the adoption of open source software, perhaps through tax breaks or some other indirect subsidy, governments can motivate the increased use of these products, thus decreasing the number of targets of cybercrime.

Open source software platforms represent a viable tool to implement effective community policing solutions against cybercrimes. Just as community policing in realspace increased the accountability of citizens and diffused the responsibility for preventing crime among the population, so too will the use of open source software in the virtual realm.

VI. CONCLUSION

The Linux penguin doesn't look like much of a crime-fighter. He's a little portly and looks as if he would be much happier sliding around the ice than chasing down criminals. Yet this logo, and the open source operating system which it represents, offer a glimpse into a powerful force for preventing crime in cyberspace. The current strategies designed to fight cybercrime are failing. The reactive, investigative model—developed over the millennia as a response to localized crimes committed by a single perpetrator against a single victim—is ill-equipped to respond to criminal acts that can span the globe in a matter of seconds and affect thousands, if not millions of victims.

Just as law enforcement officials were able to tap into urban communities as a powerful resource for developing crime-prevention strategies, the time has come to look to virtual communities as a way to stem the tide of cybercrime. Although these virtual communities exist only as a seemingly-random string of ones and zeroes beamed around the globe and reconstituted into images, pictures, and sounds on computer screens, they retain many of the same features as their tangible, realspace counterparts—most notably, a sense of common interest among their members.

The use of open source software is a unique way to apply the community policing model to cybercrime. Just as neighborhood watch programs put "eyes on the street" to deter crimes like mugging, rape, and murder, open source software allows programmers and developers to monitor the code which shapes cyberspace and deters cybercrimes.

Footnotes deleted.

InfoMarks: Make Your Mark

What is an InfoMark?

It is a single-click return ticket to any page, any result, or any search from InfoTrac College Edition.

An InfoMark is a stable URL, linked to InfoTrac College Edition articles that you have selected. InfoMarks can be used like any other URL, but they're better because they're stable – they don't change. Using an InfoMark is like performing the search again whenever you follow the link, whether the result is a single article or a list of articles.

How Do InfoMarks Work?

If you can "copy and paste," you can use InfoMarks.

When you see the InfoMark icon on a result page, its URL can be copied and pasted into your electronic document – web page, word processing document, or email. Once InfoMarks are incorporated into a document, the results are persistent (the URLs will not change) and are dynamic.

Even though the saved search is used at different times by different users, an InfoMark always functions like a brand new search. Each time a saved search is executed, it accesses the latest updated information. That means subsequent InfoMark searches might yield additional or more up-to-date information than the original search with less time and effort.

Capabilities

InfoMarks are the perfect technology tool for creating:

- Virtual online readers
- Current awareness topic sites – links to periodical or newspaper sources
- Online/distance learning courses
- Bibliographies, reference lists
- Electronic journals and periodical directories
- Student assignments
- Hot topics

302

Advantages

- Select from over 15 million articles from more than 5,000 journals and periodicals
- Update article and search lists easily
- Articles are always full-text and include bibliographic information
- All articles can be viewed online, printed, or emailed
- Saves professors and students time
- Anyone with access to InfoTrac College Edition can use it
- No other online library database offers this functionality
- FREE!

How to Use InfoMarks

There are three ways to utilize InfoMarks – in HTML documents, Word documents, and Email.

HTML Document

1. Open a new document in your HTML editor (Netscape Composer or FrontPage Express).
2. Open a new browser window and conduct your search in InfoTrac College Edition.
3. Highlight the URL of the results page or article that you would like to InfoMark.
4. Right-click the URL and click Copy. Now switch back to your HTML document.
5. In your document, type in text that describes the InfoMarked item.
6. Highlight the text and click on Insert, then on Link in the upper bar menu.
7. Click in the link box, then press the "Ctrl" and "V" keys simultaneously and click OK. This will paste the URL in the box.
8. Save your document.

Word Document

1. Open a new Word document.
2. Open a new browser window and conduct your search in InfoTrac College Edition.
3. Check items you want to add to your Marked List.
4. Click on Mark List on the right menu bar.

5. Highlight the URL, right-click on it, and click Copy. Now switch back to your Word document.
6. In your document, type in text that describes the InfoMarked item.
7. Highlight the text. Go to the upper bar menu and click on Insert, then on Hyperlink.
8. Click in the hyperlink box, then press the "Ctrl" and "V" keys simultaneously and click OK. This will paste the URL in the box.
9. Save your document.

Email

1. Open a new email window.
2. Open a new browser window and conduct your search in InfoTrac College Edition.
3. Highlight the URL of the results page or article that you would like to InfoMark.
4. Right-click the URL and click Copy. Now switch back to your email window.
5. In the email window, press the "Ctrl" and "V" keys simultaneously. This will paste the URL into your email.
6. Send the email to the recipient. By clicking on the URL, he or she will be able to view the InfoMark.